BRIDGE to
20TH CENTURY MUSIC

a programed course

Paul O. Harder

Michigan State University

Library of Congress Catalog Card Number: 72-89618

Printed in the United States of America

ACKNOWLEDGEMENTS

Ex. 3. Flathead Indians   Reprinted from Alan P. Merriam, ETHNO-MUSICOLOGY OF THE FLATHEAD INDIANS (Chicago: Aldine Publishing Company, 1967); copyright © 1967 by Wenner-Gren Foundation for Anthropological Research, Inc.

Ex. 10. Guirant de Bornelk: Alba   Reprint by permission of Arno Volk Verlag Cologne from Gennrich: Troubadours, Trouvères, Minnesang and Meistergesang, Anthology of Music Vol. 2.

F 74   © Copyright 1956 by Stainer & Bell, Ltd. All rights reserved. International copyright secured. Galaxy Music Corp., N.Y., sole U.S. agent.

F 202, 205, 208, 213, 219, 229, 232, and 260   Published with the kind permission of C.F. Peters Corporation.

F 238, 244, 249, 250, and 259   Published with the kind permission of Boosey & Hawkes, Inc.

F 276   Copyright Edward B. Marks Music Corporation. Used by permission.

F 280   Copyright Edward B. Marks Music Corporation. Used by permission.

F 287   Copyright Edward B. Marks Music Corporation. Used by permission.

F 288   Copyright Edward B. Marks Music Corporation. Used by permission.

F 289   Copyright Edward B. Marks Music Corporation. Used by permission.

F 291   © 1913, Permission for reprint granted by Durand & Cie., Paris, France, copyright owners. Elkan-Vogel, Inc., agents.

F 295   © 1947, Permission for reprint granted by Durand & Cie., Paris, France, copyright owners. Elkan-Vogel, Inc., agents.

F 300   © 1913, Permission for reprint granted by Durand & Cie., Paris, France, copyright owners. Elkan-Vogel, Inc., agents.

F 302   Copyright 1953 by Hawkes & Son (London), Ltd.

F 303   © 1904, Permission for reprint granted by Durand & Cie., Paris, France, copyright owners. Elkan-Vogel, Inc., agents.

F 305   © 1910, Permission for reprint granted by Durand & Cie., Paris, France, copyright owners. Elkan-Vogel, Inc., agents.

F 307   Copyright 1925 by Universal-Edition. Copyright assigned 1939 to Hawkes & Son (London), Ltd. for the British Empire, U.S.A., and all countries of South and Central America.

F 308   © 1904, Permission for reprint granted by Durand & Cie., Paris, France, copyright owners. Elkan-Vogel, Inc., agents.

F 311   Copyright 1953 by Hawkes & Son (London), Ltd.

F 315   © 1910, Permission for reprint granted by Durand & Cie., Paris, France, copyright owners. Elkan-Vogel, Inc., agents.

CONTENTS

PREFACE

Because this book is unlike any other in the field of music theory, it is fitting that its objectives, contents, and approaches be clearly described. The chief concern is a systematic examination of impressionist techniques. Impressionism is a style which straddles not only two centuries, but also two profoundly different aesthetic and technical eras. Coming at the end of the romantic period, impressionism retains much of the spirit of this movement; but because its unique harmonic practices thoroughly undermined older notions of tonal organization, it prepared the way for the modern musical era. Thus, impressionism forms a "bridge to twentieth-century music."

To provide a background for the study of impressionist techniques three preliminary steps are taken: (1) the principles of melodic tonality as exemplified in early monophony, as well as in primitive and non-Western music are examined, (2) various approaches to harmonic tonality taken by eighteenth- and nineteenth-century theorists are reviewed, and (3) the evolution of harmonic tonality in the classical and romantic periods is traced. In this way the sanctified position occupied by harmonic tonality during these periods is revealed, and appreciation grows for the dislocation caused by developments which first attacked, and ultimately destroyed time-honored concepts of tonal organization. It was, after all, the final rejection of harmonic tonality which led to many of the more significant technical innovations of the present century.

The musical output of the past hundred years is so vast and varied that comprehensive treatment is out of the question. Selectivity has been exercised to show major stylistic developments, with special attention given to the music of key personalities. Harmonic and tonal aspects of style are emphasized, but form, melody, and rhythm also receive attention.

As for the approaches used, programed sequences are incorporated into the text when appropriate. These sequences occur for systematic presentations, and when reinforcement is required to cultivate mastery of technical features. Programed approaches are especially useful for problems in analysis, because they direct attention to precisely those facets of the music which are important for a particular comprehension.

Unlike most theory texts, styles and technical devices are placed in an historical context, and correlations with developments in art, literature, and philosophy are traced. In this way techniques appear not as isolated phenomena, but in relation to larger aesthetic evolutions. Still, this book does not in any way substitute for one in history and literature; it is above all a theory text, but is enriched by the inclusion of subsidiary historical information.

Many approaches may be taken to the music covered in this study, much of which is highly complex. A variety of analytical tools are used as required by the objectives of the analyses. The conclusions reached are frankly neither comprehensive nor definitive; they may, however, serve as catalysts for additional--even contradictory--interpretations, which will expand comprehension of the material. In any case, the objective is to direct attention to the styles and techniques which lead to twentieth-century music, and to do so in a way that reveals major streams of evolution.

This text is designed to guide the student through his first exposure to this material. Not all questions are answered, not all problems are solved, but hopefully a basis for future, more penetrating study is established.

The author is grateful for assistance rendered by the Michigan State University Educational Development Program, Robert Davis, Director. Appreciation is extended to the following firms for permission to quote from copyrighted material: Aldine-Atherton, Inc., Arno Volk Verlag, Associated Music Publishers, Inc., Boosey and Hawkes, Inc., Durand & Cie., Elkan-Vogel, Inc., Galaxy Music Corp., J. Jobert, Edward B. Marks Music Corp., G. Schirmer, Inc., and Universal Edition. Thanks go to the students who used this material while it was being developed; their many suggestions helped shape its final form. For special assistance, thanks are also due to Wallace DePue, Frank Stewart, and M. David Lehr.

Paul Harder

ADVICE TO THE STUDENT

The programed sequences which you will encounter from time to time in this book are designed to make it easier for you to acquire technical knowledge and skills. Programed instruction is widely used today, so you probably are familiar with how it works. Briefly, it is a method which breaks up a body of knowledge into small steps called *frames*. Frames contain information you are to digest, and most call for you to make a response. Each frame builds on the preceding ones, so they should be taken in order. The first programed sequence begins on page 2. A glance at this page and those which follow will show that the page is divided into two parts by a vertical line. The main part of each frame is located to the right of this line; the answers are located to the left. You should mask the answers with a card, slip of paper, or your hand, and uncover each answer after you have recorded your response. To facilitate checking, answers are placed as near your response as possible. A bit of judicious peeking will do no harm, so don't feel guilty. In fact, there are times when the help you gain in this way may be beneficial. But there are four important points to keep in mind:

1. One reason programed instruction leads to quick, thorough learning is that you are *actively* engaged in the learning processes. Thus, it is vital that you do each of the tasks required. *The act of writing your answers contributes as much to learning as reading the information supplied by the text.*

2. Because programed material requires you to be active most of the time, you should not work for long periods without rest. A half hour of study several times a day will be more productive than several hours at one time.

3. It is important that you work near a piano in order to actually hear the examples presented. If this is impossible, play through the examples contained in the pages with which you are concerned both before and after study. At any rate, a purely intellectual approach to this subject is inadequate; full comprehension requires that aural evaluations be made.

4. To be correct, your responses need not be exactly the same as those given. Use common sense to decide if you have expressed the same meaning.

In connection with point four, it is especially important to exercise judgment when traditional harmonic analysis is required. In the field of music theory few terms and symbols are completely standardized, so the chord symbols with which you are familiar may be slightly different than the ones used here, which are the same as those in the author's *Harmonic Materials in Tonal Music* 2 vols. (Allyn and Bacon, Inc., 1968). In spite of some variations, you should be able to equate these symbols with the ones you have learned.

Larger musical examples which could not conveniently be placed in the body of the text are contained in panels located in the back of this book. As you proceed, your attention will be directed occasionally to these panels.

1

The Persistence of Tonality

After nearly three centuries of use, tonal harmonic orientations were abandoned by some composers near the beginning of the twentieth century. This was by no means a sudden, revolutionary event brought about by a single person, or even a small group; it was a natural, inevitable consequence of the long development of harmony in European music. As a prelude to surveying the evolution of tonality in the eighteenth and nineteenth centuries, and focusing particularly on the final stages of this development, we shall look at some of the various manifestations of tonality in both Western and non-Western music.

Two fundamental types of tonality are "melodic," and "harmonic." Whereas melodic tonality is universal, harmonic tonality is largely confined to Western music. Harmony is present in the music of some other cultures,[1] but no music outside Western civilization displays comparable preoccupation with a harmonic system of tone relations. Harmonic tonality is a prominent ingredient of much of the music we hear; indeed, for many of those whose listening diet consists mainly of music from the classical and romantic periods, it is indispensable and unquestioned. This is true to the extent that, for some, music which lacks obvious tonal organization, or even that based on other than the familiar major-minor system, is regarded as "unnatural," or "exotic."

In view of the vital role played by tonality (particularly harmonic tonality) in Western music, it is remarkable how poorly its concepts are understood. Our first task is to remedy this lack, and especially to establish the broadest possible view of tonality—one which includes all music in which some kind of tone system operates as an organizing force. Our point of departure will be the definition below:

> *Tonality is the tonal orientation which results from the pre-eminence of a single pitch, or pitch complex, with other pitches assuming various degrees of secondary importance.*

Because reference will frequently be made to this definition as we proceed, it is important that you digest thoroughly its meaning. The short programed sequence which follows is designed to elaborate certain of its aspects.

tonality	1. Pre-eminence of a pitch over other pitches results from various kinds of *stress*. When one pitch is stressed sufficiently to achieve pre-eminence over other pitches the result is _____ .
pitches *(or tones)*	2. Tonality is a means of organizing into a hierarchal system the _____ employed in a musical composition.

True.	3. The tonal center of a composition is that pitch which receives the maximum stress. (True/False) _____
Yes. *(This will be elaborated later.)*	4. Can tonality be conceived as imposing "structure" on tonal materials? _____
Yes. *(With no other tone to challenge it, pre-eminence is guaranteed.)*	5. Can tonality be established by a single tone alone? _____

The various means by which a particular pitch may be stressed to cause it to become a tonal center are of crucial importance. This will be our next concern.

Supporting the premise that some form of tonality is essential in music is the fact that virtually all known primitive and folk music displays at least an elementary tone system in which a hierarchy of sounds is defined. Tonality can be viewed as a common thread linking musical expression of all people, regardless of geographic location or ethnic origin. It is one of the features which elevates instinctive vocal utterances such as moans, cries, and shouts to the level of artistic expression. Tonality, then, is perhaps the simplest means by which vocal expression of pure feeling is formalized and objectified.

The examples of primitive music which follow will show some of the ways tonality is established. The first of these consists of only two pitches.

Ex. 1. Vedda[2]

In this example the music consists merely of an eight-note melodic pattern repeated indefinitely. Clearly the note B is the tonal center, A having secondary function. Three factors contribute to establishing B as the tonal center:

1. Each phrase begins and ends with B.
2. The longest notes (the last of each phrase) are B.
3. The note B is iterated more often than A.

These three items call attention to some of the means by which notes may be stressed, and stress, remember, is what causes a particular pitch to be established as a tonal center. *(Frames 6-9 refer to the three items immediately above.)*

formal *(See explanation in next frame.)*	6. Item 1 in the list above is concerned chiefly with the (rhythmic/formal) _____ aspect of music.

rhythmic   *(Other terms for this type of stress are DURATIONAL and AGOGIC.)*

7.   Because notes which begin or end phrases serve as points of departure or repose, they have special formal (structural) importance; as the initial and final pitches, such tones define the temporal limits of the phrase. Thus, the first of the three items is concerned with stress through formal placement.

Item 2, by referring to the last note of each phrase, also is concerned with formal stress, but it relates to another type of stress as well. The statement that "the longest notes are B," refers to (rhythmic/tonal/dynamic) _____ stress.

A   6

B   10

8.   Item 3 ("The note B is iterated more often than A.") refers to the most elementary type of stress: *iteration of a single pitch.* Insistent repetition of a pitch strongly establishes its pre-eminence over other, less frequently iterated pitches.

Refer, again, to Example 1. Notice that the repetition of the entire eight-note phrase is itself a form of iteration. Now, to compare the relative importance of the two notes A and B, list below the number of times each occurs (count all the notes in Example 1).

A   _____

B   _____

Yes.

9.   Is the fact that the note B occurs more often than A a factor in causing B to be heard as the tonal center? _____

When a pitch occurs more frequently than others, it tends to be stressed, and thus be heard as the tonal center. This is the principle of tonality produced by ITERATION. The next few frames will focus on this aspect of tonality.

Ex. 2.   Yecuaná Indians (Brazil)[3]

(Frames 10-14 refer to Example 2.)

10. The melody in Example 2 consists of three tones (B, D, and E). Count the occurrences of each of these tones and list in the spaces below:

B _____

D _____

E _____

B   7

D   4

E   5

---

11. The frequency of occurrence of each note, as well as the tonal material used, is indicated graphically by writing out a "weighted scale." The three notes used in the melody in Example 2 are represented below.

Observe that the note which occurs most often (B) is represented by a whole-note, and progressively smaller time values are assigned to the other two notes according to their frequency of occurrence.

Weighted scales are useful for indicating the pitches used and their relative stress through iteration, so we shall make additional use of them later. But, although the stress resulting from iteration is a strong tonality-defining factor, the note which occurs most frequently is not always the tonal center. Returning, now, to Example 2, what factor other than iteration causes B to assume the role of tonal center? (Check one.)

    (1) Accent   _____

    (2) Form   _____

    (3) Rhythm _____

---

(2) Form √ *(It would also be correct to check (3) Rhythm. See the next frame for explanation.)*

---

12. Because the phrase both begins and ends on B, and also due to the prominence of this note at the mid-point as the beginning of the second subphrase, formal structure is a more decisive factor than rhythm.

Referring again to the melody in Example 2, and also to the weighted scale in the preceding frame, which note is second in importance to B? (D or E) _____

E.

Perfect fourth.	13. What is the interval between the two principal tones? _____
	14. The perfect fourth (and its inversion the perfect fifth) frequently is a constructive element in primitive music. In Example 2, the perfect fourth B-E defines the tonal limits of the melody, with D occupying a subsidiary position as an "infix,"—contained within the structural perfect fourth. Because of its structural importance and rhythmic stress, and also because it occurs almost as many times as B, the note E has strong tonal status. In view of these considerations, can one be certain that B is the tonal center?
No. *(But the strong formal stress of B probably is decisive.)*	_____

Regardless whether B or E is heard as the center, the solid tonal orientation of the melody in Example 2 is obvious. Here, the basic structural element is the interval of the perfect fourth. Recall our original definition of tonality which states that the tonal center can be not only a single tone, but also a "pitch complex." Sometimes two or more tones function as structural factors virtually equal to one another in importance.

Example 3 shows a more elaborate melody.

Ex. 3. Flathead Indians[4]
Jumpin' Dance song

(Frames 15-16 refer to Example 3.)

15. We shall approach this melody by first constructing a weighted scale.

3   1   7   2   3   1   12   10   4

This scale shows the number of occurrences of each note in the melody. For true assessment of tonal importance, however, the occurrences of notes which are an octave apart must be combined. This produces the tabulation shown in the list below:

D   15   (12 + 3)

E   11   (10 + 1)

G   11   (7 + 4)

A   2

B   3

C   1

Frequency of occurrence alone would cause D to be the tonal center, but examine the melody in Example 3 again. Do you believe that D is indeed the tonal center?
_____

No. *(See explanation in next frame.)*

---

16. Iteration alone does not necessarily establish a pitch as the tonal center; other factors may be more decisive. In this case, formal position and rhythmic (durational) stress cause the note G to be the tonal center. This melody also demonstrates the structural importance of the perfect fourth (or perfect fifth).
    Use the numbers 1, 2, and 3 to rate the importance of the tonality-determinants below in the melody just discussed.

Iteration _____

Form   _____

Rhythm _____

Iteration   3

Form   1

Rhythm   2

The three principal determinants of melodic tonality are *iteration, rhythm,* and *form.*[5] These vary in relative importance in each case, but form generally is the strongest factor. Our approach to the next melody will pursue the matter of form a bit further.

Ex. 4. Ada-Ada (Java)[6]

We shall take a different approach to the tonal organization manifested in the melody above. To begin, let us state that the termination of phrases is particularly important to the establishment of tonality. Points of repose, in other words, have greater significance with respect to tonal orientation than the material which initiates the phrase and leads to its conclusion. This is reflected in the way vocal polyphonic compositions of the Renaissance period are classified as being in a particular mode (Dorian, Phrygian, etc.) on the basis of the final cadence alone. Also, in ultrachromatic music of the late nineteenth century, to be discussed later, cadences often provide the chief means of identifying tonal orientations.

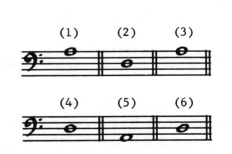

(Frames 17-21 refer to Example 4.)

17. Notice in Example 4 that six phrases have been identified.
Indicate on the staff the *final* pitch of each phrase.

Phrases: (1)   (2)   (3)   (4)   (5)   (6)

18. The analysis of phrase endings in the preceding frame reveals the tonal structure below:

Tonal Center

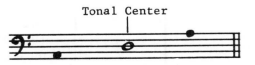

The Persistence of Tonality

The note D, rather than A, is the tonal center because the final cadence is on D. Notice, too, that the cadences on D are in most cases stronger rhythmically than those on A. (Compare phrases 2, 4, and 6 with 1 and 3.)

Look again at Example 4. Indicate below the notes which *initiate* the phrases.

Phrase		Phrase	
(1) _____		(4) _____	
(2) _____		(5) _____	
(3) _____		(6) _____	

(1) F   (4) F
(2) F   (5) C
(3) F   (6) C

---

19.   Additional light is shed on the tonal structure of this melody by including both the initial and final notes of each phrase as below:

The first four phrases begin with F and cadence alternately on A and D. The last two phrases begin with C and end first on A, then on D. The two principal structural tones are D and A. The interval between these tones is a

_____

perfect 5th *(or perfect 4th)*

---

20.   The first note of a phrase is called the *initial*; the term for the last note is the *final.* Each of these has an influence on tonality because of its formal position, but of the two, that which carries the most weight as a tonality-determinant is the _____ .

final

---

21.   One more observation will be made about the phrase initials and finals of the melody in Example 4 (see Frame 19): The example below shows that like the finals (D-A), the initials (F-C) can be arranged to form a perfect fifth.

The initials and finals produce a pattern of interlocking fifths; also, the overall pattern consists entirely of a single interval type. The successive intervals are either major or minor _____.

thirds

One final example of primitive music is shown below:

Ex. 5.   Papua (Northwest New Guinea)[7]
(after Jaap Kunst)

This melody both begins and ends with B-flat, clearly establishing this note as the tonal center. The phrase is constructed in the form of an arch rising from the initial B-flat a major seventh to A, and then dropping gradually to cadence on B-flat. But the feature which interests us most is the chain of thirds from which the melody is constructed. While perhaps not functional, chains of like intervals are a unifying and constructive factor. Such chains of either thirds or fourths are found in primitive music in widely separated parts of the world; they are common, for example, in the music of some American Indians, including the Hopi. Sachs finds interval chains to be European as well. "For actual evidence, we must turn to archaic folksongs and to melodies of the later Middle Ages, which have left us many hundreds of secular tunes in readable notation. . . . Triple and quadruple thirds are also very frequent in the knightly songs of *troubadours*, *trouvères*, and *Minnesinger*. . . . Doubtless, many troubadour, trouvère, minnesinger tunes are modal indeed; but more than half of them are tertial chains—exactly like so many Indian and Negro songs. . . ."[8]

The example below shows the kind of tertial chain to which Sachs refers:

Ex. 6.   Adam de la Halle: "On me deffent que mon coeur pas ne croie"[9]

Because the third is the basic constructive interval in Western music from about the beginning of the Renaissance period to the twentieth century, it is indeed interesting to note the similarity of its use in Examples 5 and 6. Not only does such use provide a link between widely disparate cultures, it also lends support to certain later theorists who assert the fundamental constructive properties of thirds.

We have looked at several examples of primitive music from non-Western cultures to demonstrate the fundamental nature of tonality as an organizing force. These examples show that tonal structures may result from mere iteration of one or two notes, or consist of fairly complex tone systems in which several pitches have various functional relationships to one another. In any case, the prevalence of tonal order in such music points to the instinctive turning to pitch orientations (tonality) as a fundamental method of achieving order in musical expression.

The methods we have used thus far were designed to suggest various analytical approaches, and also to reveal various ways tonality is established. Some of the examples have shown primitive manifestations of certain tonal organizations which are stressed as major premises by some Western theorists of the eighteenth and nineteenth centuries. These will be elaborated as we proceed.

Strong tonal emphasis is prevalent throughout the entire evolution of Western music to at least the beginning of the twentieth century. Several manifestations may be cited. Some of the instruments used in ancient and medieval times produced drones. Bagpipes, and the ancient Greek aulos are examples of wind instruments with drones; the lira da braccio, and hurdy-gurdy are two stringed instruments which were likewise equipped. Drones, of course, provide tonal underpinning for the melodies they accompany. Although primitive in nature, drones have persisted in compositional types such as the musette, and pieces of a pastoral or rustic nature. The pedal is a more sophisticated application of the drone principle, and is often used, significantly, by later composers to preserve tonal orientation when techniques or chromatic material threaten to cast music beyond the orbit of tonal control. Repetitive dance forms occur everywhere as a form of popular social activity. The strophic musical repetitions which naturally accompany such dances lead to tonal stress of a formal nature.

Monodic music, including secular songs, dance tunes, and most importantly the large liturgical repertoire known as plainsong, served as the material and aesthetic basis for music composed during the long evolution of vocal polyphony. This evolution began about the ninth century, and lasted until nearly the end of the sixteenth century. Thus, the character of Western music in both the medieval and Renaissance periods was affected by the principles of melodic tonality. To observe the role played by tonality in these kinds of music, two examples of Christian chant will be cited, and these will be followed by a few examples of secular monody.

Ex. 7. Ambrosian Hymn: "Aeterne rerum conditor"[10]

D.

(Frames 22-28 refer to Example 7.)

22.   Sing the melody in Example 7. What is the tonal center? _____

---

formal stress

23.   The note D is established as the tonal center because each of the four phrases ends with this note. Thus, tonality is here determined by the principle of (iteration/formal stress) _____ .

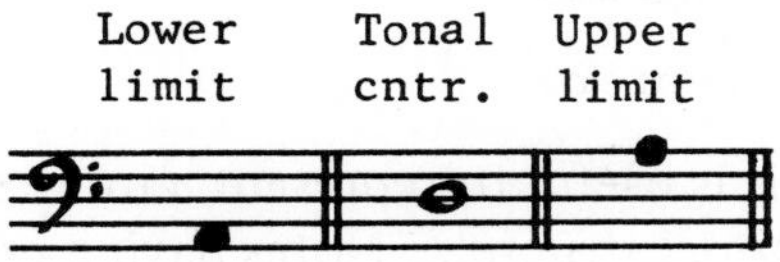

Lower limit	Tonal cntr.	Upper limit

24.   Complete the diagram below by writing notes to represent the upper and lower limits of the melody. *(Use black notes.)*

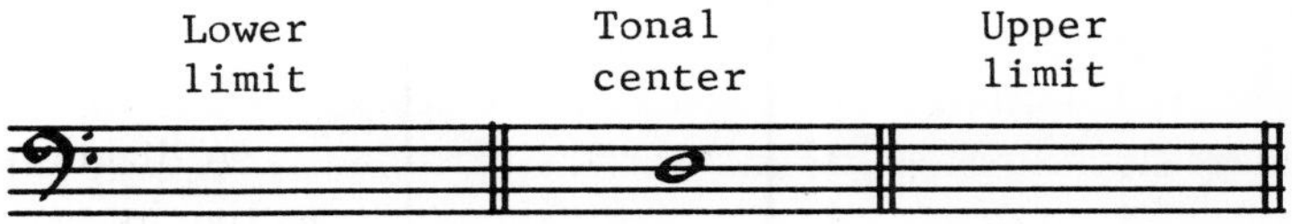

Lower limit	Tonal center	Upper limit

---

perfect fourth

25.   The upper limit is a perfect fifth above the tonal center, and the lower limit is a _____ below the tonal center.

---

26.   The frequency of occurrence for each note is shown in the form of a weighted scale below:

    1   6   11   8   5   1

   It has already been stated that the number of occurrences alone does not always indicate the tonal importance of a particular pitch; formal, or rhythmic stress often is more important. But on the other hand, such tabulations sometimes are revealing. Certainly the large number of D's contributes to the strong tonal stress for this note.

upper
lower   *(Any order.)*

   In spite of occurring only twice, the note A has special significance because it defines both the _____ and _____ limits of the melody.

G. *(If you selected another note, examine the melody again.)*

27. We shall now focus attention on another, more subtle aspect of the melody in Example 7. First, sing again the second and third phrases (measures 5-12). The note D receives formal stress by ending both of these phrases. But there is another note in addition to D which has both formal and rhythmic stress. Name this note. _____

---

28. All five occurrences of the note G are concentrated in phrases two and three. This note is stressed sufficiently for it to be established as a structural element. Thus, a more complete picture of the tonal organization is shown below:

Tonal Center

A diagram such as this is useful to represent a more subjective interpretation of tonal structure. Notes having principal structural function are given greater rhythmic value than others, and notes which have a particular relation to one another are beamed together.

The tonal diagram above shows that D is the tonal center, and that both A and G have structural importance. Whereas the note A, which marks the upper limit of the melody is a perfect fifth above the center, the note G is a perfect _____ above the tonal center.

fourth

Chants of the Catholic liturgy provide a large body of monophonic music. We shall analyze the example below:

Ex. 8. *Kyrie fons bonitatis*—Kyriale; Liber Usualis

    a. Medieval notation

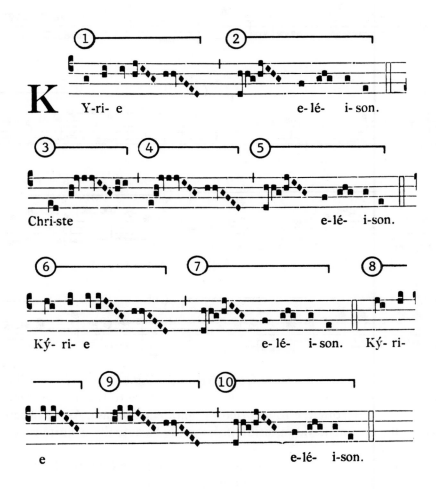

b. Transcribed in modern notation

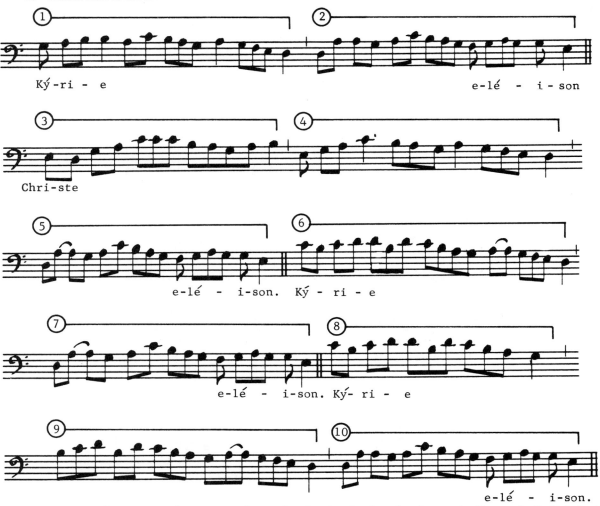

Ký-ri - e   e-lé - i - son

Chri -ste

e-lé - i -son. Ký - ri - e

e-lé - i -son. Ký- ri - e

e-lé - i -son.

This chant has a different tonal structure from that in the Ambrosian hymn in Example 7. It is in the third tone (Phrygian), but our approach will not include reference to the medieval modal system. Our purpose here will be served by charting the tonal orientation of each phrase. As we progress, you may refer to either Example 8a or 8b. The medieval notation in Example 8a actually is quite easy to interpret. Merely note the following points:

1. The top line of the four-line staff is identified as middle C by the first symbol, which is a clef sign; other pitches can be determined by relating them to this line.

2. The following symbol (called a *neume*) is interpreted by taking the lower note first:

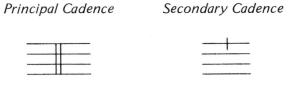

is rendered

3. Distinction between principal and secondary cadences is made as below:

Principal Cadence   *Secondary Cadence*

You should begin by singing the melody in Example 8 to observe the motives from which it is constructed. Note, too, the points of inner tonal emphasis.

E

(Frames 29-33 refer to Example 8.)
29. Each principal section (indicated by a double bar) ends with the note _____ .

30. The tonality of this chant is strongly established by the fact that each principal phrase ends on the same pitch (E). What interests us beyond this fact is how other pitches relate to the tonal center. As the first step, complete the chart below:

Phrase	Initial	Final
1	_____	_____
2	_____	E
3	_____	_____
4	_____	_____
5	_____	E
6	_____	_____
7	_____	E
8	_____	_____
9	_____	_____
10	_____	E

1 G - D
2 D - E
3 E - B
4 E - D
5 D - E
6 C - D
7 D - E
8 C - G
9 B - D
10 D - E

31. The tabulation in the preceding frame is made more meaningful by placing the notes on the staff as below:

As initials and finals of phrases, all of these notes have structural importance. Indicate the number of times each occurs (in the example above).

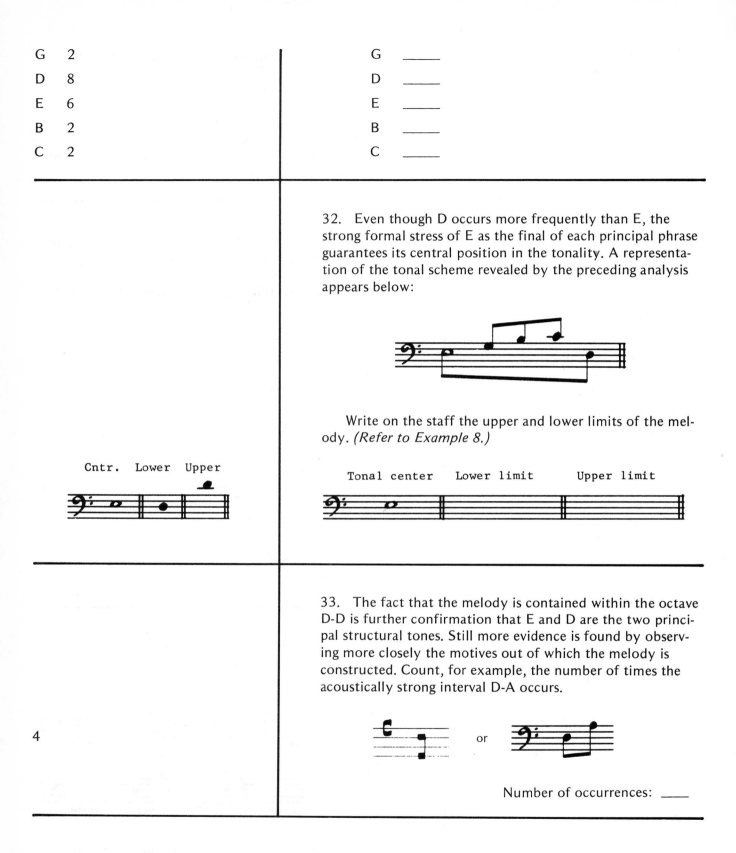

G 2
D 8
E 6
B 2
C 2

G _____
D _____
E _____
B _____
C _____

32. Even though D occurs more frequently than E, the strong formal stress of E as the final of each principal phrase guarantees its central position in the tonality. A representation of the tonal scheme revealed by the preceding analysis appears below:

    Write on the staff the upper and lower limits of the melody. *(Refer to Example 8.)*

Tonal center   Lower limit   Upper limit

Cntr. Lower Upper

4

33. The fact that the melody is contained within the octave D-D is further confirmation that E and D are the two principal structural tones. Still more evidence is found by observing more closely the motives out of which the melody is constructed. Count, for example, the number of times the acoustically strong interval D-A occurs.

or

Number of occurrences: _____

To conclude this brief glance at early Western monophonic music we shall observe two secular melodies. The first is shown in Example 9.

Ex. 9.   Goliard song: "O Roma nobilis"[11]

O Ro-ma no-bi-lis   or-bis et do-mi-na.   Cum-cta-rum ur-bi-um   ex-

cel-len-tis-si-ma.   Ro-se   o mar-ty-rum   san-qui-ne ru-be-a.   Al-

bis et li-li-is   vir-gi-num can-di-da.   Sa-lu-tem di-ci-mus   ti-

bi per om-ni-a.   Te be-ne-di-ci-mus   sal-ve per se-cu-la.

---

1. D 4. D		
2. D 5. B		
3. D 6. D		

(Frames 34-36 refer to Example 9.)

34.   The tonality of the Goliard song above centers on G, due to the formal emphasis this note receives as the final of each phrase. Indicate below the note which *initiates* each phrase.

Phrase   Phrase

1. ____   4. ____

2. ____   5. ____

3. ____   6. ____

---

rhythmic *(or durational)*

35.   The previous frame shows that the notes G and D provide the principal structural framework for this melody with B also receiving some stress. Another note which is structurally important may be discovered by looking at the mid-point of phrases 1, 2, 3, and 4. In each case the note C is elevated in importance because of _____ stress.

36. The structure of the melody is represented by the tonal diagram below:

Tonal Center

The notes which are excluded from the above example are A and E. Even though A occurs 9 times and E 8 times, neither has structural importance. Explain the reason for this (refer to Example 9):

_____

_____

_____

_____

_____

Neither initiates or terminates a phrase; also, rhythmic stress is slight. *(In your own words.)*

The final example of monody is a troubadour melody from early in the thirteenth century.

Ex. 10. Guiraut de Bornelh: "Reis glorios" *(Alba)*[12]

Reis glo-ri - os, ve - rais lums___ e clar -

tatz, Deus po - de - ros, Sen - her, si___

a vos___ platz, Al___ meu com - panh si -

atz fi - zels a - ju - da;___ Qu'eu no lo

vi,___ pos___ la   nochs   fo   ven - gu - da,

Et   a - dés   se - ra___ l'al - ba!

As in most previous examples, there is no question regarding the tonal center. The tabulation of notes below indicates that D is equaled in frequency by E, and surpassed by A; but since the melody both begins and ends on D, the role of this note as tonal center is secure.

Frequency of Notes in Example 10

D	13	A	20
E	13	B	12
F	7	C	7
G	10		

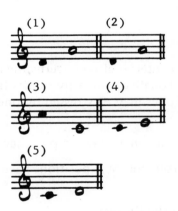

(Frames 37-40 refer to Example 10.)

37. To determine the tonal structure of the melody in Example 10, indicate the first and last notes in each phrase. *(The first is indicated; continue in like manner.)*

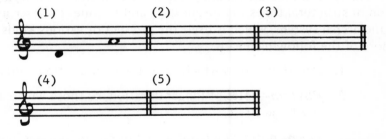

Tonal Center

(Yours may vary slightly from the one given and still be correct.)

38. On the basis of the information collected in the preceding frame, complete a tonal diagram similar to those in Frames 28, 32, and 36. Use half notes to represent principal structural tones, and eighth-notes for tones of lesser tonal value. Beams may be used to link notes which have comparable status and function.

Tonal Center

perfect fifth	39. The note A, because of its large number of occurrences (20), and also its structural use, is second in importance to the tonal center D. As in several previous examples, the interval between the principal structural tones is a _____ .
major	40. The remaining two structural notes (C and E) are each related to the tonal center by the interval of a _____ second.

Our examination of tonality in primitive music and early Western monody is now concluded. It has shown that tonality is manifested in music from several divergent cultures. So prevalent is tonality throughout the world, and so persistent are its manifestations, that it may be viewed as an instinctive expression of the human desire for order. Our particular concern here, of course, is music of Western civilization, and even the earliest recorded examples of this music give evidence of tonal structure.

Thus far, we have examined only melodic tonal structure. Melodic tonality results from various kinds of emphasis which cause one pitch to predominate over others. The approaches to tonality used here provide a simple basis for analyzing tonal phenomena in any monophonic music. These analytical tools focus on actual musical occurrences rather than rely on established historical systems such as the eight church modes in the case of liturgical chant. Thus, they provide a more nearly universal approach to tonality in monophonic music.

SUMMARY.

Analysis of melodic tonality is more than merely identifying the tonal center; it also concerns the relation of structural tones to one another, and to tones of lesser importance. Tonality ordinarily results from a hierarchal system, which is itself the product of various kinds of stress. Tones may be stressed by one or more of the following means:

1. *Iteration*—notes which are sounded more frequently than others assume added importance.

2. *Rhythm*—notes of longer duration, or those which appear in strong metrical positions have rhythmic stress.

3. *Form*—notes which initiate or terminate phrases have structural significance.

Neither √	41. Indicate the correct statement(s) by checking one of the options below: 1. Tonality is determined by the intervals contained in the melody. 2. All notes other than the tonal center are equal in importance. (1) ____ (2) ____ Both ____ Neither ____

True.	42. The tonal center is not always at the bottom of the tonal structure. (True/False) _____
Form √ *(Of course all are important, but formal stress often overrides the others.)*	43. Check the factor which ordinarily has the strongest bearing on determining tonality. Iteration _____ Rhythm _____ Form _____
melodic	44. The orientation of pitches to a tonal center in solo song is called _____ tonality.

2

Tonality As Order

The previous chapter revealed that melodic tonality derives from the stress of particular tones by the relatively primitive means of iteration, rhythm, and form. A second kind of tonality is based on the structure of a tonal complex and the function of chords within this structure. This is called *harmonic tonality*. Our purpose in this chapter is to examine the tonal order of harmonic tonality by reviewing some of the writings of theorists who approached this subject. The result should be a more thorough understanding of the underlying harmonic principles which influenced eighteenth- and nineteenth-century composers. Here is provided an introduction to the field of harmonic theory which may lead to more detailed study, or serve merely as background for the material on classical and romantic tonality which follows. The degree of emphasis is left to the discretion of those who use this book.

In view of the persistent manifestation of tonality throughout the world, it is strange that enunciation of its principles was so late in coming. Of course theorists have been concerned with tone systems (scale structures) and temperament since ancient times, but actual codification of tonality in the modern sense took place mostly in the eighteenth and nineteenth centuries.

HARMONIC THEORY

The term "tonality" was first used by the Belgian historian and theorist François Joseph Fétis in the nineteenth century.[1] But as early as 1500, composers had begun the gradual establishment of a common vocabulary of chords and tonal functions which would lead to, and make necessary, the concept of harmonic tonality. Thus, the eighteenth- and nineteenth-century view of tonality was born of harmony, and was to remain inextricably bound to it. But the establishment of harmony as an independent concept had to wait for the chord to be recognized as an harmonic entity. To clarify this point, we shall contrast the medieval and Renaissance (pre-harmonic) attitude toward vertical structures with that held by later theorists.

The *interval* was the basic constructive unit in pre-baroque composition. Focus then was upon more or less independent melodic lines which related to one another purely intervallically, for at that time the concept of "chord" did not exist. Rather, harmonic possibilities were spelled out as permissible combinations of intervals. This concept may be shown by referring to writings by the sixteenth-century theorist Gioseffo Zarlino (1517-1590). Zarlino's chief theoretical work *L'istitutioni harmoniche* is important for its summation of Renaissance compositional practices.[2] Of particular interest here is a table he supplies in which are listed the permissible intervallic combinations.[3] A few decades later, the English composer and theorist Thomas Morley included Zarlino's table in his own treatise on composition and music making *A Plaine and Easie Introduction to Practicall Musicke.*[4] This table is reproduced in Figure 1, and Example 11 shows how the rules are applied. The six chords in Example 11 are based on the *first rule* in each of the six categories in the table (*Of the Unison, Of the Third*, etc.).

A Table containing the vsuall cordes for the compostion of foure or more partes.

OF THE VNISON.

If the treble be	an vnison with the tenor
and the base	a third vnder the tenor
your *Alto* or meane shal be	a fifth or sixth aboue the base.
But if the base be	a fifth vnder the tenor
the *Alto* shal be	a third or tenth aboue the base.
Likewise if the base be	a sixt vnder the tenor,
then the Alto may be	a 3 or tenth aboue the base
And if the base be	an eight vnder the tenor,
the other parts may bee	a 3.5..6 10.or 12.aboue the base.
But if the base be	a tenth vnder the tenor,
the meane shal be	a fift or twelfth aboue the base.
Bnt if the base be	a twelfth vnder the tenor,
the Alto may be made	a 3. or 10. aboue the base.
Also the base being a	fifteenth vnder the tenor,
the other parts may be	a 3. 5. 6.10.12.and 13. aboue the base.

OF THE THIRD.

If the treble be	a third with the tenor
and the base	a third vnder it
the Alto may be	an vnison or 8.with the parts.
If the base be	a sixt vnder the tenor,
the *Altus* may be	a third or tenth aboue the base.
But if the base be	an eight vnder the tenor,
then the *Altus* shall be	a fift or sixt aboue the base.
And the base being	a tenth vnder the tenor,
then the parts may be	in the vnison or eight to the tenor or base.

OF THE FOVRTH.

When the treble shalbe	a fourth to the tenor
and the basse	a fifth vnder the tenor
then the meane shall be	a 3,or 10,aboue the base
But if the base be	a 12.vnder the tenor
the *Altus* shal be	a 10.aboue the base

OF THE FIFTH.

But if the treble shal be	a fifth aboue the tenor
and the base	an eight vnder it
the *Alto* may be	a 3 or tenth aboue the base
And if the base be	a sixt vnder the tenor,
the *Altus* shal be.	an vnison or 8 with the parts

OF THE SIXTH.

If the treble be	a sixt with the tenor
and the base	a fift vnder the tenor,
the *Altus* may be	an vnison or eight with the partes
But if the base be	a third vnder the tenor,
the *Altus* shal be	a fifth aboue be base.
Likewise if the base be	a tenth vnder the tenor,
the meane likewise shalbe	a fifth or 12.aboue the base.

OF THE EIGHT.

If the treble be	an 8. with the tenor.
and the base	a 3.vnder the tenor
the other parts shal be	a 3.5.6.10. 12.13.aboue the base
So also when the base shal be	a 5.vnder the tenor
the other parts may bee	a 3. aboue the base.
And if the base be	an eight vnder the tenor
the other parts shall bee	a 3 5 10.12.aboue the base.
Lastly if the base be	a 12.vnder the tenor
the parts shal make	a 10. or 17. aboue the base

Fig. 1. Table of chords from Morley, *A Plaine and Easie Introduction to Practicall Musicke.* Reproduced by courtesy of the Sibley Music Library, Eastman School of Music, University of Rochester.

Ex. 11.   Realizations of some of the rules in Figure 1.

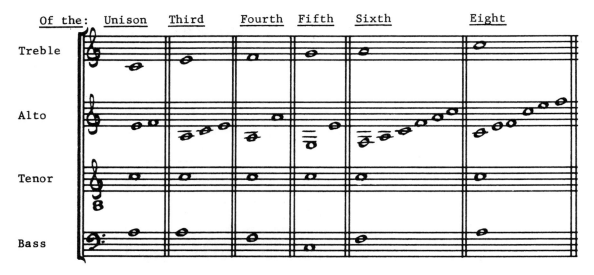

All of the sonorities which result from Zarlino's table (Figure 1) are triads in either root position or first inversion. The vital point, however, is that these are the products of intervallic associations, and the resulting sonorities are not recognized as chords in the modern sense. This, then, shows the pre-baroque attitude which employs the interval—not the chord—as the basic constructive unit.

The pivotal nature of Zarlino's theoretical writing is revealed by noting that, although his table of interval associations sums up the Renaissance approach to harmonic combinations, elsewhere his speculations lead to the first recognition of the triad as an harmonic entity. This stems from his attempt to provide a rational (mathematical) basis for music theory. Throughout his writings Zarlino explores the relations between the sciences of arithmetic, geometry, and music, with frequent allusions to Pythagoras, Euclid, Plato, and Aristotle. He attempts to explain many musical phenomena on the basis of the numbers 1-6 and the ratios between them (1:2:3:4:5:6).[5] This series he calls the *senario,* and believes it to embody the natural principle of harmony.[6] From the *senario* he derives all the consonances: unison (1:1), octave (2:1), perfect fifth (3:2), perfect fourth (4:3), major third (5:4), minor third (6:5), and major sixth (5:3).[7] This is really an extension of the Pythagorean system in which all the perfect consonances are derived from the numbers 1-4. The *senario* is also used to show that the major harmony results from the harmonic division of a string by 1, 1/2, 1/3, 1/4, 1/5, and 1/6 of its length. The result is the first six tones of the harmonic series.

Ex. 12.

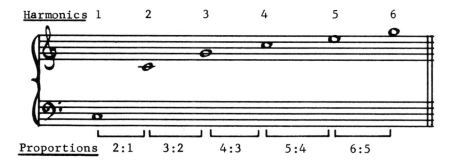

The chord which results from the combination of the first six tones of the harmonic series is called by Zarlino the *harmonia perfetta,* and is regarded by him to be the one perfect harmonic sound. This chord reduces, of course, to the three separate tones CEG, the major triad.

With his *harmonia perfetta*, Zarlino is the first theorist to recognize the triad as an harmonic entity. He thus initiates serious speculation regarding chordal structure, and aside from his valuable codification of sixteenth-century practices, this is his most significant achievement. The ground is now prepared for later theorists who begin with the triad, rather than the interval, as the basic constructive unit.

senario	45. Zarlino believed the numbers 1-6 to be the natural foundation of harmony. He called this series of numbers the _____ .
octave	46. The tones produced by two strings whose lengths are in proportion 2:1 result in the interval of a perfect _____ .
fifth	47. The tones produced by two strings whose lengths are in the proportion 3:2 result in the interval of a perfect _____ .
4:3	48. The perfect fourth results from the proportion _____:_____ .
5:4	49. The major third results from the proportion _____:_____ .
third	50. The proportion 6:5 results in the interval of a minor _____ .
major	51. The proportions of the *senario* (1:2:3:4:5:6) produce the first six tones of the harmonic series. Zarlino called this combination of tones the *harmonia perfetta*, and believed it to be the most desirable harmonic effect. The *harmonia perfetta* reduces to the _____ triad.
False. *(See the following frame.)*	52. Chords do not occur in medieval and Renaissance music. (True/False) _____

	53. Even though the *concept* of chord began with Zarlino about the middle of the sixteenth century, chords were very much a part of earlier music. After all, tones sounding simultaneously together produce chords, no matter how they are conceptualized. But the recognition given chords by Zarlino did lead to theoretical systems which caused harmony to be recognized as an independent element of music on a par with rhythm and melody.
harmonia perfetta	Harmonic theory begins with Zarlino's recognition of the major chord as an harmonic entity. His term for this "most desirable" harmonic sound is _____ .

During the seventeenth century, major and minor scales gradually superseded the liturgical modes, and composers developed a common vocabulary of chords and applied a consistent idiom of harmonic functions. It is the French composer and theorist Jean-Philippe Rameau (1683-1764) who most successfully codifies these practices. Rameau's ideas were first set forth in his treatise *Traité de l'harmonie* in 1722 and further developed in subsequent writings. Rameau's speculations laid the foundation for modern harmonic theory, and to the present day many of his principles serve as the pedagogic basis for the study of eighteenth- and nineteenth-century harmony.[8]

As the foremost eighteenth-century French composer,[9] Rameau's theoretical writings attracted wide interest and exerted a profound influence on the musical style of his own time. The focus on harmonic aspects of music, which stems primarily from Rameau, contributed to the eminent role played by harmony in the musical language of the eighteenth and nineteenth centuries. Indeed, so strong was the influence of harmonic orientations during this period that both melody and form often were delineated chiefly by harmonic functions.

What, then, are the principles laid down by Rameau? This is not an easy question to answer because his ideas were subjected to many (often contradictory) additions and revisions in his later writings. Far from static, his theories were in a dynamic state of evolution as a result not only of his own continuing investigations, but also through interaction with other musicians and writers of his time, particularly Jean Jacques Rousseau. We shall do no more here than examine briefly those aspects of his theories which are germane to the purpose of this study, which is to understand the nature of harmonic tonality and appreciate why it came to be so strong a force in music of the classical and romantic periods.

Rameau based his theory on mathematics and the observation of natural acoustical phenomena, specifically the harmonic series which is produced by vibrating strings and columns of air. Those who use such an approach are called "natural" theorists. *The initial point of departure for Rameau is the virtual identity of notes an octave removed.* The octave had long been recognized as the first and most perfect consonance after the unison, producing only a replica of the initial sound. From this identity of two notes an octave removed arises the principle of inversion, and Rameau's application of this principle produced concepts which began a new era in the history of music theory.

In contrast with prior theory in which the lower note of any interval was regarded as its fundamental, for Rameau, the minor sixth has the same harmonic foundation as the major third, *and is derived from it.* In the interval E-C, for example, the note C, not E, is considered the fundamental note. The minor sixth is not regarded as an "original" interval, but rather as derived from the major third. In like manner the perfect fourth is derived from the perfect fifth. Thus, in Rameau's view, *an "original" interval and its inversion have the same fundamental.*

(1).	54. Which is the more basic interval? _____
F	55. The fundamental note of interval (1) in the preceding frame is F; the fundamental note of interval (2) is _____ .
G	56. For both of the intervals below, the fundamental note is _____ .
octave	57. Rameau's basic premise, which leads to the principle of interval inversion, is the identity of tones the interval of a(n) _____ apart.

From the invertibility of intervals arises the still more important principle of chord inversion. The chord CEG (Zarlino's *harmonia perfetta*, called by Rameau *l'accord parfait majeur*), is the product of the proportions 4:5:6, and C is regarded as the generating tone. Because octave inversion does not alter the fundamental role of this tone, Rameau is able to assert that both the first inversion (5:6:8) and second inversion (6:8:10) are derivatives of the original chord (4:5:6); but most important of all, *each of the three versions has the same basic harmonic function.* In Figure 2 you will see reproduced a cut from the *Traité* which illustrates graphically these relations.[10]

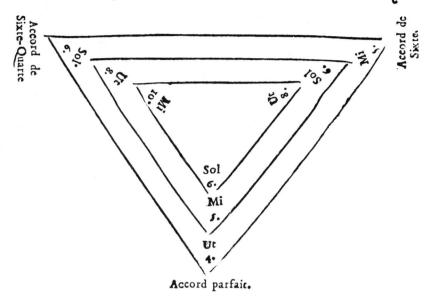

DÉMONSTRATION

De l'Accord parfait majeur, & de ses dérivez.

Fig. 2. Demonstration of the major triad and its derivatives from Rameau's *Traité de l'harmonie*. Reproduced by courtesy of the Sibley Music Library, Eastman School of Music, University of Rochester.

The lower point of the triangle in Rameau's demonstration above represents the C major triad in root position (*Ut, Mi, Sol* = CEG), and the proportions are 4:5:6; the point at the right represents the same chord in first inversion, and here the proportions 5:6:8 mean that the root has been raised an octave; the point at the left represents the second inversion, and the proportions are now 6:8:10 because both the root and third are raised an octave. But regardless of the inversion, the root (C) retains its generating function. Actual or inferred roots produce what Rameau terms the *basse-fondamentale* (fundamental bass). Example 13 shows the three positions of the C major triad, and also the fundamental of each.

Ex. 13.

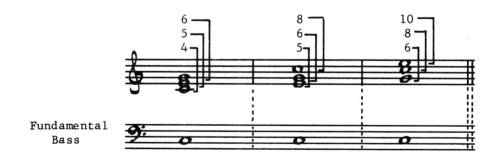

This approach to chords and their inversions is a key point in virtually all modern texts dealing with harmony; it now seems so natural, simple, and logical that it is difficult to realize how profound was the impact of this principle on harmonic theory and practice. Prior to Rameau, the greatest importance was placed on the interval itself, and theorists could not distinguish between the actual bass note and the fundamental generating note of an interval or chord. The lowest note of a chord was regarded as the fundamental regardless of its harmonic function, and chords were considered conglomerates of intervals rather than harmonic entities. But for Rameau, the generating harmonic tone is not necessarily the lowest pitch; it is the "fundamental bass," which, of course, is not always the actual sounding bass. It is the fundamental bass, however, which orders the harmonic motion, and from which harmonic function is reckoned. The fundamental bass is simply a tracing of the *roots* derived from the actual sounding harmonies. Figure 3 shows an example from the *Traité* in which the true bass *(basse-continue)* consists of an ascending and descending scale. Below this, the *basse-fondamentale* records the root of each chord.[11]

Fig. 3. Example of fundamental bass from Rameau's *Traité de l'harmonie.* Reproduced by courtesy of the Sibley Music Library, Eastman School of Music, University of Rochester.

The music in Figure 3 is shown in modern notation in Example 14 below:

Ex. 14.

Fundamental bass

Figure 3 (and Example 14) is an ideal harmonization of the ascending and descending major scale. Such a harmonization is known as the "rule of the octave," and is made as an exercise in harmonic logic. The fundamental bass supplied by Rameau is somewhat manipulated in order to "confirm" certain arbitrary concepts of chord succession, the examination of which lies beyond this study.[12] In any case, you must remember that the fundamental bass does not actually sound; it is merely a tracing of the roots.

The concepts of chord inversion and fundamental bass advanced by Rameau have far-reaching theoretical implications of tremendous importance, and have fired the furnace of harmonic speculation to the present day. But the practical benefits distilled from these principles are fairly simple; they are twofold:

1. The number of harmonic entities is notably reduced. Chords are no longer merely the product of intervallic combinations (see Figure 1); instead they fall into manageable classes of fundamental (root position) chords, and those derived from them by inversion.

2. The concept of fundamental bass leads to a simple, rational method of noting the relation of chords to one another *by means of their root relationships.* In this way the principles governing chord succession are readily codified.

In Book II of the *Traité*, Rameau attempts to discover the underlying principles which govern the progression of chords. Guided by his desire to base all his concepts on natural phenomena, he asserts that, because it is the first interval generated in the harmonic series after the octave (which causes no harmonic change), the perfect fifth produces the strongest possible root relations. Again following the harmonic series, root relations by thirds (either major or minor) are placed next in importance, whereas relations by seconds are the least desirable. In later writings Rameau greatly extends and modifies his approach to the fundamental bass, but one thing which remains unchanged is the pre-eminent position of root movements by perfect fifths.

Regardless of the complexities, impasses, and contradictions into which Rameau and others were led by their attempts to explain tonal functions on the basis of natural law, the fundamental bass remains a valuable tool for systematizing harmonic relations.

THE STRUCTURE OF TONALITY:

The remainder of this chapter will be devoted to a resumé of what Rameau and others have to say regarding tonality. As a consequence of his recognition of the fundamental nature of the perfect fifth, Rameau was able to work out a tonal structure consisting of chords based on the first, fourth, and fifth scale degrees. In this system the central chord on the first degree is attended by one a fifth above, and another a fifth below.

Chapter 2

Ex. 15.

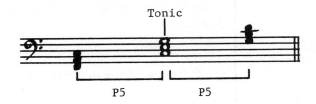

The central chord of this structure is called the *tonic*, the one a fifth above the *dominant*, and the one a fifth below the *subdominant (sous-dominante)*.[13] Rameau was the first writer to use the term "subdominant" to refer to the fourth scale degree, and recognize the symmetrical pattern implicit in the relationship between the three primary chords of a major or minor key.

Like all natural theorists, Rameau was unable to find convincing explanations for his tonal structure in either mathematics or acoustical phenomena.[14] But the fundamental nature of tonic, dominant, and subdominant harmony is a musical fact in Western music which has been reinforced by the practices of many centuries. Consider, for example, the simple, direct, often primal response elicited by music, either popular or serious, which features chord patterns limited chiefly to the tonic, dominant, and subdominant.

natural	58. Music theorists who base their principles on phenomena such as the harmonic series are called _____ theorists.
False.	59. Rameau was a natural theorist, but Zarlino was not. (True/False) _____
True.	60. Like Zarlino, Rameau used mathematics to substantiate his theoretical position. (True/False) _____
False. (The exception is chord (3).)	61. According to Rameau's principle of inversion, all of the chords below have the same root. (True/False) _____
A-flat.	62. What is the root of chord (3) in the preceding frame? _____

63. Now try your hand at writing a fundamental bass for the example below. *(Record harmonic changes at the arrows.)*

Rameau: *Pièces de Clavecin*, Book 1 (1706)

Sarabande

Fundamental bass

(Nonharmonic tone analysis will affect the fundamental bass.)

G: Dominant

C: Tonic

F: Subdominant

64. Supply the name for each of the three principal chords below: (Key of C)

P5 ⌈ G: ————————
     ⌊ C: ————————
P5 ⌈
     ⌊ F: ————————

Subdominant.

65. Which of the three terms in the preceding frame was originated by Rameau? ————————————

Rameau was by no means alone in his search for rational explanations of harmonic and tonal phenomena. Although hardly any later theorist escaped the influence of his writings, many divergent approaches were taken. A remarkable contribution was made by the Italian violinist Tartini (1692-1770), who published in 1754 his highly speculative *Trattato di musica*.[15] In this work Tartini singlemindedly pursues the study of harmony as an exact science independent of musical feeling, artistry, or the human will. Like Rameau, he bases his theories on the harmonic series, but the sciences of mathematics and geometry take top priority. He uses geometric figures such as the line, circle and square to demonstrate his theoretical concepts. Figure 4 shows three such diagrams.[16]

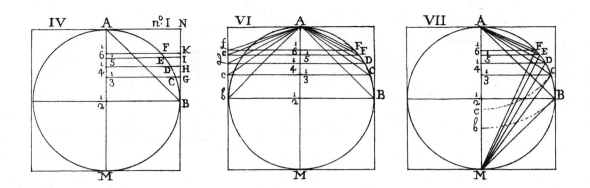

Fig. 4. Diagrams from Tartini, *Trattato di musica seconda la vera scienza dell'armonia*. Reproduced by courtesy of the Sibley Music Library, Eastman School of Music, University of Rochester.

In these figures the circle represents the unity from which Tartini feels the whole science of harmony springs. The diameter A-M represents a string which is marked off at one-half, one-third, one-fourth, one-fifth, and one-sixth of its length. From these points, sines are drawn (in diagram VII) to the circumference of the circle, and chords are drawn from these points to A and M. These dimensions are translated algebraically into sounds, and used in an attempt to prove some of his theories.[17]

But perhaps the most remarkable feature of Tartini's theory is his pioneering use of the acoustical phenomenon of difference (or combination) tones, which are sounds produced within the ear mechanism when intervals are played with sufficient volume. Tartini notes the fact that, if two adjacent tones of the harmonic series are sounded together loudly enough, a third tone *(il terzo suono)* results which is identical to the fundamental of the series.

Ex. 16.

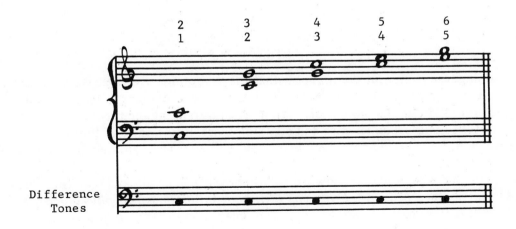

Tartini believed that the inversion of each interval in Example 16 produces the same "third tone," but in this he was mistaken in two cases. The difference tones actually produced by the major third (5:4), and the minor third (6:5) are not the fundamental, although they are closely allied to it.

Ex. 17.

Difference Tones

From the acoustical phenomenon of difference tones Tartini develops an elaborate theory of harmony in which the "third sound" is the true fundamental bass of intervals and chords. The practical results are similar to Rameau's principles of inversion and fundamental bass. Like Rameau, he sees harmony stemming from the unity expressed by the natural harmonic series, and identifies the perfect fifth as the basic determinant of the tonal harmonic system.

Another violinist and composer, Moritz Hauptmann (1792-1868) produced an equally remarkable work *Die Natur der Harmonik und der Metrik*.[18] Unlike Rameau and Tartini, Hauptmann rejects the harmonic series and mathematical proportions as the basis for his theory. He feels that it is illogical to apply the theoretically infinite harmonic series to the finite tonal material of the tempered scale. Instead he employs a philosophical approach based on Hegel's dialectical metaphysics. His basic tenet lies in the tripartite principle: *Unity-Duality-Union*. We shall cast a brief glance at his application of this principle.

The three tonal constituents of the major triad are diagramed as below:

I   III   II

C   e   G

In this diagram I = *Unity* (root), II = *Duality* (fifth), and III = *Union* (third). Thus, it is the third which unites the root and fifth into an harmonic entity.

Hauptmann sees the unity of tonality as being determined by a "triad of triads"—the tonic, dominant, and subdominant. His scheme for the tonal system established by these triads is as below:

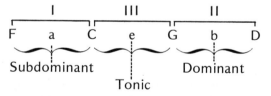

Here, his reasoning leads him to make it appear that the subdominant is the basis of the entire system whereas the tonic is the third (reuniting) element. The logic of this scheme is difficult to follow, and this is only one example of how the application of dialectical method to harmonic theory causes Hauptmann to take positions counter to musical experience and common sense. But in spite of this, his speculations are highly provocative, and they exerted considerable influence on later German theorists including Hugo Riemann.

The physicist Herman Helmholtz is renowned for establishing acoustics as a scientific study in the modern sense. His highly-regarded work *Lehre von dem Tonempfindungen als physiologische Grundlage für die Theorie der Musik* appeared in 1863.[19] Indispensable for students of acoustics, this work is of interest to music theorists as well. Helmholtz first presents a long series of experiments which establishes a firm physical foundation for the study of acoustics and musical phenomena. But there is much more. In Part III of his book, he broaches problems such as musical style, tonality, key systems, and aesthetics. Of special interest here is Helmholtz's attitude toward tonality. For him, tonality is created by the pre-eminence of a tonic plus the relations between the chords themselves. He asserts that "... *the whole mass of tones and the connection of harmonies must stand in a close and always distinctly perceptible relationship to some arbitrarily selected tonic, and that the mass of tone which forms the whole composition, must be developed from this tonic, and must finally return to it.*" (Italics are by Helmholtz.)[20] According to Helmholtz, this is "the fundamental principle for the development of the European tonal system." Thus it is a physicist who finally enunciates in a convincing manner the basic principles of tonality. Certainly this is a better statement regarding tonality than anything advanced by Fétis, who first used the term. Fétis finds tonality in "the order of melodic and harmonic facts which result from the arrangement of sounds in our major and minor scales."[21]

Zarlino, Rameau, Tartini, Hauptmann, and Helmholtz: these are five of the most important writers on harmonic theory; but there are many others who have contributed to this field. The extent of this effort is an indication of the attention given to the harmonic aspect of music during the eighteenth and nineteenth centuries. The frames which follow will check your knowledge regarding the contributions to harmonic theory which have been discussed.

Zarlino (4) Rameau (5) Tartini (3) Hauptmann (1) Helmholtz (2)	66. Write numbers in the spaces below to match each theorist with the most appropriate comment. Zarlino _____ (1) used a philosophical approach. Rameau _____ (2) based theory on scientific experiments. Tartini _____ (3) used difference tones as part of his theory. Hauptmann _____ (4) first identified the triad as an harmonic entity. Helmholtz _____ (5) first used the term "subdominant."
Rameau.	67. Name the theorist who first advanced the principle of fundamental bass. _____
False. *(The latter grows directly out of the former.)*	68. The principles of chord inversion and fundamental bass are separate notions, and have little in common. (True/False) _____
	69. Indicate the correct statement(s) by checking one of the options below: 1. Melodic and harmonic tonality are both the result of establishing the pre-eminence of a central tone.

2. Root relationships are instrumental in establishing harmonic tonality.

Both √

(1) _____ (2) _____ Both _____ Neither _____

Although none of the theorists mentioned in this chapter succeeded in giving satisfactory scientific or philosophical explanations for harmonic phenomena, there is no doubt that their work contributed to the relatively standardized dialect of harmonic functions characteristic of eighteenth- and nineteenth-century music. At any rate, their writings mirror the preoccupation with tonality and harmony so evident in this period.

We have seen some of the diverse approaches which have been taken by those who would explain the tonal order apparent in traditional music. Your attention has been directed to these writings to give you a sense of the pre-eminent role played by harmony and tonality. This is revealed not only by the amount and variety of serious speculation devoted to harmonic theory, but also by the music itself. Harmonic influence is felt in all aspects of traditional music. Melody, for example, is often little more than the linear expression of chords,[22] and form is delineated by harmonic relations in many cases. The form-defining function of harmony is so vital that a few remarks on this subject are appropriate here.

Music is divided into phrases, phrase-groups, parts, etc. in order that musical ideas occur in digestible portions. The listener's capacity for assimilation and the limitation of his attention span require punctuations of varying degrees of finality to define time lapses of varying lengths. It is within a framework of punctuations that melodic and rhythmic patterns build form through the devices of repetition, variation, and contrast. At first glance this organization appears to be largely temporal; but to this, harmonic relations add a tonal dimension. Several factors are involved: first of all, the various cadence types—final and non-final—make possible a variety of punctuation effects. Devoid of ambiguity, the limited number of cadence types available in traditional music provides the listener with frequent opportunities for orientation. This helps explain the ease with which such music is apprehended. Secondly, the structure of tonality, with the central tonic straddled by the dominant a fifth above and the subdominant a fifth below, provides for departure from the tonic (opening harmonic progression), and return to the tonic (closing harmonic progression). This principle of harmonic departure and return is expressed on all levels of the formal structure. Finally, the contrast of tonalities created by tonicization or modulation (more or less extended) contributes to an extended formal dimension.

SUMMARY.

The intent of this chapter is chiefly to underscore the importance of harmony and tonality in Western music prior to the twentieth-century. We saw in Chapter 1 that some form of tonality is present in much of the world's music. But although harmonic implications can sometimes be detected, tonality in non-Western music is mostly a melodic phenomenon. Harmonic tonality, on the other hand, at least that type in which the tonal center is defined through chords and root relationships, evolved chiefly in European music. The tonal order which results from the structure of tonality described in this chapter, plus the consistent use of basic harmonic functions, was established during the late Renaissance and early baroque eras (ca. 1550-1700); these practices were then systematized and elaborated to the level of a science by legions of music theorists in the succeeding two centuries.

Smug chauvinism and condescension toward non-Western culture was characteristic of the attitudes held by Western people prior to the twentieth century; the supremacy of harmonic music over other types was taken for granted. More recently, however, there has been ever more frequent contact with non-Western cultures. The result is growing understanding, appreciation, and acceptance of artistic modes of expression at variance with Western tradition. This is one of the factors which helped undermine the exclusive dominance of harmonic tonality near the turn of the present century. This is a matter to which we shall return in later chapters.

Comprehension of the central position of harmonic tonality in Western music since the baroque is essential to the main purpose of this study, which is to put in perspective the final abandonment of tonality, and trace the aesthetic movements and related techniques which served as a bridge to twentieth-century music.

(1) √

70. Indicate the correct statement(s) by checking one of the options below:

1. Harmonic function is a form-defining factor in most eighteenth- and nineteenth-century music.

2. Cadences provide formal divisions in harmonic music, but often are ambiguous as to tonality.

(1) _____ (2) _____ Both _____ Neither _____

3

Classical Tonality

Preparatory to investigating tonality in music of the classical period, we shall look at one earlier example. The purpose is to show that, long before the principles of harmonic tonality were enunciated by music theorists, some European composers ordered their music in such a way that patterns of harmonic tonal structure were created. As early as the latter part of the sixteenth century a tonal plan based on the tonic-dominant relationship is apparent in many works. English composers seem to have taken the lead in this respect, and one of those whose music clearly anticipates future harmonic preoccupations is Thomas Morley. For evidence of "progressive" harmonic tendencies in Morley's music, turn to his canzonet "Sweet Nymph Come To Thy Lover,"[1] contained in Panel 1 found at the back of this book.

	(Frames 71-77 refer to Panel 1.)
	71. The opening measures, as well as the final cadence, clearly establish the tonal center of this composition as
F	_____ .

		72. Disregarding repeats, there are six principal cadences; these are identified by the circled numbers (① , ② , etc.). Indicate with a letter the tonal orientation established by each cadence.	
1. F	4. C	1. _____	4. _____
2. C	5. F	2. _____	5. _____
3. F	6. F	3. _____	6. _____

	73. The six cadences cause the tonal pendulum to swing between F and C (tonic and dominant). Due to the tonicization caused by the B-natural, cadence 2 can be analyzed in the key of C major; cadence 4, however, is in the key of
minor	C _____ .

74. The cadences in Morley's canzonet establish a macro-tonal* scheme of tonic-dominant, the same relationship which is prevalent in later music. In addition to the basic tonic-dominant emphasis, the smaller chord-to-chord harmonic relations point to usages which become virtually standard practice in eighteenth- and nineteenth-century music. To see this, we shall analyze the harmonic implications of the first phrase, utilizing symbols developed much later to represent harmonic function.

Complete the harmonic analysis of phrase 1.

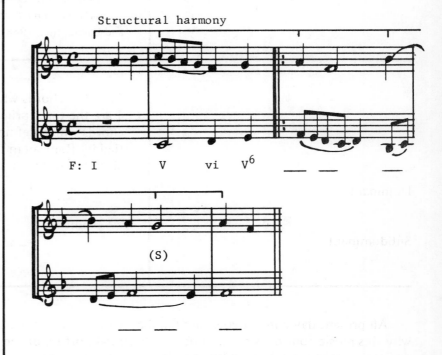

---

*The term "macro-tonal" refers to larger tonal relations produced by cadences, and the tonality of parts, sections, movements, etc.

75. Of course the harmonic implications of two-part writing are often ambiguous, so chords other than those identified in the preceding frame could be named. The next-to-the-last chord, for example, could be analyzed as vii° as well as V^6. Such alternates, however, would not affect the purpose of this analysis, which is to show the clear harmonic organization underlying the music.

List the number of occurrences for each chord as analyzed in the preceding frame.

I _____   V _____

IV _____   vi _____

I   4   V   3
IV 1   vi 2

I-V-I-IV-V-I

76. Frequency of occurrence (iteration) is an important factor for the establishment of tonal structure, but even more significant is the choice of those chords which perform a structural role.* In Frame 74, the six chords having structural significance are identified; write Roman numerals for these in the order they occur.

___ ___ ___ ___ ___ ___

_____

*For information concerning structural harmony consult the author's *Harmonic Materials in Tonal Music,* 2 vols. (Boston: Allyn and Bacon, Inc., 1968), I:204-09.

Dominant

Subdominant

77. The chords which have structural importance in phrase 1 are the three primary chords (I, IV, and V). These are the chords which define the structure of tonality ultimately codified by Rameau in the eighteenth century. Complete the chart below by writing the names for the two missing chords.

Tonic —
⎡ _____
⎢ (P 5th above)
⎣ _____
(P 5th below)

All present-day concert goers are familiar with music of the baroque and classical periods. The reasons why this music continues to comprise a substantial portion of the recital and concert repertoire are not difficult to understand. In addition to its vigor, melodic charm, and generally optimistic character, its fairly limited tonal and rhythmic vocabulary make it easy to apprehend—relatively simple demands are made on the listener, and total involvement is not required. But most important is the high degree of orderliness built into every aspect of the music. A superior degree of orderliness is especially characteristic of music from the classical period (ca. 1750-1830). In this music, form dominates content and the ideals of clarity, precision, and restraint take precedence over the expression of individual emotions. Such is the spirit of classicism. Music, which is by nature abstract, is rendered more concrete—thus easier to assimilate —by the order and symmetry basic to the classical ideal.

We shall now consider the various ways harmony and tonality contribute to order in classical music. The following six points have a bearing on this matter; examine each carefully.

HARMONIC ORDER IN CLASSICAL MUSIC

1. The structure of tonality is itself a form of order.
2. The limited number of cadence types facilitates tonal and functional orientation.
3. Consistent root relationships establish clear harmonic functions which result in a high degree of predictability.
4. The limited (mostly diatonic) chord vocabulary is easily assimilated.
5. Mostly diatonic root relationships with relatively infrequent modulations to distant keys are used.

6. Melodic chromaticism which is incidental to generally diatonic harmony is more prevalent than harmonic chromaticism. Most harmonic chromaticism is embellishing or nonfunctional.

To further your understanding of classical harmonic tonality, we shall analyze a typical example (Panel 2), with particular reference to the six points stated above.

A	*(Frames 78-100 refer to Panel 2.)* 78. The composition in Panel 2 is a simple ternary form with coda. The major formal divisions (A-B-A′) are shown, and the 22 principal cadences are identified by the circled numbers. Begin the analysis by examining the tonality established in the first few measures, and also by the final cadence (22). It is evident that the principal tonality of this composition is _____ major.
F♯ minor	79. The middle section (B) begins at measure 17. The tonality at this point is _____ .
A major	80. The final section of the ternary form (A′) begins at measure 44. The tonality here is _____ .
	81. We now have identified tentatively the macro-tonal organization as A - f♯ - A. To verify this and to observe further subtleties, we must analyze in greater detail. Because cadences provide points of tonal organization, we shall direct our attention to the 22 principal cadences which have been identified in Panel 2. Complete the list below (use abbreviations such as PA for perfect authentic, IA for imperfect authentic, H for half, etc.).

PART ONE (A)

			Cadence	Key	Type
1	A	H	1	A	H
2	A	PA	2	_____	_____
3	A	H	3	_____	_____
4	A	PA	4	_____	_____

dominant

5	f♯	H
6	D	PA
7	D	PA
8	e	IA
9	f♯	IA
10	f♯	IA
11	f♯	H
12	f♯	PA
13	f♯	PA
14	A	IA

F♯ minor

15	A	H
16	A	PA
17	A	H
18	A	PA
19	A	PA
20	A	PA
21	A	PA
22	A	PA

82. Although cadence 3 in the preceding frame could be analyzed as PA in E major, tonicization of E (V_3^4/V) is the preferred analysis. The analysis in the preceding frame shows that the opening section is entirely in the key of A major, and that the principal harmonic motion fluctuates between tonic and _____.

83. Tabulate the cadences in part two.

PART TWO (B)

Cadence	Key	Type
5	f♯	H
6	_____	_____
7	_____	_____
8	_____	_____
9	_____	_____
10	_____	_____
11	_____	_____
12	_____	_____
13	_____	_____
14	_____	_____

84. The analysis in the preceding frame reveals that the most prevalent key in part two is _____.

85. Tabulate the cadences in the remainder of the composition.

PART THREE (A') and CODA

Cadence	Key	Type
15	_____	_____
16	_____	_____
17	_____	_____
18	_____	_____
19	_____	_____
20	_____	_____
21	_____	_____
22	_____	_____

86. Our analysis of cadences has revealed only three types of cadences. Check the type which occurs most frequently in the composition as a whole (Frames 81, 83 and 85).

Perfect authentic _____

Imperfect authentic _____

Half _____

---

closely *(or nearly)*

87. The number of times the various cadences occur in each key is shown below:

	PA	IA	H	Total
A	8	1	4	13
f♯	2	2	2	6
D	2	-	-	2
e	-	1	-	1

The prevalence of cadences in the tonic key of A major, and the close relation of all other keys produce a tightly knit tonal structure. The keys other than A major all occur on diatonic scale degrees of the central tonality; such keys are called _____ related keys.

---

relative

88. The analysis of tonalities through cadences confirms the macro-tonal scheme of A - f♯ - A. The example below represents more completely the tonal organization.

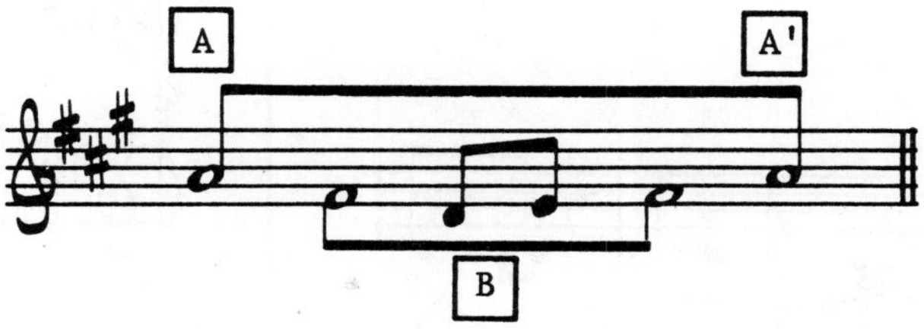

Simple, balanced structures such as this are typical of classical tonality. Clarity, symmetry, and easily apprehended relationships are in accord with classical ideals of formal balance.

The principal key of the middle section (F-sharp minor) is called the _____ minor key of A major.

---

89. Now that the macro-tonal organization has been laid bare, a few phrases will be analyzed in detail to observe the

smaller chord-by-chord function of the harmony. The first eight measures constitute a two-phrase period. The cadences already have been analyzed, so these chords are shown in the example which follows. Complete the harmonic analysis by writing appropriate chord symbols in the spaces provided.

Mozart: *Sonata,* K. 576

A: I V$^4_3$ V$^4_2$ I^6 V$^6_5$

I IV I$^6_4$ V

I V$^4_3$ V$^4_2$ I^6 vii$^{d7}_{}$/vi vii^{d7}/V

I$^6_4$ V^7 I

(No response required.)

90. The number of occurrences for each chord as analyzed in the preceding frame is shown below:

I	8
V and V^7	7
IV	1
vii^{d7}/vi	1
vii^{d7}/V	1

Not only do tonic and dominant harmonies predominate to a marked degree, but they occur in important structural positions. The latter is an example of "formal" stress; the former is stress by "iteration."

The above tabulation shows the extent of tonic-dominant harmony in this phrase.

91. Supply the Roman numeral analysis for the following example. *(Remember that you have already analyzed the cadence of the second phrase as perfect authentic in D major. Thus, a modulation is involved in this example.)*

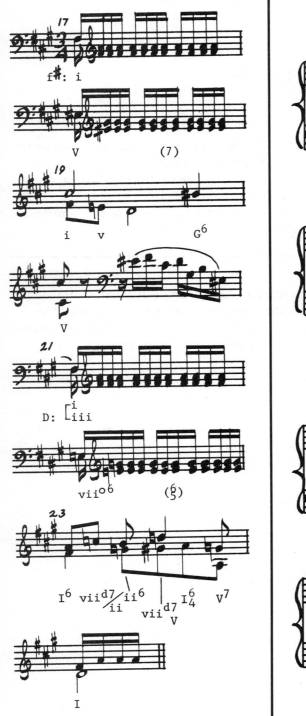

Mozart: *Sonata,* K. 576

92. The two phrases in the preceding frame contain greater harmonic variety than the phrases in Frame 89. We shall look closely at the harmonic structure of each phrase.

Chapter 3

2. *(See the next frame.)*

Which tonal diagram below best portrays the harmonic structure of the first phrase in Frame 91? (1 or 2) _____

No. *(Other factors such as rhythmic position and surrounding chords are usually more important.)*

93. Diagram 2 in the preceding frame is best, because it visually represents the harmonic function of the second chord which is to embellish the tonic. Also, the incidental passing role of the v⁶ chord in measure 19 is better portrayed than in diagram 1.

Is the structural importance of a chord determined by its duration? _____

(No response required.)

94. Further reduction of diagram 2 in Frame 92 reveals the three chords which constitute the harmonic backbone of the phrase.

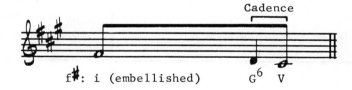

Thus the basic harmonic structure here is tonic (embellished) followed by a cadence (G^6 - V).

---

1. *(See the next frame.)*

95. Which diagram below best portrays the harmonic structure of the second phrase in Frame 91? (1 or 2) _____

(1)

D: iii   vii°⁶ I⁶ vii^d7/ii ii⁶ vii^d7/V V⁷ I

(2)

D: iii   vii°⁶ I⁶ vii^d7/ii ii⁶ vii^d7/V I⁶₄ V⁷ I

96. Tonal diagram 2 in the preceding frame is undesirable because it overstresses the importance of chords which have embellishing rather than structural importance. The two secondary dominants and the tonic six-four chord merely serve to embellish the chords which follow. Further reduction shows the harmonic substructure of the phrase.

D: iii–I⁶   ii⁶   V⁷   I

    Mindful of the close relation between the supertonic and subdominant chords, the diagram above suggests a basic tonic-subdominant-dominant-tonic organization. This harmonic pattern is very prevalent in the music of classical composers, particularly Haydn and Mozart.

(No response required.)

97. Tones which are not included in the diatonic scale are called *chromatic* alterations. In music of the classical era, such tones occur chiefly as melodic embellishments of diatonic tones, or as constituents of harmonies which serve as embellishments to structural (usually diatonic) chords. Functional uses of chromatic tones occurred more frequently as the harmonic idiom evolved during the nineteenth century, and these uses will be examined later. The Mozart *Adagio* which we are now analyzing contains several instances of both melodic and harmonic chromaticism. Circle each note in the example below which is *not* included in the A major scale.

Adagio

A:

D♯

passing tone

---

98. List the chromatic note(s) you circled in the preceding frame which have melodic (not harmonic) function. _____

99. The note D♯ (measure 7) merely fills in the whole-step E–D, and has no influence on the harmony. This note is a nonharmonic tone; specifically it is called a chromatic
_____ _____.

100. All chromatic notes other than D♯ in Frame 97 have harmonic function. These are shown below with the analysis which already has been made (Frame 89).

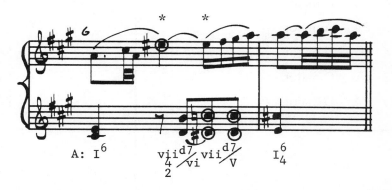

A: I⁶   vii°$^{d7}_{4\ 2}$/vi vii°^{d7}/V   I⁶₄

	The two chords (at the asterisks) in which chromatic notes appear have (structural/embellishing) _____ function.
embellishing	

The composition in Panel 3 is a "Menuetto" from Haydn's *Sonata No. 15* in D Major for piano. This piece is in ternary form (ABA), and each of the three parts consists of a smaller ternary form. The formal analysis is indicated in the example. Our concern is to assess the contribution of tonality to the formal design and to note the harmonic construction of smaller units (phrases and periods).

	(Frames 101-116 refer to Panel 3.) 101. The Menuetto (A) both begins and ends in the key of D major; this, then, is the principal tonality. The Trio (B) both begins and ends in the key of _____.
D minor	

	102. Even if we should stop at this point, the principal tonal relationship between Parts A and B has been observed.
	
	   Menuetto *Trio* *Menuetto (D.C.)*
	     [A] [B] [A]
	  D major D minor D major
	
	The principal contrast between A and B is not that of different tonalities, but rather change of _____.

mode	

			103. But there are keys in addition to D major and D minor which contribute to the formal design and remain to be discovered. To do this, complete the list of cadences and keys contained in the Menuetto (A).
			Measure *Cadence* *Key*
4	IA	D major	4 IA D major
8	PA	A major	8 _____ _____
14	H	D major	14 _____ _____
18	IA	D major	18 _____ _____
22	PA	D major	22 _____ _____

104. In the preceding frame you may have analyzed measure 8 as a half cadence in D major (preceded by three measures

of dominant tonicization). Indeed, the A major triad in measure 8 serves as the dominant of D major when the period is repeated; but it also serves as the tonic in A major when proceeding to the following phrase. As in all such situations, the choice between tonicization and modulation is arbitrary. In either case, the key of D major is enlarged by a gesture toward the dominant tonal area.

The second part (b) of the Menuetto (measures 9-14) begins in the key of _____.

A major

---

105. Complete the list of cadences and keys contained in the Trio (B).

Measure	Cadence	Key
28	PA	D minor
37	_____	_____
45	_____	_____
55	_____	_____

28 PA D minor
37 PA F major
45 H D minor
55 PA D minor

---

106. Whereas the two keys employed in the Menuetto (A) have a tonic-dominant relationship, the two keys employed in the Trio (B) have a tonic-_____ relationship.

mediant

---

107. The relation between the tonalities and form is shown in the diagram below:

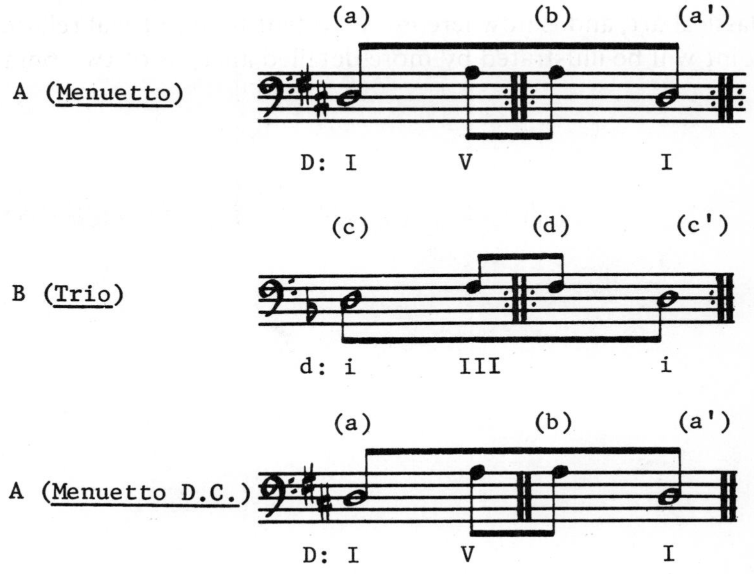

(No response required.)

108. Within each of the three principal parts (ABA), a new key is established *before* the contrasting section begins. Thus, there is a mild conflict between form and tonality. It is significant, however, that each of the contrasting middle sections (a*b*a and c*d*c) is in a key *other than the "tonic."*

Another representation of the tonalities shows the relation of each to the central key of D major.

All of these are closely-related keys. (True/False)
_____

False. *(See the next frame.)*

---

109. The means by which the foreign keys of D minor and F major are brought into the tonal orbit of D major are typical of harmonic practice during the classical era. Although not closely related, the parallel keys of D major and D minor are closely identified through their common tonic note (change of mode is not a modulation, a new tonic note is not established). But change of mode opens up a new set of closely-related keys all of which are foreign to the original tonic.

(No response required.)

Our analysis has revealed a symmetrical pattern of key relations which closely parallels the larger formal units, and only slightly less so the smaller units. This sort of formal and tonal balance is a hallmark of classical tonal practices. The concern for balance, and easily-perceived structures is apparent in all aspects of classical art, and is nowhere more evident than in tonal relations and harmonic configurations. The latter point will be illustrated by more detailed analysis of two phrases taken from Panel 3.

110. The final two phrases of Haydn's Menuetto are shown below along with a harmonic analysis.

Haydn: *Sonata No. 15* in D Major ("Menuetto")

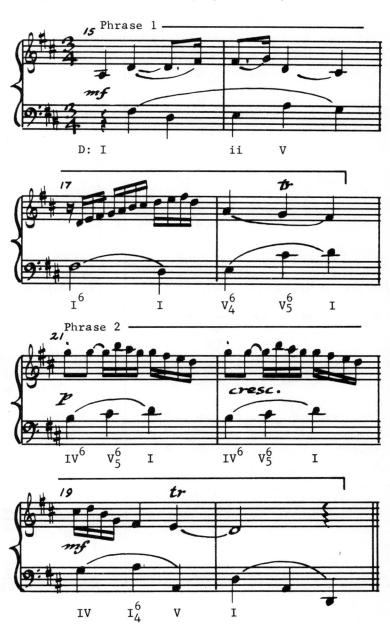

List (by chord symbol) the initial and final chord of each phrase.

	Initial	Final
Phrase 1	_____	_____
Phrase 2	_____	_____

D: (bracket spanning Phrase 1 and Phrase 2)

1. I - I
2. IV⁶ - I

---

111.   The two phrases quoted in the preceding frame contain four different chords. To indicate the relative importance of these chords, the *number of beats* each sounds is tabulated below:

	No. of Beats
I	13
ii	1
IV	3
$V^{(7)}$	7

This reveals once again the importance of the tonic-dominant axis in classical tonality. Even the subdominant chord fails in most cases to come close to these two in either frequency or structural use. But the two phrases just analyzed close out the Menuetto, and also the entire composition. Strong tonal orientation is to be expected at such a location in the form. To see another facet of classical harmonic practice, let us look at two phrases which occur at the time the ear is led from the key of F major back to the key of D minor, a place tonal instability is to be expected.

(No response required.)

112.   The first phrase is analyzed in F major and the second in D minor. These two phrases serve to re-establish the key of D minor after an excursion into F major.

Haydn: *Sonata No. 15* in D major ("Menuetto")

Phrase 2

vii$\frac{d7}{iii}$ iii   ⎡vi$^6_4$

d: ⎣i$^6_4$ V^7

VI   ii$^{\circ4}_3$ V

During the first phrase the harmony becomes (more/less)
_____ functional in F major.

less

---

113.   After the unambiguous initial tonic chord, the harmony moves first to the supertonic, and then to the mediant
chords (both tonicized). By the use of several tones not in
the key, and also by the avoidance of primary chords, tonal
feeling in F major is weakened.
    With regard to phrase 2, would it be correct to describe
the harmonic function as a prolonged dominant emphasis in
D minor? _____

Yes.

---

114.   The harmonic function of phrase 2 in Frame 112 is to
prepare for the key of D minor by stressing the dominant.
Notice that, except in the third measure, the note A is
stressed in the bass. The first chord (tonic six-four) merely
retards the appearance of the dominant seventh which follows, and the harmony in the third measure (VI-ii$^{\circ4}_3$) serves

nonharmonic	an embellishing function. As in the preceding phrase, there are several altered tones (G$\sharp$, F$\sharp$, and D$\sharp$). These tones have (harmonic/nonharmonic) _____ function.
dominant	115. The two phrases quoted in Frame 112 contrast with those in Frame 110 by containing a higher percentage of secondary triads, less functional harmony, and more altered tones. In this way tonal fluidity is produced. Here, the tonality of F major is undermined and that of D minor gradually established. One additional subtlety remains to be noted. Observe that phrase 1 in Frame 112 closes with the mediant triad in F; this is the same as the minor _____ chord in D minor.
This is a thought-provoking question for which there is no single correct answer. Any of the measures in the second phrase could be cited.	116. The chord referred to in the preceding frame could well be analyzed as a common chord (F: iii = d: v). This chord is not quite the *major* dominant which eventually is used to propel the music into D minor, but it certainly serves as a link between the two keys, and contributes to the smooth harmonic transition. At what point in these two phrases do you feel a firm commitment has been made for the return to D minor? _____

SUMMARY.

We have seen that varying degrees of tonal stability serve different formal purposes. Such fluctuations also call forth a variety of emotional responses. Thus, the interplay of tonal stability and instability contributes to the ebb and flow of dramatic tensions—a vital feature of classical music's rhetoric. Because of the relatively modest dimension of the harmonic environment, and also the points of tonal reference supplied by frequent cadences, it is easy for the listener to chart the music's course. Typically, periods of tonal ambiguity are quite short; merely for fleeting moments the listener is cast adrift, uncertain where the next tonal landfall will appear.

117.   Although incomplete, the various analyses we have made in this chapter should be sufficient to test the validity of the six points concerning harmonic order in classical music listed on pages 57-58. Check below whether or not you believe each point has been verified.

		Yes	No
1.	Harmonic structure employed as a constructive device	____	____
2.	Limited cadence types	____	____
3.	Consistent harmonic functions	____	____
4.	Mostly diatonic chord vocabulary	____	____
5.	Mostly diatonic root relations	____	____
6.	Mostly melodic or non-functional chromaticism	____	____

Yes, in all cases.
(Of course, you are entitled to disagree.)

The analyses conducted in this chapter highlight the simple tonal order, which, along with form, provides the structural basis of classical music. Certainly, much more complex tonal relations occur. But rare is the case in which the fundamental role of tonic, subdominant, and dominant harmonies is not clearly evident, or in which chromaticism performs other than an embellishing role. Such is the nature of classical harmonic tonality. But the harmonic idiom practiced by classical composers served merely as the basis for an extraordinary development. By the end of the classical era, tonal harmony was far from exhausted; vast resources remained to be discovered and exploited during the succeeding decades.

Classicism waned soon after 1800, and was followed by the movement called romanticism. We shall observe in the next chapter how classical tonality expanded as a result of the need, generated by romantic ideals, for a richer palette of harmonic colors.

4

Expanded Tonality

Romanticism was spawned by the social upheavals of the late eighteenth century, particularly the French revolution which began in 1789. The concepts of liberty and individual worth find expression in all romantic art forms including literature, art, and music. Jean Jacques Rousseau (1712-1778) is generally regarded as the father of romanticism, and his works show the preoccupation with nature, and the rebellion against established social and political order which are essential features of romanticism.[1] Other early manifestations occur in the works of the German poets and dramatists Schiller (1759-1805) and Goethe (1749-1832). With its emphasis on imagination and emotional expression, romanticism was a reaction against classicism. Rather than classic symmetry, equilibrium, and perfection, romantic artists cherished the expression of individual passion; the result was growing freedom from formal restraint and heightened expression.

In music, the romantic era saw dramatic expansion of tonal and technical resources. Although classical forms such as the symphony and sonata continued to be used, they were greatly distended to accommodate more varied and higher-charged emotional display. Also, new forms evolved. The *symphonic poem,* for example, was developed by Liszt as a vehicle for music with dramatic or programmatic content, and the *concert overture* supplied the need for an orchestral "character piece." Color resources, too, were enlarged by introducing new instruments into the orchestra, and by improving the technical capacities of the others. The orchestra was the favored medium of romantic composers; in their hands it became ever larger, and the instruments were treated with more pronounced individuality. The peculiar tonal and technical characteristics of each instrument were exploited for greater expressive effect.

But our concern here is with harmonic resources. We wish to observe briefly the evolution of harmony in the romantic era. In this connection, Beethoven (1770-1827) has special importance. His works bridge the gap between classicism and romanticism. For him, as well as for virtually all nineteenth-century composers, harmony continued to be an essential ingredient, and supplied abundantly the fresh tonal resources needed for the ever more personal and subjective expression called forth by the romantic ideal.

The four points below summarize the evolution of the harmonic idiom during the romantic era:

1. Although tonality was as strong a force as in classical music, its boundaries were continually expanded. This was accomplished by more frequent tonicizations (secondary dominants and modulations) to more distant keys.

2. The harmonic vocabulary was enlarged by more frequent use of altered chords and extended tertian sonorities (7th, 9th, 11th, and 13th chords). A larger proportion of active (dissonant) sonorities was used. This caused a higher tension level and greater sense of unrest.

3. Chromaticism was used more extensively not only melodically, but also within the harmony.

4. Root relations were less diatonic than in classical music; they reflect the greater use of altered chords. There was also greater use of third-relation harmony (both diatonic and chromatic).

Several examples will now be examined to illuminate various features of harmonic tonality in romantic music.

(Frames 118-126 refer to Panel 4.)

118. The composition in Panel 4 consists of an independent phrase (which serves as an introduction) followed by three additional phrases—a small ternary form.

Introduction 𝄆 A 𝄆 B A′ 𝄇

In Panel 4, the form is shown as well as a harmonic analysis of all but part B. You will be asked later to supply the analysis for this phrase. To begin, note the tonal relation between the first two phrases.

The change from C-sharp minor in the introduction to D-flat major in part A is best described as (change of key/modulation/change of mode) _____ .

change of mode

119. Enharmonic change here is merely for simpler notation. The aural effect is of a modal shift from minor to major; the tonal center remains the same.

Use Roman numerals to indicate the principal harmonic movement in the first two phrases (section A and B).

c♯ : i - V
D♭: I - V

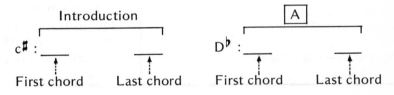

Introduction | A |

c♯ : ___ ___   D♭ : ___ ___
First chord Last chord   First chord Last chord

120. Chords which are tonicized by secondary dominants have added harmonic significance.[2] Expand the analysis of the preceding frame by writing on the staff *the roots of those chords which are tonicized* (preceded either by a dominant or leading-tone chord); supply also the appropriate Roman numeral for each chord.

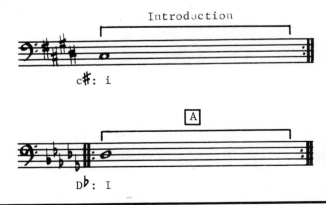

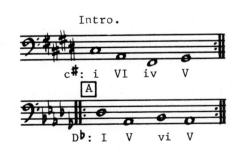 Intro.
c♯: i VI iv V
| A |
D♭: I V vi V

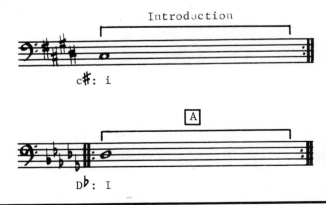 Introduction
c♯: i
| A |
D♭: I

(Answer is located below the example in Panel 4.)

121. Because the activity of secondary dominants has specific direction, these chords impart a high degree of motivation to the harmony. Part of the forward thrust of Schumann's composition results from frequent tonicizations.

Your task now is to supply the chord symbols for part B. Begin by covering the solution to this analysis, which for your convenience is placed at the bottom of Panel 4. Note: *Analyze in the keys indicated in Panel 4.*

122. Your analysis in the preceding frame may differ somewhat from the one supplied and yet be equally valid. Choice of chord symbols frequently depends on how nonharmonic tones are interpreted, and there are few absolute criteria to rely upon. As analyzed, there is a total of 16 chord symbols in part B. Of these, nine represent chords which have dominant function. (This includes secondary dominants and diatonic dominant and leading tone chords.) Thus, more than half of the chords in part B are active; they have dominant function. Increased use of active chords and spread of dominant functions throughout the phrase is a hallmark of much romantic music. Even casual reference to the classical examples quoted earlier will show how much more persistent dominant function is in romantic music. Of course, no new process is involved here; it is simply a matter of increased emphasis on active harmonic entities.

(No response required.)

123. The example below shows the harmonic structure of the entire composition.

This diagram reveals that each part begins and ends with either tonic or _____ harmony.

dominant

---

124. In the example below, all but the most essential structural harmony has been stripped away.

From this, you can appreciate the degree of influence tonic and dominant harmony continues to exert on the shaping of tonal structure. But there is another important point to be made: part B closes with the F major triad ($b^\flat$:V). If analyzed in D-flat major, this chord is a(n) (diatonic/altered) _____ mediant triad.

altered

125.   Refer again to Panel 4. Notice that the climax of the entire composition occurs at the end of part B (measure 24). At this point the highest pitch is reached, *and the most colorful harmony is sounded.* The F major triad can be analyzed in D-flat major as a *chromatic mediant.*[3] This chord has a slightly dissonant relation with the chord which follows.

The notes which produce the false relation dissonance are _____ in chord 1, and _____ in chord 2.

Chord 1:   A♮
Chord 2:   A♭

126.   In the Schumann composition (Panel 4), the potential chromatic mediant (D♭:III) is followed immediately by the dominant seventh chord. This emphasizes the dissonant relation of these chords. The root movement here is up by the interval of a minor _____ .

third

Our analysis of the composition in Panel 4 has shown three things:

1.   Tonic and dominant harmony continues to play a major role in establishing tonality.
2.   Tonicization provided by secondary dominants is generally more extensive in romantic music than in music of the classical era.
3.   Third-relation harmony is used at a crucial moment in the composition. This points to the importance of such harmony in the tonal vocabulary of the romantic period.

Beginning with Beethoven, nineteenth-century composers showed an increasing interest in third-relation harmony (both diatonic and chromatic). Such harmony is manifested both in large tonal relationships (modulation, and between large formal units), and also in root movements within the phrase. Chromatic mediant relationships, in particular, result in expanded tonal resources and undermine somewhat the pre-eminent functional role of fifth-related harmonies.

To continue our demonstration of the expansion of tonality during the romantic era, we shall turn to a composition by Frederic Chopin.

(Frames 127-135 refer to Panel 5.)
127.   The small one-part form of the composition in Panel 5 divides into three four-measure phrases; the beginning of each phrase is identified by a circled number. In phrases one and two, the melody sets out from the note B to trace an arch curve; in the third phrase, an ascending line is traced from B to the tonic E. Each phrase begins with the same chord. (True/False) _____

True.

Phrase 1.

128. Rather than pose a problem in analysis, our purpose here is to make observations regarding harmonic relations. Thus, an harmonic analysis is supplied. Of course, in music as chromatic as this, a variety of approaches may be taken. The analysis given is but one of several possibilities, and will be qualified somewhat as we move on.

In which phrase occurs the simplest (most diatonic) harmonic expression of the tonic key of E major? (Phrase 1, 2, or 3) _____

---

129. Even those composers who exploited chromaticism to a notable degree (Chopin and Liszt, for example) generally affirm the tonality near the beginning of a work with strong, unambiguous harmony.* In this case, the first phrase leaves no doubt as to the tonality; very few altered tones are used, and tonic, dominant, and subdominant harmonies dominate the phrase.

The analysis shows a shift of tonality to A-flat major in measure seven and a return to E major in the following measure. The two keys are represented below:

E   A♭

True.
$(A^\flat \, C \, E^\flat = G^\sharp \, B^\sharp \, D^\sharp)$

These two keys bear a chromatic mediant relationship to one another. (True/False) _____

---
*But see Frame 136.

---

130. The modulation to A-flat constitutes a tonicization of the third scale degree of E major (with enharmonic change), and occurs at the climax of the composition (measure 8). This is identical to the tonal structure observed in Panel 4. Also similar to the Schumann example is the hasty return to the tonic key through the dominant chord (at the end of measure 8). The harmonic movement in measure 8 from $A^\flat$:I to E:V^7 is an example of chromatic third-relation harmony. (True/False) _____

True.

---

131. Third-relation harmony is used extensively in this work and contributes greatly to the expansion of tonality. We shall now focus our attention on this aspect. The example

below shows a reduced and simplified version of the principal chords in phrase 2. *(The chords are all shown in root position.)*

Chord 3 is analyzed as a secondary dominant because it serves to tonicize the chord which follows. Its relation to the preceding chord (V), however, is that of a chromatic _____ .

mediant

---

132.   Because it is tonicized, the C-major chord (4) has increased status. It could, in fact, be analyzed as a temporary tonic. But what is important here is its relation to the tonic key of E major.

The relationship between these two chords is the same as that between chords 2 and 3 in Frame 131.   (True/False)

_____

True.

---

133.   In each of the two chromatic mediant relationships noted thus far, the chord roots are a major third apart (B-G, and E-C). Another chromatic mediant relationship occurs between chords 4 and 5 (Frame 131). In this case the roots are a _____ third apart.

minor

134. The first five chords in Frame 131 are arranged below to reveal the symmetrical tonal structure which they produce.

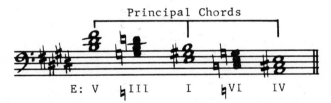

The perfect fifth relationships of tonic-dominant and tonic-subdominant provide the foundation of this structure; and chromaticism of the altered chords contributes color without disturbing the tonal equilibrium. How many new tones are brought into the tonal orbit of E by the two chromatic mediants? _____

Three.
(G♮, C♮, and D♮)

---

135. Any major scale contains seven of the twelve tones of the chromatic scale. The two altered chords shown in the diagram of the preceding frame increase to ten the number of tones which are absorbed into the tonal system.

Chopin's *Prelude* (Panel 5) contains a considerable amount of chromaticism (especially in phrases 2 and 3). This chromaticism results mostly from (harmonic/melodic) _____ action.

harmonic

In addition to his dazzling career as a virtuoso pianist, Franz Liszt (1811-1886) produced a large number of compositions. The most important of these are for piano or orchestra. His music is an amalgamation of several influences: his Hungarian heritage of national (Gypsy) melodies, early classical training in Vienna under the direction of Czerny and Salieri, and the literary-motivated romanticism of his age. He was also allied with Wagner in the radical artistic movement called *Zukunftsmusik* (music of the future). This refers mainly to the synthesis of the arts, which, for Liszt, meant the liberalization of form to accommodate literary or philosophical programmatic elements. In fact, most of his music is programmatic in either a literal or emotive sense. He is the creator of the symphonic poem, perhaps the most characteristic orchestral form of the romantic period.

Liszt extended still further the harmonic innovations made by Chopin. In his music, the tonal horizon is pushed still further away; more altered chords are used, modulations occur more frequently, and tonally ambiguous passages are more numerous and extended. Some of his late works, in particular, show that he was close to abandoning tonality in favor of free tonal associations dictated by the music's emotive course. In this, Liszt's achievements have revolutionary significance. By stressing harmony's purely coloristic role he helped weaken classical functional relationships, and thereby provided a stepping-stone to impressionism, and ultimately to twentieth-century music.

To observe some of Liszt's harmonic usages, we shall look at a few brief examples. The first is an excerpt from the *Sonetto del Petrarca*, No. 104, which is in Panel 6.

Diminished seventh chord.

(Frames 136-146 refer to Panel 6.)
136. In Liszt's *Sonetto del Petrarca,* the basic tonality of E major is not fully established until measure seven. The material leading up to this point reveals some novel aspects of Liszt's harmonic style, so we will begin by observing how the introductory measures are constructed. A glance at the first four measures reveals the sequential structure which is employed. The example below shows only the lefthand part, and the notes which occur *on the beats* are indicated by the arrows.

Name the chord type which is formed by the indicated notes. _____

Mm⁷
(The major-minor seventh chord is also called a dominant seventh. Here it is in 2nd inversion.)

---

137. The sequence units are related by minor thirds to produce a diminished seventh chord. But in addition to this, the diminished seventh chord is used vertically to begin each sequence unit. Each sequence unit contains two chords. The first unit is shown in the example below, and the quality of the first chord is indicated. Indicate in the space provided the *quality* of the second chord.

d⁷ _____

---

138. The major-minor seventh chord is active and normally requires resolution. The first four measures contain six such chords. Indicate the keys into which each of these chords would resolve *if they were to function as dominant seventh chords.*

Chapter 4

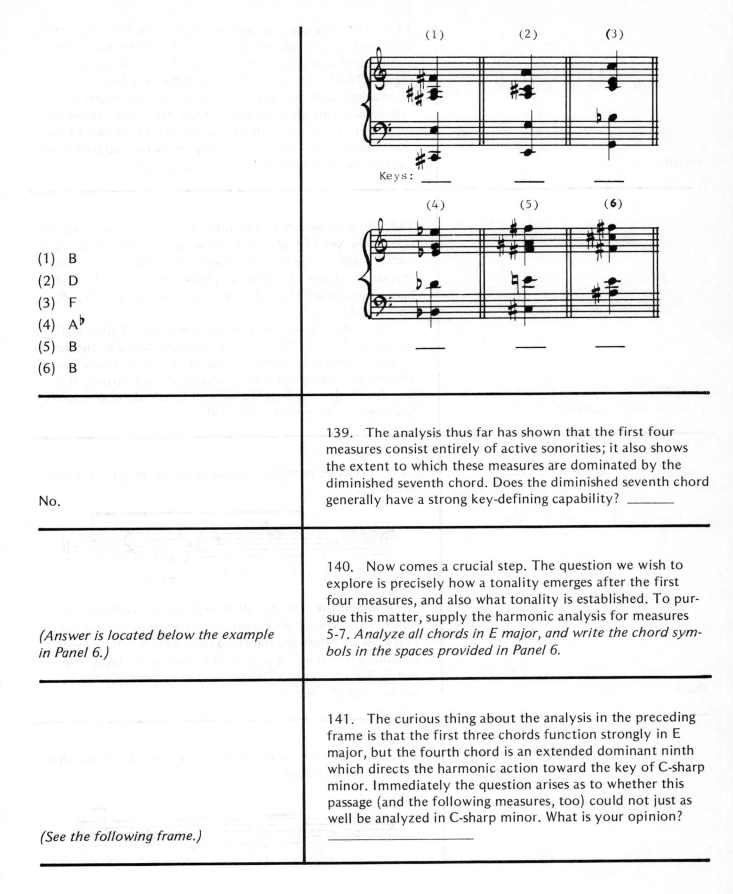

Keys: ____ ____ ____

(1) B

(2) D

(3) F

(4) A♭

(5) B

(6) B

____ ____ ____

No.

139. The analysis thus far has shown that the first four measures consist entirely of active sonorities; it also shows the extent to which these measures are dominated by the diminished seventh chord. Does the diminished seventh chord generally have a strong key-defining capability? _____

(Answer is located below the example in Panel 6.)

140. Now comes a crucial step. The question we wish to explore is precisely how a tonality emerges after the first four measures, and also what tonality is established. To pursue this matter, supply the harmonic analysis for measures 5-7. *Analyze all chords in E major, and write the chord symbols in the spaces provided in Panel 6.*

(See the following frame.)

141. The curious thing about the analysis in the preceding frame is that the first three chords function strongly in E major, but the fourth chord is an extended dominant ninth which directs the harmonic action toward the key of C-sharp minor. Immediately the question arises as to whether this passage (and the following measures, too) could not just as well be analyzed in C-sharp minor. What is your opinion?

_____

142. These measures as well as much of the opening section could indeed be analyzed in the key of C-sharp minor. One of the most significant aspects of this harmony is tonal ambiguity. Neither E major nor C-sharp minor achieves complete dominance over the other. Some persons might hear one tonal orientation, some the other. Here, the expansion of tonality to include two keys is the significant fact to note. The two keys (E major and C-sharp minor) are related to one another as a major and its _____ minor.

relative

(No response required.)

143. In spite of tonal ambiguity, we shall continue to analyze in the key of E major. There is strong evidence to support E major as the central tonality: the composition ends in this key, and several important phrases begin with E major harmony (consult the complete score, measures 7, 21, 38, 45, and 68).

An analysis is supplied for the remainder of the opening section in Panel 6. This analysis keeps all chords in the key of E major. Obviously, other approaches could be taken. Tonicizations, for example, could be shown as modulations. But this does little to change the view of tonal relations—merely the degree of emphasis is affected.

144. The basic harmonic action of measures 7-14 is shown below:

E: I   vi   ii   ♮III   V⁷   I

Roots of the principal structural chords are shown as half notes. These chords are identified as having structural importance because they are tonicized (preceded by chords with dominant function); any chord thus treated is elevated in status. Both the vi and ♮III are related to the tonic (E) by the interval of a minor _____.

third

145. The harmony of measures 15-21 is much simpler than that which precedes it.

E: III   ii⁷   III   ii⁷   V⁷   I

(1) active sonorities
(There are more than twice as many.)

The first two chords have relatively weak functional value. This, as well as the repetition, low spacing, and thinner texture, contributes to the languid mood of this phrase.

With respect to all the chords in the first 21 measures, which predominates: (1) active sonorities, or (2) inactive sonorities? _____

(No response required.)

146. The inventory of chords below indicates the wide variety of sonorities used in measures 5-21 (once a tonality begins to be established).

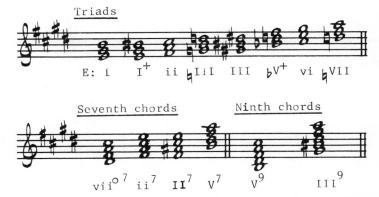

---

147. The example below is from the final section of Liszt's *Sonetto del Petrarca*.

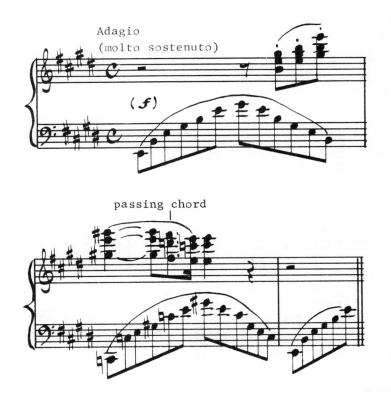

(1) major (2) augmented (3) major	Each measure contains a single triad. Indicate the *quality* of each. (1) _____ (2) _____ (3) _____

CDEF♯ G♯

148.   The example in the preceding frame shows once again Liszt's preference for the augmented triad. It also demonstrates influence of the whole-tone scale.* Name the notes of the whole-tone scale (on C) which are present in the second measure of the example above. _____
_____ _____

   *Composed of major seconds only, the whole-tone scale tends to produce undifferentiated tonal effects. See Chapter 10, Frames 368-384.

149.   In the second measure of the example in Frame 147, all the tones but one (A♯) of a whole-tone scale on C are used. Notice that the bass notes in this example are a major third apart (E-C♯).

   This example shows three aspects of Liszt's harmonic style; (1) preference for the augmented triad, (2) whole-tone scale influence, and (3) chromatic mediant relation of roots. The latter of these three points is further demonstrated below. Supply a Roman numeral analysis for this example.

Liszt: *Trois Études de Concert,* No. 3 ("Un Sospiro")

Allegro affettuoso (piu lento)

150. All of the chords in the preceding example are in root position. This makes it easy to analyze root relations. Record the number of occurrences for each relation below:

2nd - 2

3rd - 5

5th - 0

Root movements by 2nd   _____

Root movements by 3rd   _____

Root movements by 5th   _____

---

151. The analysis in the preceding frame reveals that in this example root movements by thirds predominate to a marked degree; moreover, fifth relationships are completely lacking. One of the three primary triads is not included in this passage. This is the _____ chord.

dominant

---

152. We have already noted whole-tone scale influence (Frames 147-149). The example which follows shows a still more systematic use of this scale.

Liszt: *Trois Études de Concert,* No. 1 ("Il Lamento")

The bass in the first four measures forms a scale which begins and ends on E-flat. This is a complete whole-tone scale. (True/False) _____

True.

153. The passage quoted in the preceding frame ends with the tonic chord in A-flat major. The chords which sound above the whole-tone scale are somewhat obscured by non-harmonic tones (and nonharmonic chords). An important fact, however, is that the series of chords both begins and ends with the dominant seventh chord in A-flat major. Thus we have merely an elaborated authentic cadence.

$$E^{\flat 7} \quad (E^6_4 \ B^7 \ c^6_4 \ G^9 \ c^6_4 \ G^9 \ A^{\flat 6}_4) \quad E^{\flat 7} \quad A^{\flat}$$

$$A^{\flat}: \qquad \qquad \qquad V^7 \qquad \qquad \qquad I$$

The chords enclosed by the two dominant seventh chords have (high/low) _____ functional value.

low

SUMMARY.

The examples analyzed in this chapter indicate the chief harmonic development in the nineteenth century: *expanded tonality.* This is the product of evolutions in harmonic practice which are summarized in the four items below:

1. *Less consistency in root movement:* third relationships, in particular, assume added importance; there is greater use of nonfunctional harmony.

2. *Enlarged chord vocabulary:* there is greater use of active chords (including the augmented triad) with dominant function; there also is higher incidence of all types of altered chords, and expanded tertian sonorities (diatonic and altered).

3. *Expanded tonal horizon:* there are more frequent tonicizations and modulations to more distant keys.

4. *Increased chromaticism:* there is greater use of nondiatonic tones as chord constituents, and also in harmonic relationships.

Besides producing restless, highly-colored harmonic effects, these evolutions caused a loosening of tonal order. Incapable of unlimited expansion, tonality was much closer to total destruction than could have been realized at the mid-point of the nineteenth century. But the seeds of destruction were not sown by outside protagonists; they were planted by composers who still accepted tonality as an *a priori* condition of music, but who developed new harmonic resources to express their personal response to the romantic ideals of their time.

Our study has led us to that vital point in harmonic evolution where the gravitational pull of the tonic barely is able to hold in its orbit chords spinning at the farthest reaches of the tonal universe. What follows is an extremely fascinating development. As we proceed, we will often be poised on the razor's edge between functional harmonic tonality, and the various rejections of tonality and traditional harmonic practice which follow.

5

Ultrachromaticism (I)

This is the first of two chapters which deal with extreme chromaticism. Actually, no sharp distinction can be made between expanded tonality, the subject of the preceding chapter, and ultrachromaticism—the difference is mainly of degree. Many altered chords and frequent modulations (especially to foreign keys) produce expanded tonality; ultrachromaticism results from prevalent use—both harmonically and melodically—of the twelve tones of the chromatic scale. Consistent use of the total chromatic spectrum produces rich tonal variety, but tends to undermine the effect of a tonal center. It is this aspect of ultrachromaticism which is of most immediate concern here. Consequently, we shall focus on the effect of ultrachromaticism on tonality, and observe the extent to which chromaticism gains eminence over diatonicism during the second half of the nineteenth century.

Richard Wagner (1813-83) brought German romantic opera to the apogee of its development. By redefining the relation of drama to music, he established a new operatic style. To convey his huge dramatic visions, he created a new form: the music drama. But important as this innovation was, his influence on evolving harmonic practices was even more far-reaching. He was, indeed, a pivotal figure in the evolution of harmony, and scarcely any of his contemporaries and successors were untouched by the force of his overwhelming musical personality. Wagner intensified the role of harmony as a conveyor of dramatic and philosophical ideas. All aspects of harmony, including the chord vocabulary, root relations, tonal stability/instability, and chromaticism were exploited to further the dramatic element. Chromaticism, in particular, was used to portray dramatic stresses such as longing, grief, and remorse.

Unlike many romantic composers such as Chopin and Liszt, in whose music chromaticism was used largely for expressive detail, Wagner used chromaticism both as detail and as the structural basis for tonality. For his opera *Tristan und Isolde,* he created a truly new harmonic language. The principal theme of this opera, unrequited love, is expressed by the sonorities used, nonharmonic action, and also by harmonic functions. *Tristan und Isolde* was composed during the years 1856-59 but did not receive its first performance until 1865 in Munich. An earlier attempt at the Court Opera in Vienna was abandoned after 77 rehearsals; the opera was given up as "impractical." This attests to the revolutionary nature of this work, in which the ultrachromaticism at times approaches the negation of tonality. In this respect, it is a precursor of musical styles to appear several decades later. Not until nearly 1900, were the implications of Wagner's chromaticism and tonal evasion fully realized.

Turn, now, to Panel 7, which contains two brief examples taken from the "Prelude" to *Tristan und Isolde.*

Major-minor seventh.
(or dominant seventh)

(Frames 154-171 refer to Panel 7.)
154.   The opening measures in Example *a* contain several short phrases separated from one another by rests. Our first concern will be the tonal relations between these phrases. Each of the first three phrases ends with the same type chord (at the asterisks). Indicate the quality of these chords.

_____

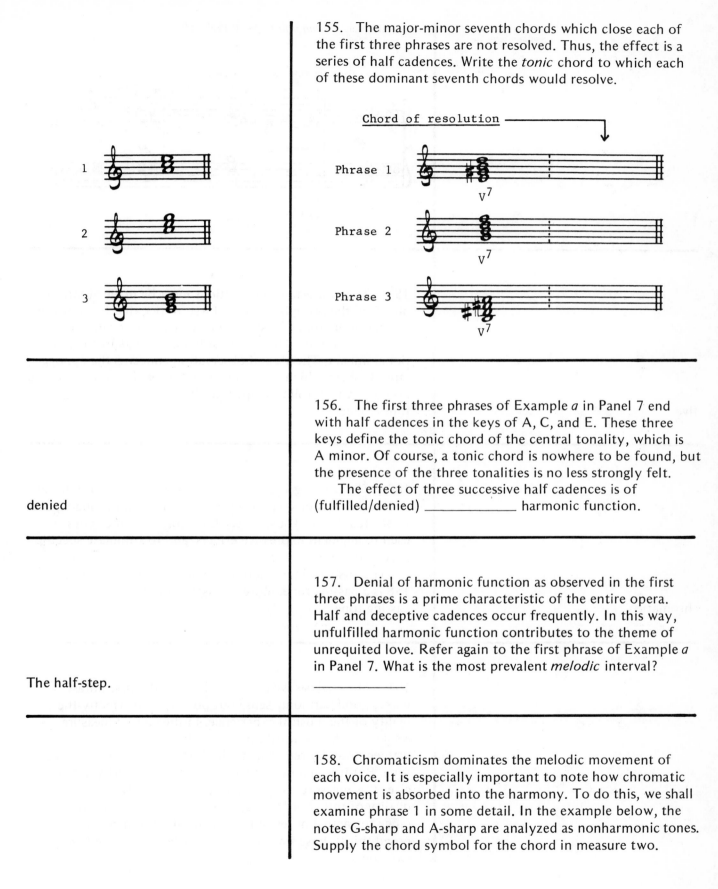

155. The major-minor seventh chords which close each of the first three phrases are not resolved. Thus, the effect is a series of half cadences. Write the *tonic* chord to which each of these dominant seventh chords would resolve.

Chord of resolution ⟶

Phrase 1

V⁷

Phrase 2

V⁷

Phrase 3

V⁷

1

2

3

---

denied

156. The first three phrases of Example *a* in Panel 7 end with half cadences in the keys of A, C, and E. These three keys define the tonic chord of the central tonality, which is A minor. Of course, a tonic chord is nowhere to be found, but the presence of the three tonalities is no less strongly felt.

The effect of three successive half cadences is of (fulfilled/denied) _____ harmonic function.

The half-step.

157. Denial of harmonic function as observed in the first three phrases is a prime characteristic of the entire opera. Half and deceptive cadences occur frequently. In this way, unfulfilled harmonic function contributes to the theme of unrequited love. Refer again to the first phrase of Example *a* in Panel 7. What is the most prevalent *melodic* interval?

_____

---

158. Chromaticism dominates the melodic movement of each voice. It is especially important to note how chromatic movement is absorbed into the harmony. To do this, we shall examine phrase 1 in some detail. In the example below, the notes G-sharp and A-sharp are analyzed as nonharmonic tones. Supply the chord symbol for the chord in measure two.

Wagner: *Tristan und Isolde* ("Prelude")

F⁶

159. Two important observations must be made about the phrase in the preceding frame. First, notice that both of the nonharmonic tones (G-sharp and A-sharp) occur in strong metrical positions. This makes still more poignant their emotional impact. The second observation concerns the appoggiatura G-sharp which is considerably longer than the harmonic note (A) which follows. Specifically, it is _____ times longer.

five

160. The prolonged appoggiatura with consequent deferral of resolution is in keeping with the expression of longing and frustrated desire. Thus, we see how nonharmonic tones are used to augment expressive effects, and to stimulate specific psychological responses.

The A-sharp in measure three of the example in Frame 158 is a passing tone. More precisely, it is a _____ passing tone.

chromatic

161. The analysis we have supplied for the first phrase makes good harmonic sense but portrays imperfectly the reality of the musical experience. In the second measure a sonority that is heard for five of the six beats is explained away by recognizing the G-sharp as a nonharmonic tone. But it is precisely the quality of this sonority which gives this measure its special aural character. What is the quality of this chord? To answer this question, first rearrange the actual notes to form a chord built of superimposed thirds. Base the chord on F *(enharmonic spellings must be used).*

diminished-minor	**162.** Now identify the quality of the chord in the preceding frame. It is a _____-_____ seventh chord.
tritone	**163.** Because of its relatively long duration, the diminished-minor seventh chord contributes most to the establishment of the "characteristic timbre" of this passage. But even though its actual quality must be recognized, it is nevertheless best analyzed as the result of nonharmonic action. The other nonharmonic tone in this phrase (A-sharp) has been analyzed as a chromatic passing tone. Proper assessment of its tonal effect must take into account its relation to the root of the E major-minor seventh chord with which it is associated. This relation is a _____.
French	**164.** Even though the A-sharp has but short duration, and is unequivocally a nonharmonic tone, the sonority it produces is worth noting. If the note A-sharp is respelled as B-flat and the notes redistributed the chord below results. As respelled above, the chord can be analyzed as a _____ sixth chord.
	165. Our analysis has revealed that the first phrase, regardless how it is analyzed contains the following types of sonorities: *Chord Type* *Duration* dm⁷ 5 beats Mm⁷ 3 beats F⁶ 2 beats Thus, every sonority in this phrase is active, and the most prevalent sound is the diminished-minor seventh

chord. This chord affects most listeners as having a particularly wistful, yearning effect.

Are the second and third phrases in Example *a* of Panel 7 constructed exactly the same as the first? _____

No.

---

166. The sonorities of the second phrase are the same as the first, but phrase 3 is slightly different. Even so, the prevailing sounds still are the diminished-minor seventh and the dominant seventh chords. The fourth phrase restates the third an octave higher.

New harmonic interest begins in measure 16, from which point the music proceeds in a more continuous manner. The harmonic analysis which is supplied for these measures indicates the tonal fluidity. Here there is greater variety of sonorities, and the keys of A minor, C major, and D minor are at least skirted. The last cadence shown in this example is a _____ cadence.

half

---

167. Example *b* of Panel 7 shows a passage which occurs somewhat later in the Prelude. It consists of six statements of a motive, each one of which ends on a dominant seventh (or ninth) chord. Indicate the key implied by each of these phrases.

Phrases	Key
1 and 2	F
3 and 4	G
5 and 6	E

Do any of these chords resolve to their expected tonic? _____

No.

---

168. Here, again, we have the effect of yearning produced by avoiding expected harmonic functions. But, most important, is the weakening of tonality which results. When not a single tonic is fully established, and when chords active in different keys succeed one another, the dissolution of tonality is well advanced.

Analyze the harmony which precedes the dominant seventh chord in phrase 1.

Chapter 5

Wagner: *Tristan und Isolde* ("Prelude")

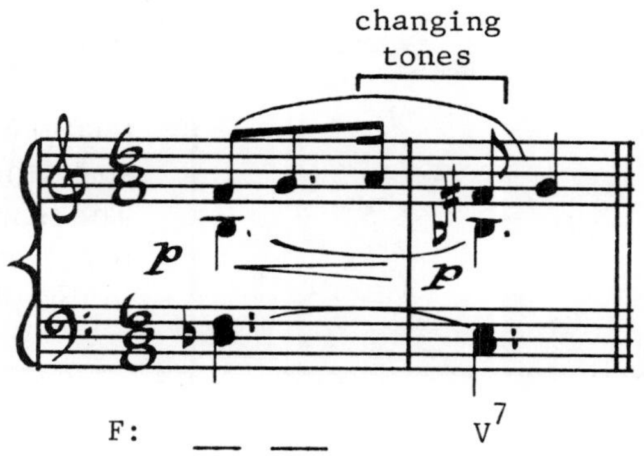

F: It⁶ F⁶

---

169. In each of the six phrases, the harmonic motion is augmented sixth to dominant. Is it true that in this entire passage there is not a single stable sonority? ______

Yes.

---

170. All of the notes which occur during the first three beats of the example in Frame 168 are written as a scale on the staff below:

Except for one missing note (E-flat), we have a ______ ______ scale.

whole-tone

---

171. The salient features of Example *b* in Panel 7 are summarized below:

1. Only active sonorities are used.
2. Several keys are implied, but none established.
3. Whole-tone scale influence is felt.

The harmony is best described as (fulfilled/unfulfilled) __________ functional expectations.

unfulfilled

Two additional excerpts from Wagner's *Tristan* are shown in Panel 8.

172. The basic harmonic movement in Example *a* is very simple, as indicated by the chord symbols which have been supplied. Here, the tonality is not in doubt. The chromaticism is largely melodic, and the few chromatic harmonic relations have embellishing function. Reduced to its simplest state, the harmonic structure is merely I (embellished)-V-I. The significant feature, though, is the extent to which dominant function predominates. There is a total of nine measures in this phrase; of these, _____ have dominant function.

six

---

173. Spread of dominant (active) function over much of the phrase is characteristic of late romanticism. The result is increased tension. In this case, delayed resolution stimulates feelings of desire and expectation. Melodic chromaticism occurs in all the upper voices, but is particularly evident in the inner voices.

The harmony of this example is best described as non-functional. (True/False) _____

False.

---

174. Observe, now, Example *b* in Panel 8. The highly chromatic nature of this passage is obvious, but to understand its construction we must examine it closely. The middle part has been left unanalyzed, but the chord symbols which are supplied reveal a simple harmonic movement from A-flat major to a half cadence in F minor.* However, the most interesting part of this phrase is the material which lies between the iv^7 and G^6 chords. Note first of all the repetitious melodic pattern beginning on the third beat of measure one and ending on the first beat of measure four. This kind of writing is called a _____ .

sequence

---

*Nonharmonic tones cloud the picture here, as is often the case in such music. Other, equally valid, interpretations might result in a slightly different analysis.

Shortly, we shall look more closely at the harmonic aspects of the sequence noted in the preceding frame. But first it is necessary to explain a method of labeling chords which will be used frequently as we proceed. If chords have little functional value, or occur in passages of indeterminate tonality, Roman numerals have little meaning. In such cases, letters which indicate the root and triad type, plus numerals to show sevenths, ninths, etc., are simpler, and more revealing. Note the following principles:

1. Letters identify the root in all cases.

2. *Triad* qualities are shown as below:

$$A = \text{major} \qquad A^+ = \text{augmented}$$
$$a = \text{minor} \qquad a^\circ = \text{diminished}$$

3. Sevenths, ninths, elevenths, and thirteenths are shown by adding the appropriate numeral (A^7, A^9, A^{11}, or A^{13}).

4. Inversions are indicated by the usual figured bass symbols.

Such symbols are not, in all cases, precise (the quality of the seventh, ninth, etc. is not identified), but they do reveal at a glance three important things: (1) root, (2) triad quality, an (3) the extent of tertian extension.

---

minor

No.

---

175. Now to continue, the harmonic sequence in Example *b* (Panel 8) is shown below with symbols such as those described above.

The lower-case letters indicate that all sonorities are based on _____ triads.

176. The first chord ($b^{\flat 7}$) in the sequence is labeled f:iv^7 in Panel 8. The next chord analyzed is a German sixth. *Now for the crucial point:* Are the chords which lie between iv^7 and G^6 (under the bracket) *functional* in F minor? _____

177. The sequence we are examining is called a "real" sequence because intervallic relations are exactly the same in each stage.* Notice in Frame 175 that the highest voice moves consistently in a pattern of a half-step up and a minor third down. Also, the tracing of roots in the example below shows a pattern of a major third down and a major second up.

---

*By "stage" is meant each appearance of the sequence unit.

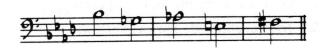

Real sequences rarely produce functional harmony in a single key because each stage of the sequence establishes a new tonal orientation. The result is tonal ambiguity. In such passages, tonality is suspended until a new, more permanent orientation is established. Much of Wagner's ultrachromatic, coloristic harmony is the result of real sequences.

The harmonic effect of Example *b* in Panel 8 is represented below:

$$A^\flat: I^6 \begin{bmatrix} ii^7 \\ f: iv^7 \end{bmatrix} \text{(suspended tonality)} \quad G^6 \ V^7$$

(No response required.)

Panel 9 contains two additional examples of Wagner's chromatic writing.

(Frames 178-188 refer to Panel 9.)

178. In Example *a*, the brackets indicate a *real* sequence. The first stage begins in G major, the second in E-flat (a chromatic mediant relation). The phrase ends (at the asterisk) with a half cadence in the key of _____.

D minor

---

179. The basic harmonic movement in the first five measures is represented below:

G: I   E♭: I   d: V

The final two brief phrases are interesting because they show the substitution of the dominant seventh chord on F-sharp in the final phrase for the dominant triad on A which closes the next-to-the-last phrase. This is yet another example of third-relation harmony. The final chord in the example is a dominant seventh chord in the key of _____.

B

---

180. A closer look at the harmony reveals the chromatic nature of the relationships and the contrast between functional and nonfunctional harmony. In the example below, all nonharmonic tones have been eliminated and a possible analysis supplied:

The augmented triads (at the asterisks) are nonfunctional; all other chords may be regarded as functional in that they help establish feeling for the keys of G, E-flat, D (minor), and B. In the entire example, root relations are limited to three intervals: (1) major seconds, (2) minor seconds, and (3) _____.

minor thirds

181. Example *b* in Panel 9 contains mostly chromatic movement in all the voices (the lower two consist *entirely* of half-step movement). This is indeed an example of ultrachromaticism! To attempt an explanation of the harmonic implications, we shall try a rather novel approach. One thing which is fairly certain is that the final chord is at least potentially a dominant seventh in the key of C. The preceding chord (at the asterisk) is a _____ sixth chord.

French

half	182. The progression F^6 - V^7 produces a _____ cadence in the key of C.

---

183. The cadence, as usual, provides tonal orientation. But what else in this passage is tonally certain? We will endeavor to answer this question in the next few frames.

Except for three tones, which are unequivocally non-harmonic (these are identified in the example), the coincidence of the voices produces familiar, traditional sonorities. Each of these chords is numbered in the example, and the quality is listed below:

1.	dm^7	8.	F^6
2.	d^7	9.	dm^7
3.	Mm^7	10.	d^7
4.	dm^7	11.	d^7
5.	dm^7	12.	dm^7
6.	Mm^7	13.	F^6
7.	d^7	14.	Mm^7

Without exception, each chord in this list is an active sonority. (True/False) _____

True.

---

184. The exclusive use of active sonorities is certain to result in a fairly high level of tension, and restless harmonic activity. Tonality, however, need not be threatened. If active chords occur mostly as diatonic seventh chords, or as tonicization agents, and if structural harmonic relations are evident, tonal orientation may still be clear. We must look closely at the chords of our example to see if they behave in a familiar, functional manner.

We are now approaching the crucial feature of this analysis. To assist you in the next step, a reminder of the "functional" uses of each chord type in the phrase under consideration is supplied below:

Chord Type	Functional Uses
dm^7	ii$^{\circ 7}$, vii$^{\circ 7}$, vii$^{\circ 7}$/?
d^7	vii^{d7}, vii^{d7}/?
Mm^7	V^7, V^7/?
F^6	Altered II^7 (progressing to V or V^7)

In addition to these uses, strong root movement (down a fifth, for example) may produce functional harmony regardless of other factors.

(No response required.)

185. Examine each chord in Example *b* of Panel 9 and indicate below whether or not it moves to the succeeding chord in a *functional* manner.

		Functional Use	
Chord	Type	Yes	No
1	dm⁷	_____	_____
2	d⁷	_____	_____
3	Mm⁷	_____	_____
4	dm⁷	_____	_____
5	dm⁷	_____	_____
6	Mm⁷	_____	_____
7	d⁷	_____	_____
8	F⁶	_____	_____
9	dm⁷	_____	_____
10	d⁷	_____	_____
11	d⁷	_____	_____
12	dm⁷	_____	_____
13	F⁶	_____	_____

1 No
2 No
3 No
4 Yes
5 Yes
6 No
7 No
8 No
9 No
10 No
11 No
12 No
13 Yes

186. It is not expected that all agree with the findings recorded in the preceding frame. But nevertheless, it should be quite clear that few chords have familiar, tonality-defining function. In spite of the fact that all the chords are traditional sonorities, their use fails for the most part to establish a tonality. All are potential tonality builders, but this potentiality is willfully ignored. Instead, one active chord progresses to another merely for the sake of the color effect. *The result is nontonal harmony; until the cadence is reached, tonality is suspended.*
Could a Roman numeral analysis be made of this phrase?
_____

Yes.

187. Of course a Roman numeral analysis could be made, but it would reveal little more than has already been discovered: that most functional implications are avoided.
One final aspect of this phrase needs to be stressed: In spite of the apparent freedom of harmonic movement, the effect of the music is highly integrated, and the influence of some kind of hidden logic is felt. What are the factors which prevent this passage from sounding haphazard? One thing which contributes to the sense of unity is the limited number of chord types. The entire phrase has but four types of chords. The number of occurrences for each type is listed below:

Chord Type	Occurrences
dm^7	5
d^7	4
Mm^7	3
F^6	2

In addition to limited chord types, there is a partial sequence in the second and third measures which contributes to cohesiveness. The upper two parts are free, but the lower two reveal the sequential relation between these two measures. Is the sequence in the lower voices a "real" sequence?

Yes.

_____

188.   The third, and most important factor is the prevailing chromaticism itself. The lower two voices move only by half-step, and chromaticism is predominant in the upper voices as well. The tabulation of all *melodic intervals* is revealing (major and minor sevenths are grouped with their corresponding inversion).

	m2	*M2*	*m6*	*P8*
Soprano	10	2	1	1
Alto	4	2	0	0
Tenor	8	0	0	0
Bass	9	0	0	0
Total	31	4	1	1

More than 83 percent of all melodic movement is by half-step! Thus a consistent chromatic character is imparted to the melodic lines which is a significant element in the aesthetic effect.

(No response required.)

Wagner's ultrachromaticism sometimes results in nonfunctional use of familiar chord types. The effect of this evasion is tonal uncertainty bordering on atonality. But such passages are usually fairly brief patches of color within a prevailing tonal landscape. His most prevalent use of tonally ambiguous harmony is in *Tristan,* which has been singled out by some writers as the work which contributed more than any other to the dissolution of tonality.[1] Even here, however, one does not sense a rejection of tonality, but rather an expanded tonality with frequent points of tonal orientation (cadences, in particular). The areas of suspended tonality serve to heighten dramatic and emotional effects when needed and stand in contrast to tonally stable passages.

SUMMARY.

Ultrachromaticism is the prevalent use of the twelve tones of the chromatic scale. The aspects of Wagner's chromaticism which concern us here are summarized by the following points:

1. Active sonorities, including seventh, and ninth chords, etc., as well as augmented-sixth chords, are used extensively.
2. Traditional "functional" resolutions of active chords are often evaded.
3. Chromatic third-relation harmony is an important aspect of the harmonic idiom.
4. Chromatic melodic movement prevails in many passages.
5. The cadence is the chief tonality-defining factor in many cases.
6. "Real" sequences lead to tonal fluidity.

	189. Indicate the correct statement(s) by checking one of the options below: 1. Ultrachromaticism results mainly from melodic embellishment. 2. Third-relation harmony may be either diatonic or chromatic. (1) ____ (2) ____ Both ____ Neither ____
(2) √	
mediants	190. *Chromatic* third-relation harmony produces chords which are called chromatic _____ .

6

Ultrachromaticism (II)

Wagner's harmonic innovations were taken up almost immediately by other composers. Anton Bruckner (1824-96), for example, transferred Wagner's idiom to the symphony. As a token of his respect, Bruckner dedicated his third symphony (1873) to Wagner. Richard Strauss (1864-1949) not only inherited Wagner's operatic mantel,[1] but continued in his own way to expand tonal horizons and enlarge the chord vocabulary. Ultrachromaticism is our subject here, and we shall observe this feature in a few examples from works by composers who were influenced to some degree by Wagner's music.

The music of César Franck (1822-90) has a gothic aura even though modern elements are sometimes evident. A prominent characteristic of his music is tonal restlessness, which, when used to excess, erodes the foundations of tonal order. Although his aesthetic stance was quite irreconcilable with that of Wagner,[2] many ultrachromatic passages in his works can be seen as influenced by Wagner's harmonic concepts. Franck's most important orchestral work is the *Symphony in D Minor* (first performed in 1889). We shall begin by looking at a few examples from this work.

191.   The voices in the example below move almost entirely by half-step.

Franck: *Symphony in D Minor*

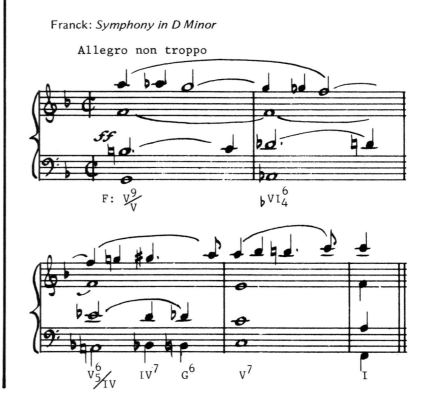

functional	Judging on the basis of the Roman numeral analysis which is supplied, the harmonic movement of this example is mostly (functional/nonfunctional) _____ .
melodic	192. Except for the movement of the first chord to the second, all harmonic relations have strong tonality-defining function. The chromaticism in this case is mainly (harmonic/melodic/both harmonic and melodic) _____ .
Three. *(Mea. 2, second beat; mea. 4, last eighth; mea. 5.)*	193. Ultrachromaticism which is the result of melodic (often nonharmonic) movement contributes to linear activity and a feeling of restlessness, but does not necessarily result in tonal ambiguity. It does, however, produce highly colored effects and enlarges the tonal material to include all the tones of the chromatic scale. The result is a saturated, over-ripe kind of tonality. Music of this type is associated with the later stages of tonal harmonic evolution. Look closely at each sonority produced by the melodic movement in the example in Frame 191. How many *inactive* chords (major or minor triads) do you find? _____
	194. Another example of Franck's ultrachromaticism is shown below: Franck: *Symphony in D Minor*

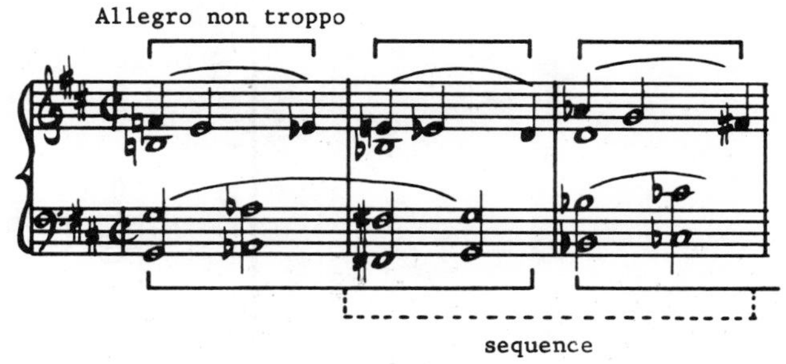

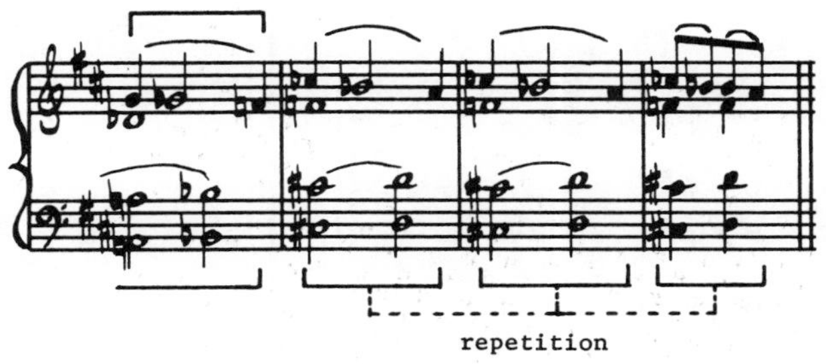

As is frequently the case in such passages, sequence plays an important part. The first two brackets drawn *beneath* the staff indicate a two-measure sequence unit; the brackets drawn *above* show a sequence within a sequence.

Several steps will be required to explain the tonal organization of this passage. First, indicate the tonality which emerges at the end. _____

D minor.

---

195.   Although D minor is quite strongly established in the last three measures, the rest is not so clear. Let us proceed by examining the construction of the sequence unit in the first two measures.

The bass begins and ends on the note G.

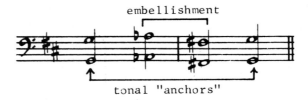

The chromatic embellishing notes A-flat and F-sharp can be considered "nonharmonic" tones; if analyzed as such they would be called _____ tones.

changing

---

196.   It is easy to accept the note G as the tonal basis for the first two measures, but what harmony is created by the upper voices? To find out, we shall analyze each chord produced by the coincidence of the voices. Eight sonorities occur; indicate each of these below. (The first two are shown as examples. You will also have to contend with enharmonic equivalents; be guided by the actual aural effect of the notes.)

1. G⁷   5. F♯ ⁷

2. e⁶   6. e♭ ⁶

3. E⁶   7. E♭ ⁶

4. a♭   8. g

1. G⁷   5. _____

2. e⁶   6. _____

3. _____   7. _____

4. _____   8. _____

197. To make the harmonic relations explored in the preceding frame still clearer, the *roots* are traced on the staff below:

$\bigcirc$ = major $\bullet$ = minor

This example clearly reveals the harmonic sequence (chords 1-4, and 5-8). This is an example of (functional/nonfunctional) _____ harmony.

nonfunctional

---

198. The analysis we have just made reveals the nonfunctional aspect of the micro-harmony, and once this fact is known the purpose of the analysis has been realized. Such harmony serves an embellishing, color function, and it is fruitless to assign Roman numerals to each chord, or even to try to determine a key in the traditional sense. But there is a kind of tonal order evident here. First of all, root movement by thirds predominates, and the passage both begins and ends with a chord whose root is _____.

G

---

199. So now we have discovered the essential tonal order of the first two measures.

(nonfunctional harmony)

$\bullet$ = major $\bullet$ = minor

(No response required.)

---

200. It remains for us to find some kind of order in the larger harmonic relations of the example in Frame 194. Since the third and fourth measures are a real sequence of the first two, all that has been ascertained thus far applies here too. At the beginning, we determined that the last three measures were in the key of D minor. With these facts in hand, we can diagram the basic harmonic movement of the entire passage.

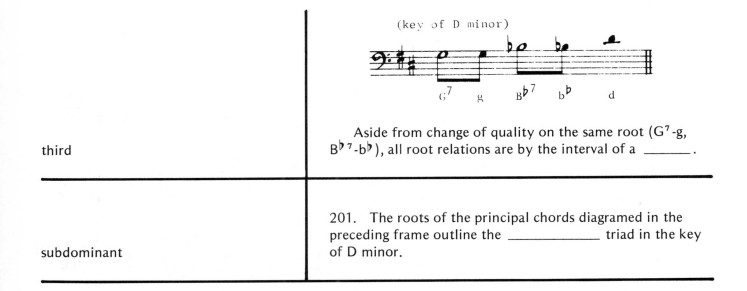

(key of D minor)

G^7　g　$B^{\flat 7}$　$b^\flat$　d

third

Aside from change of quality on the same root (G^7-g, $B^{\flat 7}$-$b^\flat$), all root relations are by the interval of a _____ .

subdominant

201. The roots of the principal chords diagramed in the preceding frame outline the _____ triad in the key of D minor.

Whereas Franck was influenced by Wagner more or less against his will, Richard Strauss embraced whole-heartedly Wagner's modern harmonic tendencies. Strauss' early musical education, however, was supervised by his conservative father, and his first compositions show the influence of Mendelssohn and Brahms. But in 1885-86, while conducting at Meiningen as von Bülow's successor he became associated with the poet and musician Alexander Ritter. From him, Strauss absorbed the aesthetics of the Liszt-Wagner revolution *(Zukunftsmusik)* in which music is integrally linked with poetic, dramatic, and philosophical expression. Under Ritter's influence, Strauss turned to the composition of frankly programmatic music. He also adopted, and extended Wagner's vocabulary of chromatic harmony. His early orchestral works, the symphonic poems *Don Juan* (1889), *Tod und Verklärung* (1890), *Till Eulenspiegel's lustige Streiche* (1895), *Also sprach Zarathustra* (1896), and *Don Quixote* (1898) established Strauss as one of the most gifted and versatile German composers of his time. A brilliant orchestral craftsman, he advanced the technical resources of orchestral musicians by placing what seemed then to be impossible demands. But in spite of his unique contributions to the orchestral repertoire, his most lasting works are probably the operas in which Strauss carries on the Wagnerian ideal of *Musik aus Ausdruck* (music as expression). Also, like Wagner, Strauss uses the *Leitmotif* as an expressive and unifying device. Some of Strauss' most advanced writing occurs in *Salome* (1905) and *Elektra* (1909). The latter, in particular, represents his most advanced stride towards rejection of tonality. His most popular opera, *Der Rosenkavalier* (1911), while often highly chromatic, is a step backward toward more stable tonal ground.

We shall look at several examples of chromaticism in Strauss' music. The first is from the symphonic poem *Till Eulenspiegel's lustige Streiche.*

202. The example below consists of the "Eulenspiegel" motif stated twice in the upper part.

Strauss: *Till Eulenspiegel's lustige Streiche*

Beginning with the first full measure, the bass moves entirely by _____ -steps.

half

203. The melodic line is in the key of F major. Does the chromatic bass line contribute in any way to the establishment of an F tonality? _____

No.

204. A line which is almost totally chromatic is bound to be ambiguous with respect to tonality. Notice that the last note of the bass is B, a tritone removed from the tonic F.

Of course, the chromatic intervals give a particular character to the bass line itself, but this line does nothing to confirm the tonality of the melody.

The chords which begin and end each of the two phrases are shown below:

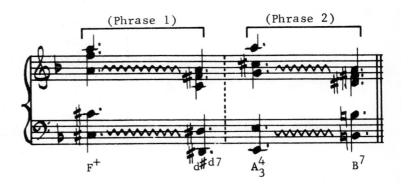

These chords have structural importance; do they contribute to the feeling of F major? _____

---

205. Still trying to find functional harmonic order, observe that each chord is rewritten in root position below. This is to make more evident possible functional root relationships. *(Some enharmonic conversions are made to produce tertian spellings.)*

Strauss: *Till Eulenspiegel's lustige Streiche* (altered)

Used by permission of C. F. Peters Corporation.

Does this aggregate of chords contribute to the definition of any specific tonality? _____

---

206. All of the chords in the preceding frame are in root position; thus root movements are easily traced by following the bass line. The intervallic relations of the roots are summarized below:

	Up	*Down*	*Total*
Fifth	0	1	1
Third	5	0	5
Second	3	2	5
Tritone	-	-	3

Chapter 6

No.	Do these root movements suggest functional harmonic use in the traditional sense? _____
	207. Our examination of the example first presented in Frame 202 leads to the following conclusions:
	1. The tonality of the melody (F major) is in no way confirmed by the harmony.
	2. The mostly chromatic bass is a unifying factor, but has no tonal significance.
	3. Chords are familiar types (triads and seventh chords), but bear little functional relation to one another. The choice of these chords apparently is dictated largely by the interval between the chromatic bass and the melody at any specific moment.
(No response required.)	Harmony such as this produces intriguing splashes of color, but is nontonal in spite of the familiar character of the sonorities. This type of chord use is aptly called "color" harmony.
	208. Another example by Strauss, this time from *Don Quixote*, is shown below:

Strauss: *Don Quixote*, Op. 35

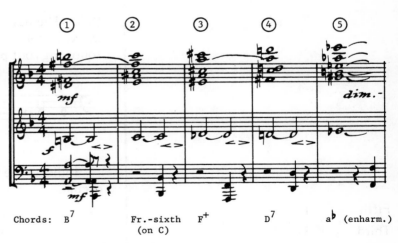

Chords: B⁷   Fr.-sixth   F⁺   D⁷   a♭ (enharm.)
                          (on C)

(cont'd)

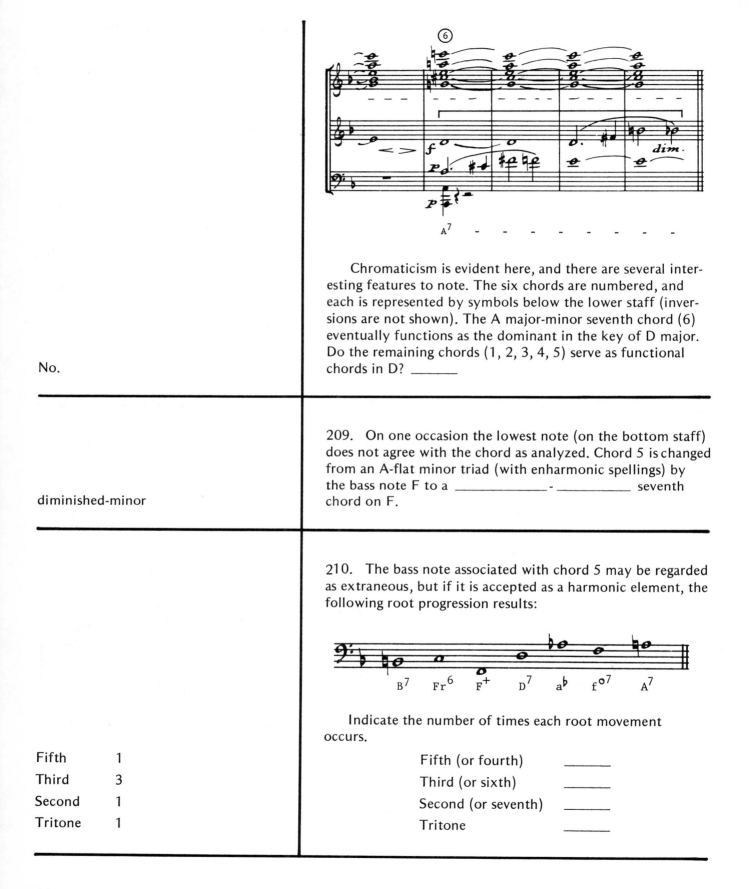

Chromaticism is evident here, and there are several interesting features to note. The six chords are numbered, and each is represented by symbols below the lower staff (inversions are not shown). The A major-minor seventh chord (6) eventually functions as the dominant in the key of D major. Do the remaining chords (1, 2, 3, 4, 5) serve as functional chords in D? _____

No.

209. On one occasion the lowest note (on the bottom staff) does not agree with the chord as analyzed. Chord 5 is changed from an A-flat minor triad (with enharmonic spellings) by the bass note F to a _____ - _____ seventh chord on F.

diminished-minor

210. The bass note associated with chord 5 may be regarded as extraneous, but if it is accepted as a harmonic element, the following root progression results:

Indicate the number of times each root movement occurs.

Fifth (or fourth)	_____
Third (or sixth)	_____
Second (or seventh)	_____
Tritone	_____

Fifth	1
Third	3
Second	1
Tritone	1

211. The tabulation of root movements in the preceding frame shows once again that highly chromatic music is often associated with root movements by thirds.

One final observation concerns the voice written on the middle staff of the example in Frame 208. All the notes of this voice fall into the chords as analyzed *until chord 6.* Here, the notes (under the bracket) do not agree with the chord. These notes suggest the tonic which soon is to be established. Thus, we have a combination of A (dominant) and _____ (tonic) harmony.

D

(No response required.)

212. Except for the final chord which has functional value as the dominant in D major, all the chords in the passage just analyzed are used for the sake of their color potential; they have but slight functional relation to one another. Although not completely atonal, tonality in the classic sense is barely discernible. The accommodation of chromaticism in several parts, and the exploitation of chords for their color effects are the chief criteria for the selection of chords, not the establishment of tonal order.

Hugo Wolf (1860-1903) is known primarily as the composer of about 300 songs which extend the artistic lineage of Schubert and Schumann. An Austrian, he spent most of his short life in Vienna, where as music critic for the "Wiener Salonblatt," he sided with the Wagner-Bruckner clique against Brahms. So vehement were his attacks on Brahms that he antagonized the influential but conservative Hanslick. This had the effect of retarding the acceptance of his own music. Although Wolf wrote a number of instrumental works including a symphonic poem and a string quartet, his natural affinity was for song composition. He was a staunch admirer of Wagner, and is justly called "the Wagner of the Lied." Within the intimate form of the art song, he marvelously realized Wagner's ideal of the union of poetry and music. He also adopted Wagner's conception of harmony and tonality, and wrote many passages which feature both melodic and harmonic ultrachromaticism. Three examples follow which show some aspects of Wolf's chromatic harmonic style.

213. In the example below, the chords seem almost to be accidental occurrences caused by the chromatic movement of the voices. Yet the two phrases complement one another and the harmonies convey the impression of structural design. But wherein does this lie? How can one make sense out of these harmonies?

First it is essential that you play the example several times, listening particularly for those harmonies which have *structural* function.

Wolf: *Mörike-Lieder* ("Frage und Antwort")

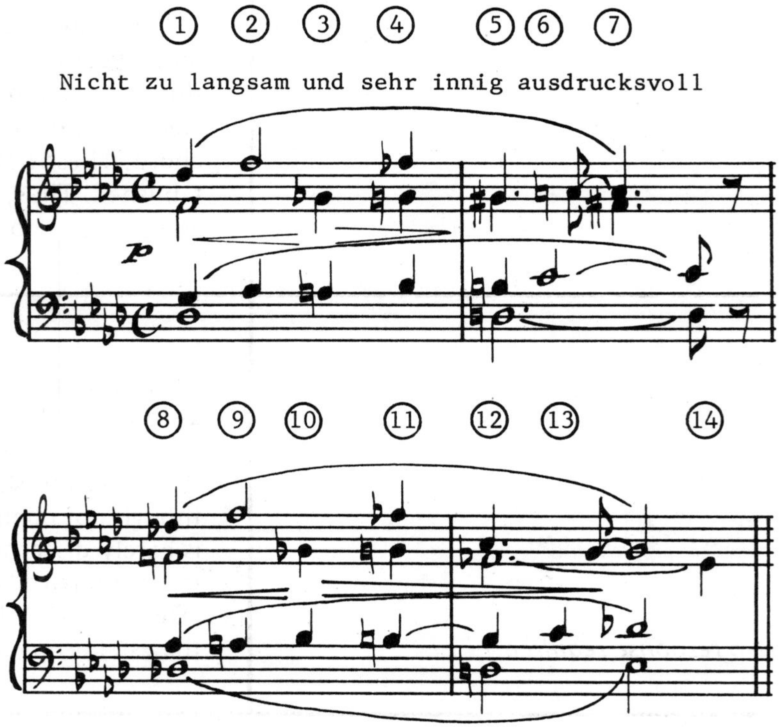

1 2 3 4 5 6 7
Nicht zu langsam und sehr innig ausdrucksvoll
p
8 9 10 11 12 13 14

What is the tonality of this example? ____________

D-flat major.

---

214. With reference to concepts developed earlier in this study, what approach can you suggest to identify the structural harmony in the example of the previous frame?

____

____

____

(See the following frame for explication.)

---

215. The question in the preceding frame has many answers. You may indeed follow your own approach to see where it leads. But the method with which we shall continue here is to let the formal structure of the phrases help identify the structural harmony. In other words, we shall focus our attention on the chords which *begin* and *end* each phrase. Write on the staff the four structural chords as defined above. *(Use whole notes.)*

1   2

Phrase 1   Phrase 2

(Write where arrows point.)

216.   There is a subtlety connected with the initial chord of the first phrase: the note G in the "tenor" may be heard as an appoggiatura which resolves to A-flat (look, again, at the example in Frame 213). If analyzed in this way, the first phrase begins with a D-flat major triad as does the second phrase. The *quality* of the final chord of each phrase is the same.   (True/False) _____

True.

217.   The chords within each phrase (other than the ones identified as structural chords) are little more than accidents of voice leading. Still, their sonorities help create the "character" of the musical effect, and it is revealing to analyze their quality even though they have little functional significance. In this kind of music there are usually several ways to interpret nonharmonic tones, so the chords can be variously analyzed. The list below records the chord qualities at the numbers inscribed in the example in Frame 213:

CHORD TYPES	CHORD NO.
Triads	
M	2, 8
A	9
d	5
Seventh chords	
Mm^7	7, 12, 14
dm^7	6, 11
d^7	4
mM^7	3
M^7	10
Whole-tone chords	1, 13

Most of the chords in this list are (active/inactive) _____.

active

218. The fourteen sonorities identified in the example of Frame 213 comprise nine different types; the result is harmonic variety pushed to an extreme. Here Wolf is painting with a harmonic palette dripping with color. Though this music is tonal, chord function often is uncertain, and the ear quickly becomes saturated with the excess of tonal variety.

Each of the two phrases in Frame 213 terminates with a _____ cadence.

half

219. Another aspect of Wolf's harmonic style is shown in the next example.

Wolf: *Goethe-Lieder* ("Grenzen der Menschheit")

In this example, most chords change at the rate of one per measure. The chord in measure 1 is a major triad. *The*

Augmented.

chords in all the remaining measures have the same quality.
Name the quality of these chords. _____

---

220. Augmented triads dominate the harmonic material in the preceding frame. Of the nine measures in this example, seven consist of augmented triads. No doubt their use here was suggested by the somewhat mystical text. The important thing, though, is their effect on tonality. Because the augmented triad divides the octave into equal intervals (major thirds), it is impossible to differentiate aurally between the chord members. Not one of the three tones has the aural effect of a root; thus augmented triads are, in themselves, incapable of defining a tonality. Harmonies dominated by augmented triads generally result in a state of *suspended tonality.*

    Discounting differences of notation, only four augmented triads exist (CEG♯, D♭FA, DF♯A♯, and E♭GB). The passage in Frame 219 utilizes the complete repertoire of augmented triads. (True/False) _____

True.

---

221. The chords in measures 2, 3, 4, and 5 state in descending chromatic order the four possible augmented triads. This is shown in the example below (enharmonic spellings are used):

    These four chords include all the notes of the chromatic scale. (True/False) _____

True.

---

222. The voice part and also the notes played by the right hand move down mostly in chromatic motion in accordance with the chords as written in the preceding frame. The notes played by the left hand, however, ascend with each chord change. This produces an effective pattern of symmetrical motion.

Measures

Note that the upper voice descends in minor seconds
while the lower voice ascends consistently in _____
thirds.

minor

---

223. Look now at the lowest notes of the accompaniment
in measures 6-9 (Frame 219). What is the relation between
these notes and the corresponding notes in measures 2-5?

_____

_____

_____

Again, ascending minor 3rds, this
time starting on E.

---

224. Your attention is called to the symmetrical aspects
of the passage in Frame 219 because symmetricality renders
obscure—at times obliterates completely—tonal orientation.
But consider this question: Does the use of consistent intervallic relations such as those discovered in the preceding few
frames help compensate for the lack of tonal order? _____

Yes.

---

225. The materials and techniques which attack tonality
often themselves supply new forms of structural tonal logic.
This will be observed on numerous occasions as we progress
in this study.
    The final example should satisfy the most ravenous ap-
petite for chromaticism. In all, there are only six melodic
intervals larger than a half-step (one major third, one minor
third, and four major seconds).

Wolf: *Goethe-Lieder* ("Harfenspieler" II)

Langsam, aber nicht zu schleppend

Yet, in spite of mostly chromatic movement, this passage is clearly tonal. The melody emphasizes the note C in the first two measures, and descends to G in the fourth measure where the lower notes cooperate to produce a _____ cadence in the key of C minor.

---

half

---

226. The melody of the example in the preceding frame clearly establishes the key of C minor. Except for the cadence, however, the lower two voices lend no support. In the first three measures the lower voices move entirely in parallel motion (symmetricality, again); the interval between these two voices (measures 1-3) is consistently a _____ third.

---

minor

---

227. Parallel minor thirds is the prevalent feature of the lower two voices until the fourth measure where these voices move in parallel _____ thirds.

---

major

---

228. Most of the sonorities produced by the sliding chromatic lines are simple triads, with diminished quality prevalent. This, plus the tonic-dominant emphasis of the melody, and especially the clear tonal implication of the half cadence (c: iv⁶ - V) makes the entire passage sound less radical than one would expect. So ultrachromaticism need not necessarily

False. *(Only the cadence chords have structural value.)*

lead to dissolution of tonality provided structural tonal relations are stressed, or tonal orientation is provided by the cadences.

The tonality of the example in Frame 225 is not in question. Most of the chords have structural importance. (True/False) _____

SUMMARY.

Although the ultrachromaticism of late romantic music caused progressive erosion of tonality, chords were no less important. Music of this period was, in fact, chord dominated—particular chord types were exploited for the sake of their unique emotive impact. Augmented triads, for example, figure prominently in Liszt's music, whereas Wagner favored dominant seventh and ninth chords as well as the diminished-minor seventh chord and the French-sixth. Chords, however, can be used in nontonal ways, and in this chapter we have noted several passages in which tonality is either ambiguous or temporarily suspended. But the music of Liszt, Wagner, Franck, Strauss, and Wolf is in the main clearly tonal; these composers did not completely abandon traditional concepts of harmonic order. Chromatic as it often is, their music does not complete the evolution of harmonic tonality. The chapters which follow will continue to trace this evolution with particular attention given to the progressive dissolution of structural harmonic tonality.

7

Denial of Harmonic Function

To this point much has been made of the nature and evolution of harmonic tonality. Special attention has been given to the expansion of tonality and the diminishing emphasis on functional root relations brought about by increased use of chromaticism in the romantic era. Our focus now will be on various conscious rejections of harmonic tonality. The bridge to twentieth-century music was engineered by those composers who turned from the established order and rhetoric of harmony, and, one way or another, redefined their tonal materials and methods. This was accomplished partly by "rediscovering" archaic materials such as the liturgical modes, but also by absorbing certain non-Western influences as we shall see later.

This chapter is devoted to the Russian pianist and composer Alexander Scriabin (1872-1915), whose musical evolution led eventually to the complete denial of harmonic function. His early works show the influence of Chopin and Liszt; later he absorbed some of the stylistic traits of Debussy and Ravel, but his mature style was formulated chiefly by his passionate interest in Wagner's music. He not only carried forward Wagner's harmonic language (especially that of *Tristan*), but he extended the Wagnerian principle of *Gesamtkunstwerk* to include the projection of colored lights in his symphonic poem *Prometheus: The Poem of Fire.* An adumbration of today's "psychedelic" effects, these projections were to be played from a color keyboard with a specific color associated with each note (for example, C = red, G = orange, D = brilliant yellow, etc.). Unfortunately, the construction of an instrument to produce these effects proved too difficult, so the first performance (1911) was without the color organ.

First contact with Scriabin's music often is baffling. His later works, in particular, impart a sense of "floating" sonorities with few points of contact with stable tonal ground. The effect is a continuous state of spiritual exaltation. To gain an inkling of Scriabin's purpose and an understanding of his methods, one must consider his mystical, visionary nature. He was, in fact, absorbed in theosophy, which is the union of religion and philosophy. A primary concern of theosophy is to penetrate the heart of divine nature and define the forces of creation and life within a unitary system.[1] Scriabin's intellectual and aesthetic evolution led to a final grandiose conception. It was a work, never completed, to be called *Mysterium.* This was to be an all-encompassing work including music, poetry, dancing, colored lights, and scents—a mass dance of ecstasy in which all would participate. Indeed, Scriabin felt himself to be a kind of messiah who was to "sound the final chord of our race, reuniting it with the Spirit." From theosophic notions of unity stems Scriabin's technique of fusing chord and scale, harmony and melody. In some of his works a single set of notes generates all of the tonal material. It is this aspect of his style plus the unique chords he evolved which we shall investigate now.

229. The strongest influence on Scriabin was that of Wagner. The brief example below is reminiscent of the opening measures of *Tristan*.

The melody begins by outlining the B-flat minor triad, but the harmony does little to reinforce this feeling. The whole passage shows whole-tone scale influence. The last chord, for example, contains all the notes of a whole-tone scale. Can the first chord also be analyzed as stemming from a whole-tone scale? _____

Yes.

230. If the B-flat in the first measure and the C in the second are analyzed as appoggiaturas, all the notes fall into the same whole-tone scale. Thus, the total effect is of completely static harmony. What is the intervallic relation between the bass notes of the two chords? A _____.

tritone   (or *dim. 5th*)

231. If the B-flat in the first measure of the example in Frame 229 is accepted as the chord tone, the result is a dominant ninth chord. In any case, the harmony fails to establish tonal feeling because the tonal implications of the first chord are in no way satisfied in the second.

   To carry one step further the notion that the chord in the first two measures is an extended dominant structure, both the A and C (at the asterisks) can be analyzed as part of the chord. The A can be considered the eleventh and C the _____ of a dominant chord on E-flat.

thirteenth

232. The example in Frame 229 shows several features of Scriabin's style. These are (1) whole-tone scale influence, (2) static harmony, (3) tritone use, and (4) sequence. Another typical passage is shown below:

Scriabin: *Etude,* Op. 56, No. 4

tritone

What is the interval between the bass notes in each of the first three measures (the bracketed notes)? A _____ .

False.
(Each chord suggests a different key, but none is established.)

233.   Each of the chords in the first three measures of the example in the preceding frame shows whole-tone influence. The aural effect in each case is a dominant ninth, eleventh, or thirteenth chord. Because of this, these measures have clear tonal orientation.   (True/False) _____

---

234.   The first six chords of the example in Frame 232 are shown in simplified notation below:

All six of these chords are similar; each has the effect of a dominant ninth, eleventh, or thirteenth chord. But when one active chord moves to another having similar activity, the result is static, usually nonfunctional harmony. The above succession of chords produces the effect of suspended tonality, and contains a (high/low) _____ degree of harmonic variety.

low

---

perfect

---

235. Whereas the chords in the preceding frame have low functional value in spite of their obvious activity, the final two chords of the example in Frame 232 do establish a tonality, and bear a functional relation to one another. To discover the reason for this, first answer this question: What interval separates the roots of the final two chords?
A _____ fifth.

$G^\flat$: V^{13} - I^{13}

---

236. The first six chords are related mostly by tritones so the functional effect is slight. The final two chords on the other hand, are related by roots a perfect fifth apart. This accounts for the stronger functional effect.

The effect here is something like an authentic cadence (dominant-tonic), but there is an important difference. To spotlight the nature of this difference, first indicate the precise chord symbol for each chord *(both are expanded tertian sonorities).*

$G^\flat$: _____   _____

(No response required.)

---

237. The first chord analyzed in the preceding frame is a dominant thirteenth with the fifth and eleventh omitted. The second is a tonic thirteenth with all tones present except the ninth ($A^\flat$). Thus, both chords contain practically the same tones. The only note in the second chord not contained in the first is G-flat. This causes the effect of harmonic change to be minimized. Remember that a complete thirteenth chord contains all seven tones of a scale. Thus, movement from one diatonic thirteenth chord to another merely involves redistributing the same notes.

---

238. Another example of limited harmonic variety is shown below:

Scriabin: *Sonata No. 5*, Op. 53

The sequential basis of this passage is immediately apparent. The pattern traced by the bass notes is E♭-A-F-B♮. Here again the tritone is stressed; also, all of these notes fall into the same _____ - _____ scale.

whole-tone

A.

239. Chord 1 consists of five notes. Only one additional note is needed to complete a whole-tone scale. Name the missing note. _____

False.

240. Chord 2 consists of exactly the same interval pattern as chord 1. (True/False) _____

Rhythm.

241. Although chords 2 and 4 are built up slightly differently than chords 1 and 3, the aural effect is very much the same in all cases. All four chords consist of notes contained in a single whole-tone scale.

Since there is practically no harmonic variety in this passage, we must look elsewhere for the musical interest. Which musical element carries the chief burden of interest in the example of Frame 238? _____

242. An especially fascinating aspect of Scriabin's style is his concept of chords as "magical columns of sound." In his later works he turns away from triadic harmony and builds chords in a variety of intervals. The so-called "mystic chord" consists of perfect, diminished and augmented fourths.

This chord supplies the basic harmonic material for his orchestral work *Prometheus: The Poem of Fire,* and other works too. Sometimes it is altered as we shall see shortly.

Scriabin's harmony is generally colored by liberal use of tritone relations, and the mystic chord is no exception. How many tritones does the chord above contain?

Two.
(C-F♯ ; B♭-E)

---

243. There are several interesting features about Scriabin's mystic chord. Although it is usually spelled in fourths, it may also be arranged in thirds and considered an altered thirteenth with fifth omitted.

The mystic chord contains all four triad types: major (DF♯A), minor (ACE), diminished (F♯AC), and augmented (B♭DF♯). Thus, this one chord is capable of supplying a wide variety of chords. But as actually used by Scriabin, there is little fluctuation of tension, and an almost total lack of harmonic movement; this leads to monotonous, static tonal effects.

The actual aural effect of the mystic chord is of an altered dominant _____ chord.

thirteenth

---

244. In the *Sonata No. 7* for piano, the mystic chord is altered by lowering the sixth note from D to D♭, and at times by extending the series of fourths to include a G.

The opening measures are shown in the next example.

Scriabin: *Sonata No. 7, Op. 64*

Are there any notes under the bracket which are not part of the chord as notated above this example? _____

No.

245.   The preceding frame shows that all the melodic and harmonic material for several beats derives from the "ground" chord.* The last chord (at the asterisk) has special importance throughout the sonata. The notation hinders assessment of its construction, so simpler notation is used below:

*By ground chord is meant the set of notes which generates much of the harmonic and melodic material. The ground chord gives a composition its unique aural character.

minor

This notation makes more comprehensible what is an interesting—but fairly simple—audible effect. The chord is actually based on D. Above this note there is a major third (F♯), and a _____ third (F♮).

---

246.   The presence of both major and minor thirds produces an iridescent and ambiguous quality, aptly suited for Scriabin's visionary pursuit of an exalted state of being. Chords with split thirds will be encountered in other contexts as we proceed. In all cases, the term "split third" is used to refer to simultaneous associations of major and minor quality.

In spite of the tension provided by the F-natural and F-sharp in the chord as notated in the preceding frame, the chord possesses stability because of the perfect fourths (A-D). Which tone in this chord is heard as the root? _____

D.

---

247.   The example below shows how the ground chord generates the split third chord.

The upper four notes (bracketed) appear to form a B-flat seventh chord. But close scrutiny reveals that the actual aural effect is of a split third chord the *sounding* root of which is the note _____.

F-sharp

---

248.   To discover another interesting feature of the chord discussed in the preceding frame analyze the intervals between notes 1-2, 2-3, and 3-4 as directed below. *(Note in (b) that an enharmonic spelling is used.)*

(a) m3   (b) P4   (c) m3

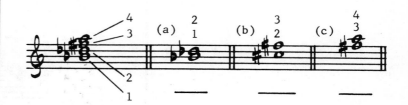

(a) 2/1   (b) 3/2   (c) 4/3

---

249. The split-third chord as spaced by Scriabin in the seventh sonata turns out to be a symmetrical structure consisting of a perfect fourth with a minor third both above and below.

$$m^3$$
$$|$$
$$P4$$
$$|$$
$$m^3$$

The passage below features exploitation of this sonority. Here we have on the upper staff a parallel stream of identical sonorities.

Scriabin: *Sonata No. 7, Op. 64*

G-sharp
(or A-flat)

The first chord on the upper staff (C E♭ G♯ B) is a split third chord. The *sounding* root of this chord is _____ .

---

250. The example below contains one of Scriabin's most remarkable chords.

Denial of Harmonic Function

113

Scriabin: *Sonata No. 7, Op. 64*

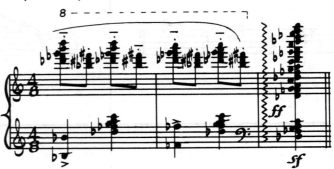

This towering chord consists of 25 notes covering a span of five octaves. The tonal structure is the same in each octave, so we shall examine one unit to observe its makeup. To facilitate our approach, the notes are respelled.

Like the chords discussed in Frames 245-249, the chord above contains both major and minor thirds. But, in addition, this chord has the interval of a _____ above the sounding root A.

seventh

We shall continue by analyzing in greater detail how both melodic and harmonic material is derived from a ground chord.

(Frames 251-259 refer to Panel 10.)

251.   Begin by looking at the first three measures of Example *a* in Panel 10. To discover the relation between the notes in this example and the ground chord you must do two things: (1) identify each note by writing into the example the numbers assigned to the chord tones below, (2) draw a circle around those notes which are *not* included in the chord. *(Write on Panel 10 [first three measures only], then check the correct solution at the left of this frame.)*

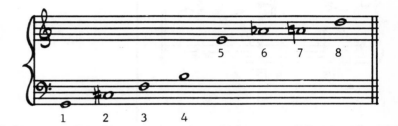

252. Continue in the same fashion with measures 4, 5, and 6.

Chapter 7

253. Continue as before with measures 7, 8, and 9.

254. What is the relation between measures 9 and 10?

_____

_____

Measure 10 is a sequence of measure 9.

255. Measure 10 is exactly the same as measure 9 except that it is transposed up a minor third. Thus, analysis would produce the same numbers if the ground chord is adjusted to the new pitch level.

Our analysis has revealed the fact that most notes are derived from the ground chord (only five are not, and these tones can be interpreted as having "nonharmonic" function). Also, some number series tend to recur (2-3-4, 3-6-8, and 4-1-3, for example).[2]

In the whole of this example there is not a single sonority which does not contain a tritone. (True/False) _____

False.
(But there is only one [m. 6], and here there is a M^7 to preserve the prevailing high level of tension.)

256. Turn now to Example *b* in Panel 10. Begin by applying number analysis to the notes on the first beat only *(lower bracket)*. *(Write on Panel 10, then check the correct solution at the left of this frame.)*

Yes.

257. Now with respect to the example as a whole, the pattern of thirty-second notes is stated six times *(upper brackets)*. Are the intervals in this pattern exactly the same in each case? _____

tritone

258. The passage in Example *b* is a sequence having several symmetrical characteristics. The intervals in each of the six groups of thirty-second notes make the pattern: m 2nd - m 3rd - M 2nd - m 3rd; the three-note chords on the bass staff are composed of tritones, m 7ths, and M 10ths; finally, the sequence moves up a _____ for each stage.

259. The final measures of the sonata are shown below:

Scriabin: *Sonata No. 6, Op. 62*

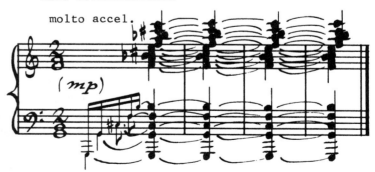

This chord includes most of the tones of the ground chord, and confirms the incipient G tonality. For the sake of simplicity, octave doublings are eliminated below:

Thus, the sonata ends with a piling up of the first six notes of the ground chord. It is the mystic chord based on G with the uppermost note lowered a (major/minor) _____ second.

minor

Our approach to Scriabin's music has focused on his preoccupation with harmony. For him, chords had special mystical significance related to his unorthodox blend of philosophy and religion. His mature harmonic style (represented by Sonatas 6-10) features virtually constant tension; the tritone is omnipresent, and the prevailing effect is of altered dominants which constantly evade resolution. Highly saturated with both melodic and harmonic chromaticism, this music causes one to feel sated with overripe sonorities. In spite of the exotic colors, the harmony is static; tonal variety is actually quite limited because particular sonorities dominate the tonal structure, and harmonic tension is constant.

Although pushed to the brink of atonality, tonal order is not completely lacking. It is true, though, that Scriabin goes beyond tertian harmonic structures to build chords with a variety of intervals, apparently selected from the higher reaches of the harmonic series;[3] also, functional root relations are mostly lacking.

Scriabin's style is most effective when limited to small works such as *Prelude* Op. 74 No. 1, which is reproduced in Panel 11. This piece contains many features of his mature style, and careful examination would be rewarding. But space forbids detailed analysis here, so we will point out only a few of the more significant features.

(Frames 260-271 refer to Panel 11.)
260. The harmony is dominated by the mystic chord (with the sixth note lowered). But this chord is often obscured by chromatic embellishing notes which can be likened to non-harmonic tones. Notation, too, sometimes makes analysis difficult. The example below shows how the ground chord can be extracted at No. 1.

Scriabin: *Prelude*, Op. 74, No. 1

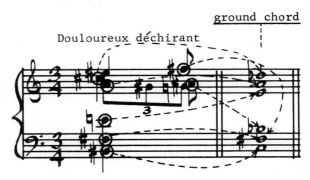

Denial of Harmonic Function

	Only three of the ten notes present during this beat are not included in the chord; these serve a(n) _____ function.
embellishing *(or nonharmonic)*	

	261. Arrange the notes included at No. 2 to represent the ground chord (as above) on A.

	262. The ground chord can be extracted from the notes at No. 3. Upon which note is the chord based (F♯, C, or G)? _____
C.	

	263. The chord at No. 4 is a mystic chord (with the sixth note lowered) based on C. (True/False) _____
True.	

	264. The same type chord occurs at No. 5. In this case it is based on the note _____.
E-flat	

	265. The chord at No. 7 is based on the note _____.
F-sharp	

	266. At No. 11, the ground chord can be spelled equally well on B-sharp and F-sharp. (True/False) _____
False. *(F♯ is the "root.")*	

	267. Of the six chords analyzed thus far, five (1, 2, 4, 7, and, 11) are in "root" position. The chord at No. 3 is based on C even though F-sharp is the actual bass note. The mystic chord most often appears with the ground note in the bass and the second note immediately above. The remaining notes may appear in any order as required by the movement of the voices.
(No response required.)	

tritone

268. The material beginning at [B] is the same as the opening measures ([A]). What is the intervallic relation between these two passages? A _____ .

F-sharp is emphasized by prolongation, and formal placement. Most important, F-sharp is the ground of the final chord. *(In your own words.)*

269.   The tonal orientation of the first part ([A]) is C, whereas the composition ends on F-sharp, a tritone removed. Notice, too, the exploitation of the tritone in the cadence-like progressions in the final seven measures (chords 6-7, 8-9, and 10-11). Here the tritone replaces the perfect fifth to produce a cadence effect. Scriabin, in effect, asks an unstable interval to perform the function of a stable one, a departure from traditional practice. In spite of the ambiguous root relation, F-sharp is clearly felt to be the tonal center at the end. Explain the reasons why this is so.

_____

_____

_____

_____

Your answer may include any of these points:
1.   lower tessitura
2.   simpler texture
3.   lower dynamic level

270.   The final chord (No. 12) contains a further alteration of the mystic chord. Here, not only the uppermost (sixth) note is lowered, but also the fifth note. This merely changes its quality; the tension level is much the same. In the entire composition there is not a single stable sonority. How, then, is the earlier tension relaxed at the close?

_____

_____

_____

(No response required.)

271.   Our approaches to the composition in Panel 11 have revealed the following aspects of Scriabin's style:

    1.   The mystic chord (with the sixth note lowered) provides the basis for most of the harmonic material.

    2.   Notes not included in the ground chord often have the character of nonharmonic tones.

    3.   The ground chord is most often in "root" position.

    4.   The two principal parts of the form are related by a tritone.

    5.   Cadences are formed by chords related by tritones.

    6.   Melodic lines contain mostly chromatic movement.

SUMMARY.

Totally chromatic, yet not quite atonal, Scriabin's mature style is a way station close to the frontier of complete rejection. Scriabin was obsessed with the creation of new chords, the most famous of which is the so-called mystic chord, built in fourths—augmented, diminished, and perfect. Often a single chord serves as the basis for a complete composition. Such a chord is "a tonal field which is equally chord and scale."[4] Even though his is a chord-dominated style in which much of the emotive effect resides in the unique quality of the sonorities, harmonic function is almost completely denied. Most chords are dominant-type sonorities which constantly evade resolution; the prevailing impression is tonally static. Harmonic motion, after all, requires not only an *active* sonority, but also resolution to a relatively *inactive* one. Scriabin, however, conceived a composition to be part of a continuum without beginning or end—an expression in sound of an all-encompassing unity. Harmonic motion, thus, was unwanted.

Scriabin's style is a personal idiom shaped by his philosophical speculations. Intriguing though it may be, it did not lend itself to further development. Nevertheless, through his rejection of tertian structures and functional harmonic relations, Scriabin contributed to the final dissolution of harmonic tonality. The direct line of descent with respect to extreme chromaticism leads through Liszt, Wagner, Strauss, and Wolf to Schoenberg and the second Viennese school, and this development the author intends tracing in a later volume. But now, to continue this study of the evolutions which led to twentieth-century music, we shall turn back a few years.

Scriabin's mature style dates from about 1905, and by this time other composers already had opened new gates to reveal vast unexploited tonal resources. Whereas Scriabin's style stems directly from Liszt and Wagner—thus strongly influenced by German aesthetics—the movement we shall follow next is a conscious reaction against German music in general, and Wagner's influence in particular. This development is called impressionism, and its central figure is Claude Debussy.

8

New Tonal Freedoms

The term impressionism was first applied to the works of a small group of late nineteenth-century artists. It was suggested by the title of a painting by Monet "Impression: Sunrise" (1872). As in the case of most new artistic movements, impressionism was rooted in antagonism. The rebellion in this case was against the world of academic art which perpetuated ideals inherited from Renaissance masters, as well as the excessive emotionalism of romanticism.

The ideals of impressionism are best expressed in works by Monet, Renoir, Sisley, and Pissaro. These painters were primarily concerned with optical perception and the movement of light. Much of their work was done out-of-doors, a radical departure from the accepted practice of the time which was to bring sketches into the studio where the real work was done. The impressionists, however, wished to transfer directly to the canvas their perception of the changing influence of light and shade. As their desire was to capture a fleeting moment of reality, they turned to a highly analytical examination of the visual sensation of light, and insisted on the "scientific" nature of their discoveries.

The optical discoveries of which so much was written include these three principles: (1) transfer of color, (2) simultaneous contrast, and (3) the optical mixture of color. It was Edouard Manet (1832-1882), generally regarded as the originator of impressionism, who discarded the classic principle of local color in which the color of each object remains separate from that of surrounding objects. He observed that reflected light transfers color from one object to another, and painted the transferred colors in a naturalistic way, or sometimes in an arbitrary way to heighten the visual impact.

As for the principle of simultaneous contrast, it can be proved that any hue modifies its neighboring color by producing an aureole of a tone which is its own complement. For example, red placed next to yellow (if red is quantitatively greater) produces not only the sensation of orange, their intermediate color, but also of green, the complementary color of red. With this knowledge, painters intensified the brilliance of their chromatic effects by actually painting in the complementary to a given color.

The principle of optical mixture is closely related to the preceding one. It was found that small areas of pure color are mixed by the eye to produce an intensified sensation. Impressionist painters broke up light into its constituent primary hues and covered their canvases with mosaics of color spots, which, when viewed from a distance, blend together to produce a more brilliant color sensation than could be obtained by mixing paint on the palette. This is perhaps the most striking feature of impressionist technique, and its most rigorous application may be observed in the works of Georges Seurat, who is sometimes referred to as a scientific impressionist. This technique is called divisionism or pointillism, and it is paralleled by an analogous practice in music in which tones are separated from one another by silences, and drastic contrasts of pitch, timbre, and dynamics are exploited.

In spite of all their theorizing, impressionists were the least intellectual of painters; they apprehended life not through the mind, but through the senses. They interpreted nature with tenderness, and their paintings reflect a world enchanting to the eye. There also is a prevailing cheerfulness in their work; the inhabitants of their paintings are generally engaged in the pursuit of pleasure. Preoccupied with the depiction of nature, the impressionists concerned themselves little with class struggle or ideology. Because of this, and also their concern with surface appearance, impressionist art is vulnerable to the charge of superficiality. But this art, though poorly regarded at the time of its creation, today enjoys an immense popularity. Most important of all, in spite of its limitations and its relatively short life as an active movement, impressionism established new ways of observing and recording reality.

Coincident with impressionism in art, a group of poets known as "symbolists" attacked similar problems in the field of literature. Rimbaud, Verlaine, Maeterlinck, and Mallarmé are the principal figures of this school. Theirs was a revolt against the realistic novel with its minute descriptions of objective reality. Uninterested in narrative and description, the symbolists attempted to recreate the subtle states of the human psyche. Poetry, they thought, should suggest meaning, evoke sensations, and thus rise above the level of mere description. For them, the symbol and the metaphor—even the mere sounds of words—were more valuable than clearly stated meaning for the expression of the inner life of the soul. Sometimes obscure and esoteric, with little conventional versification, the intent of this poetry was to arouse emotional responses and to suggest states of mind. Its abstract nature brings it close to the most abstract art of all—music. Symbolist poetry did, in fact, exert an important influence on music. Claude Debussy (1862-1918), the composer most intimately associated with impressionism in music, was included in the circle of symbolist writers, and was particularly fascinated by Mallarmé.

Debussy received thorough musical training at the Paris Conservatoire to which he was admitted at the age of eleven. At the Conservatoire his study was marked by constant conflict with his teachers because of his unwillingness to "abide by the rules." He was from the beginning a musical rebel. When he was twenty-two—after several unsuccessful attempts—his cantata *L'Enfant prodigue* (The Prodigal Son) won for him the coveted *Prix de Rome,* which entitled him to live at the Villa Medici in Rome at government expense, with no obligation other than an annual work to demonstrate his progress. At the end of the second year he sent back the symphonic suite *Le Printemps* (Spring) for orchestra and wordless chorus. This work displeased the professors at the Conservatoire, who cautioned him to "beware of that vague impressionism which is one of the most dangerous enemies of truth in art." This was the first application of the term impressionism to music, and henceforth Debussy was identified with this artistic style. Actually, Debussy objected strenuously to the label as being too limiting, but was unable to shake himself loose from it. And regardless of Debussy's objection, there is an obvious parallel between the blurred outlines and pastel hues characteristic of much impressionist art, and the fragmentary phrase structure, indefinite cadences, and diffuse harmonies of his music. This is a music which understates; like impressionist art, it suggests rather than explains.

Debussy's position as a pivotal figure bridging the music of the nineteenth and twentieth centuries cannot be overstated. For this reason it is desirable that some of the influences on his musical development be noted. First of all, he was early enamored with the music of Wagner, and even made pilgrimages to Bayreuth. But later his interest in Wagner waned, and he became violently antagonistic to Wagner's ideas. He strove to escape from Germanic influences which then were especially strong in France. His goal was to establish a truly French musical style. Still, the influence of Wagner's harmonic style (particularly that of *Tristan*) is evident in Debussy's music, especially in his use of unresolved dissonance, the avoidance of cadence function, and also the use of chords for their expressive impact.

Another early influence occurred when Debussy was employed by Mme. Nadezhda von Meck, Tcchaikovsky's patroness, as a piano teacher for her children. Traveling with the family in Switzerland, Italy, and later in Russia, Debussy became acquainted with the music of Borodin and Mussorgsky, the influence of which showed up later in his own music. Still another important influence occurred at the Universal Exposition staged in Paris in 1889 to celebrate the century of progress that followed the French Revolution. For this exposition the Eiffel Tower was built to demonstrate the practicality of steel for the construction of tall buildings, and the scientific, industrial, and artistic accomplishments of France were displayed. From the French colonies were brought examples of native culture, and Debussy was especially taken with the exotic timbres, rhythms, and scales of the Javanese gamelan. Oriental influences play an important role in impressionist music as we shall see later. These, then, are the chief influences which helped shape Debussy's style. We shall take note how they are translated into technical devices as we continue.

Special attention has been given to Debussy because not only is he the originator of impressionism in music, but his works express better than those of any other composer the ideals of impressionism. But other composers are also involved with this movement, and they will be met in due course.

We shall begin our examination of impressionist technique with a few references to Debussy's composition for orchestra *Prélude à l'après-midi d'un faune* (The Afternoon of a Faun), the first composition in impressionist style to attract wide attention. This work was begun in 1892 and first performed in Paris on December 22, 1894. It is based on a symbolist poem by Mallarmé concerning the amorous recollections of a faun (a deity of the woods, half-human, with pointed ears and goat's feet) in which the distinction between illusion and actuality is uncertain. In 1912, Debussy's Prelude served as the basis of a ballet presented by Diaghilev's Ballets Russes. This ballet greatly offended Parisian taste and led to the first "Ballets Russes scandal." This was Nijinsky's first choreographic effort, and in this he was influenced by the rhythmic concepts of Jacques Dalcroze. The effect was largely static—the dancers moving stiffly and rhythmically, resembling figures on a classical bas-relief. Also, some of Nijinsky's movements were regarded as being obscene.[1]

L'après-midi d'un faune opens with a passage for solo flute which immediately establishes a languid, exotic mood. More important, this deceptively simple passage shatters the familiar order of traditional tonality. The frames which follow will show the new tonal freedoms established by this, and other passages in Debussy's revolutionary work.

272. The opening melody is shown below with a simplified version in which most of the nonessential notes have been stripped away. This is to reveal the basic tonal structure.

Debussy: *Prélude à l'après-midi d'un faune*

The structural tones in the first two measures show an oscillation between two tones which are the interval of a _____ apart.

tritone *(or A 4th)*

273. The structural exploitation of the tritone in the first two measures denies classical tonality which is based on the tonic-dominant axis of a perfect fifth. The result is a feeling of "unnatural," or ambiguous tonality, in keeping with the spirit of the music. Because the tritone divides the octave

into two equal parts, it produces a symmetrical, static effect. Also symmetrical is the exact repetition of the first measure in the second. Immediate repetition of a small fragment is a characteristic feature of impressionist music. Symmetrical devices such as those observed here give the music a sense of static balance, and create a timeless, motionless effect.

The chord outlined in the third measure may be interpreted either as an E major triad with added sixth,[2] or a seventh chord whose root is _____ .

C-sharp

---

274.   Even though there may be some ambiguity, the chord in measure three will be regarded here as an E major triad with added sixth. The example below suggests a possible interpretation of the basic tonal structure of the entire phrase.

The relative stable sonority on E is both preceded and followed by ambiguous tonal relations. The cadence note (A♯) is related to the tonal center by the interval of a _____ .

tritone *(or A 4th)*

---

275.   The tonal structure of the melody in Frame 272 incorporates two tritones (C♯-G and E-A♯). The exploitation of tritone relations is an important part of impressionist technique, and we shall encounter many other examples. Here in the very first measures of *l'après-midi,* tonal relations are stressed which flaunt traditional style; hardly a hint of tonic-dominant functionality exists here. This, then, is the revolution accomplished by this simple melodic line, and the entire work consists mostly of coloristic harmony in which chords have little urgency to move in a particular direction; they are used for their sound values as unique entities with no established relation to their neighbors. A parallel between this use of chords and the symbolist poets' use of words for their suggestive value is obvious.

The melody we have just examined appears several times as the work progresses; it undergoes transformations, and is given a variety of harmonizations. We shall look at a few of these to observe the harmonic relations just described.

(No response required.)

276. The principal melody of *l'après-midi* appears in harmonized form first in measure eleven. This statement is shown in the example below. To approach the harmonic structure of this phrase, analyze nine of the chords in the spaces provided. *Do not use Roman numerals.* Instead, use symbols such as C^7, a^7, $b^{\circ 7}$, D^{13}, etc. *(Inversions need not be shown. Be alert for enharmonic spellings.)*

Debussy: *Prélude à l'après-midi d'un faune*

1. D^7 2. G^7
3. D^7 4. G^7
5. $d\sharp^{\circ 7}$ 6. B^{13}
7. E^{Add6} 8. $C\sharp^7$
9. $A\sharp^7$
(See the following frame.)

---

fourth

277. Chords 2 and 4 in the preceding frame are identified as seventh chords on G. They are actually spelled as German-sixth chords and may be analyzed as such. If D major is accepted as a momentary tonic, these German-sixth chords are built on the _____ scale degree.

---

278. The nature of this music calls for a variety of approaches. In all cases, analysis is designed to direct your attention to certain selected features in the music, and symbols are chosen which are appropriate to the purpose served. The symbols used in the preceding frame are not absolutely precise, but they do identify the chord roots, and also the quality in most cases. Your own symbols need not always be exactly the same as the ones supplied provided you understand the reason for the variations. Try, however, to adapt to the symbols used.

The example below traces the roots as analyzed above, and also indicates an interpretation of the structural importance of each chord.

This passage contains mostly color harmony. There is, however, one strong, unequivocally functional progression. It is from chord _____ to chord _____ .

6 (to) 7
(dominant-tonic)

279. The only clear tonal orientation is in the third measure of the example in Frame 276. The harmony both before and after does little to affirm an E tonality. Notice that this passage contains not a single simple triad—most chords are seventh chords. Do most of the sevenths of these seventh chords resolve in a normal manner (down by step)? _____

No.
(Most resolve upward.)

280. An important aspect of the new tonal freedom associated with impressionism is indifference to the resolution of dissonance; active chords, like inactive ones, are often treated as color entities *without obligation to either a structural system or functional movement.* But functional harmony and strong tonal orientation are by no means completely abandoned, as will be seen in the next example. Our melody appears again at measure 21 in somewhat altered form. Analyze the chords at the places indicated in the same manner as in Frame 276.

Debussy: *Prélude à l'après-midi d'un faune*

leggiero e espr.

1. E^Add6   2. C

3. E^{Add6}   4. E⁹
5. e°⁷   6. B⁹

---

281. In the example below, the analysis of the preceding frame is transferred to staff notation.

This diagram shows the strong tonal emphasis on E. The phrase is even based on the tonic-dominant axis provided by the first and last chords. So functional harmony does occur in impressionist music, but its role is often secondary to purely coloristic effects.

Chord 2 is a chromatic mediant in E major; it produces an effect which can best be described as (ultrachromaticism/ expanded tonality) _____.

expanded tonality

True.
(The tritone E - B♭ is the reason.)

282. Chord 5 in Frame 280 more seriously undermines the feeling of an E tonality than chord 2. (True/False) _____

(Answer is located at bottom of Panel 12.)

283. Omitting several other appearances, the example in Panel 12 shows a setting which occurs at measure 100. This is the last complete occurrence and leads to the principal tonality of E major. Like the others, this example consists of both functional and nonfunctional harmony. Analyze the chords as before. *(Write on the example in Panel 12. For your convenience, the correct solution is shown below the example.)*

---

major-minor
(or dominant)

284. Chords 1, 2, 3, 4, and 5 (in Panel 12) are all of the same type. These chords are _____ - _____ seventh chords.

No.

285. Although obscured by enharmonic spellings, chords 1-5 are all in second inversion. Do any of these chords resolve as dominant seventh chords? _____

286. The diagram below traces the root relations of the chords as analyzed in Panel 12.

The chords in the first part of this passage have low functional value. But the latter part provides very strong cadence affirmation of the principal tonality of E. Which chord is the *first* to have high functional value in E? _____

10. *(There is certain to be some difference of opinion.)*

287. A Roman numeral analysis of chords 10-13 is meaningful; it reveals the functional nature of these chords which is in contrast to the preceding nonfunctional harmony. Supply chord symbols for the chords below:

Debussy: *Prélude à l'après-midi d'un faune*

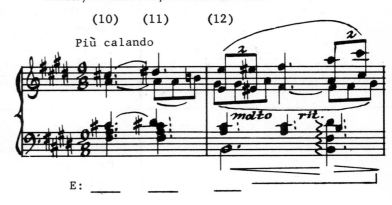

E: ii vii°$^6_5$ V^{13}

I

288. Chord 12 has been analyzed as a dominant thirteenth. Although this is the simplest interpretation, others are possible. The spacing of notes and the melodic lines produce an aural effect of several chords sounding together.

Debussy: *Prélude à l'après-midi d'un faune*

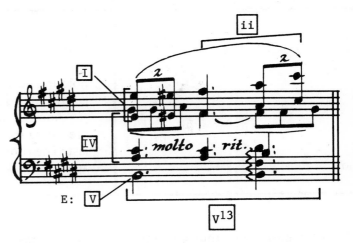

(No response required.)

Because every degree of the scale is present in a complete thirteenth chord, the harmonic effect is determined by the spacing. Any note placed in the bass tends to act as the root. Thus, the prolonged B in the lowest voice of the example above asserts itself and has strong tonal function as the dominant of E.

---

289.   One final example is a small fragment derived from the first part of our melody. This occurs in the coda at measure 107.

Debussy: *Prélude à l'après-midi d'un faune*

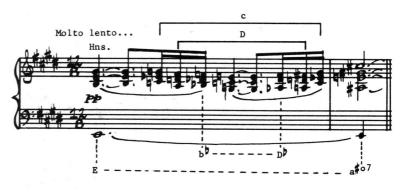

The example is designed to show the nearly symmetrical structure of this phrase. The brackets *above* the staff link identical chords, while the dotted lines below the staff link chords which are unlike. This is an example of color harmony which has no functional value whatever. Its static effect is reinforced by the sustained note in the bass which can be called a _____ .

pedal

---

290.   The pedal is often used to give tonal stability to passages which feature nonfunctional harmonic relations; they hold in check tonality-destroying forces, even though they contribute to motionless harmonic effects.

Another symmetrical feature of the example in the preceding frame is the relation of the first chord to the last. The roots of these chords are the interval of a _____ apart.

tritone

The examples shown thus far were selected to contrast functional and nonfunctional harmony. In impressionist music, traditional tonic-dominant relations are minimized, but not abandoned altogether. Still,

Chapter 8

the prevailing effect is of floating harmonic color rather than movement. This static effect is heightened by the use of pedals, and symmetrical relations such as the immediate repetition of short phrases, the exploitation of the tritone, and balanced harmonic and melodic patterns.

Another of the new tonal freedoms of impressionism is the extensive use of altered chords, especially chromatic mediants and altered dominant structures. The result is tonality expanded to include chords which have little functional relation to one another.

291.   In the example below, the tonality of C is clearly established by the recurring figure on the lower staff. Many of the triads in the intervening passages, however, are chromatic mediants which greatly expand the color resources of the tonality.

Debussy: *Préludes,* Vol. II, No. 6 ("‘General Lavine'—eccentric")

Most of the triads are related to one another by the interval of a _____.

third

292.   As unrelated as the triads seem, they are held to the tonal orbit of C major by being either diatonic triads or chromatic mediants related to I, IV or V.

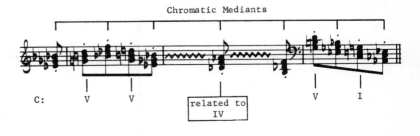

New Tonal Freedoms

Attention already has been called to the penchant for symmetrical writing in impressionist music. This example contains several interesting features. The first five chords in the example above form a pyramid which is a palindrome.[3] With reference now to the example in Frame 291, what other symmetrical element do you find in measures 1-4?

_____

_____

_____

Measures 3-4 are an exact repetition of 1-2.

---

293. Still another type of symmetrical writing may be discovered by listing the quality of each triad in the example below *(write your answers on the appropriate horizontal lines):*

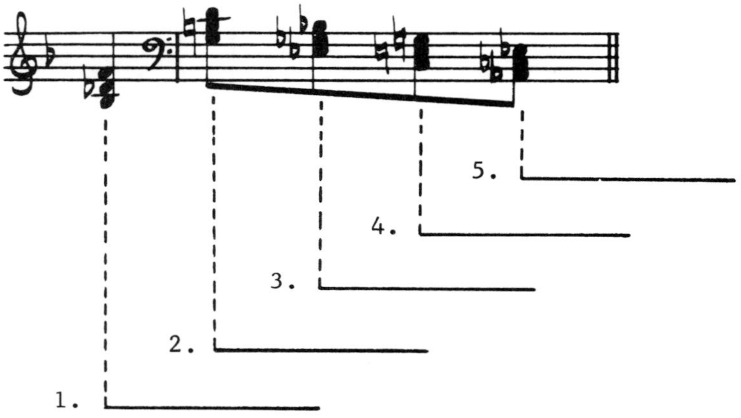

1. minor
2. major
3. minor
4. major
5. minor

---

294. The analysis in the preceding frame shows that triads alternate between major and minor. Another glance at the original example in Frame 291 will show that this is true of the entire phrase. Such arbitrary symmetrical relations add a new tonal dimension to music. Check the term which best applies to this example.

1. Expanded tonality _____

2. Ultrachromaticism _____

1. √

---

295. Another example of chords with chromatic mediant relationships is shown below. Indicate the quality of each chord in the spaces provided.

Debussy: *Estampes* ("Jardins sous la pluie")

(All chords are major triads.)

296. To see more clearly the relation of the chords in the preceding frame, write on the staff below the *root* of each chord. *(The first is given as an example.)*

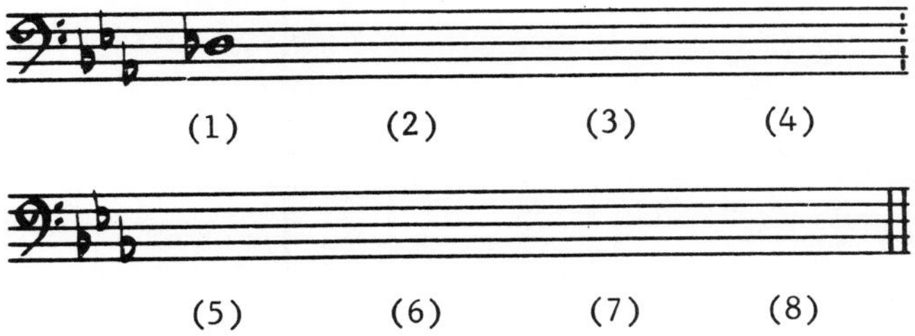

---

real

297. The roots recorded in the preceding frame reveal that chords 5-8 constitute a sequence of chords 1-4. The sequence is (real/tonal) _____.

No.

298. Do the chords in this example establish a tonality? _____

299. In contrast to the example in Frame 291, the example in Frame 295 establishes no sense of tonality. This is often true in the case of real sequence. The use of major triads only is a type of symmetrical harmony. (True/False)

_____

True.

---

300. Tonal orientation is a bit stronger in the next example. The last two chords are a perfect fourth apart, and this is a strong root relation. Nevertheless, the tonality is ambiguous. The last chord, for example, is it a tonic or dominant? One cannot be certain. List the quality of each triad in the spaces provided.

Debussy: _Préludes_, Vol. II, No. 2 ("Feuilles mortes")

1. major
2. minor
3. major
4. minor
5. major

---

301. Again we see the symmetrical alternation of major and minor triads. This, plus the prevailing third-relation root movement contributes to nontonal feeling.

    Much of the unique aural charm of chromatic mediant progressions is due to the false relations which usually occur. Between chords 1 and 2 in the preceding frame, for example, there are two false relations. One is listed below, indicate the other.

2. F♯ - F♮

302.   Our next example shows the colorful effect of a chromatic mediant in an otherwise diatonic passage. The composer in this case is Frederick Delius (1862-1934) who was born in England of German parentage. Strongly influenced by French music, he is often referred to as the English impressionist.

Since this passage is quite tonal, a Roman numeral analysis is pertinent. Supply the proper chord symbols. *(Show inversions.)*

Delius: *Irmelin,* Act I ("Prelude")

303.   Two of the chords in the preceding frame are in second inversion. Second inversions figure prominently in impressionist music. Because of their relatively weak sonority, they contribute somewhat to loosening of the tonal fabric.

All of the chords in the example below are in second inversion.   (True/False) _____

True.

New Tonal Freedoms

Debussy: *Masques*

2.

304. The example in the preceding frame leaves no doubt as to the tonality of F-sharp. Still, the exclusive use of second inversion chords produces a weaker, more diffuse tonal effect than would a variety of chord positions, including some with the root in the bass.

Refer, again, to the example above. Notice that two chords are numbered. Both of these are altered chords in F-sharp major. Which has a chromatic mediant relation to the surrounding chords? _____

305. Only major triads are used in the final demonstration of chromatic mediants below:

Debussy: *Préludes,* Vol. I, No. 7 ("Ce qu'a vu le vent d'Ouest")

In addition to chromatic mediant relations, this example features another tonality-defeating harmonic relation. The chords at the asterisks are preceded and followed by chords the interval of a _____ removed.

tritone
(d5 or A4)

---

306. The chords in the first three measures of the above example (under the bracket) produce a symmetrical structure which is called a _____ .

palindrome

---

307. In impressionist music, dominant chords are altered in various ways to produce more colorful effects. The chords at the asterisks below are altered dominants. A simplified notation of these chords is shown at the right.

Delius: *Five Piano Pieces*, No. 1 ("Mazurka")

Of course the highest note C (in the reduced chord) could be analyzed as a nonharmonic tone; if this note is accepted as a chord member the analysis would be a dominant thirteenth chord with lowered _____ .

fifth

308. Many altered dominants (including the one in the preceding frame) show influence of the whole-tone scale. They are often called "whole-tone dominants." Except for the final chord, all of the sonorities in the next example are derived from the whole-tone scale on D-flat.

Debussy: *Masques*

$V^{\natural 9}_{5}$

The first six measures in this example consist entirely of whole-tone dominants. In spite of the tension generated by each of these, the effect is harmonically static. Because these chords are all derived from the same whole-tone scale, everything is an arpeggiation on the same chord (scale). The cadence, however, creates harmonic motion. We shall look now at the final four measures. Supply the chord symbol for the chord in measures 7-8 (at the asterisk).

---

raised

309. The chord analyzed in the preceding frame may be called a dominant ninth chord with (raised/lowered) _____ fifth.

(No response required.)

310. The harmony in measure 9 of Frame 308 needs further explanation. Analyzed as a tonic in G-flat major, the notes F, A-natural, and C-natural obviously are not included in the harmony—they comprise what is sometimes called an "appoggiatura chord." This chord resolves nicely into the G-flat triad in measure 10. But another explanation for measure 9 is to recognize two chords sounding simultaneously—F over G-flat—this is called a "polychord."[4]

---

311. Altered dominants occur in measure 3 of the example below:

Delius: *Irmelin*, Act I ("Prelude")

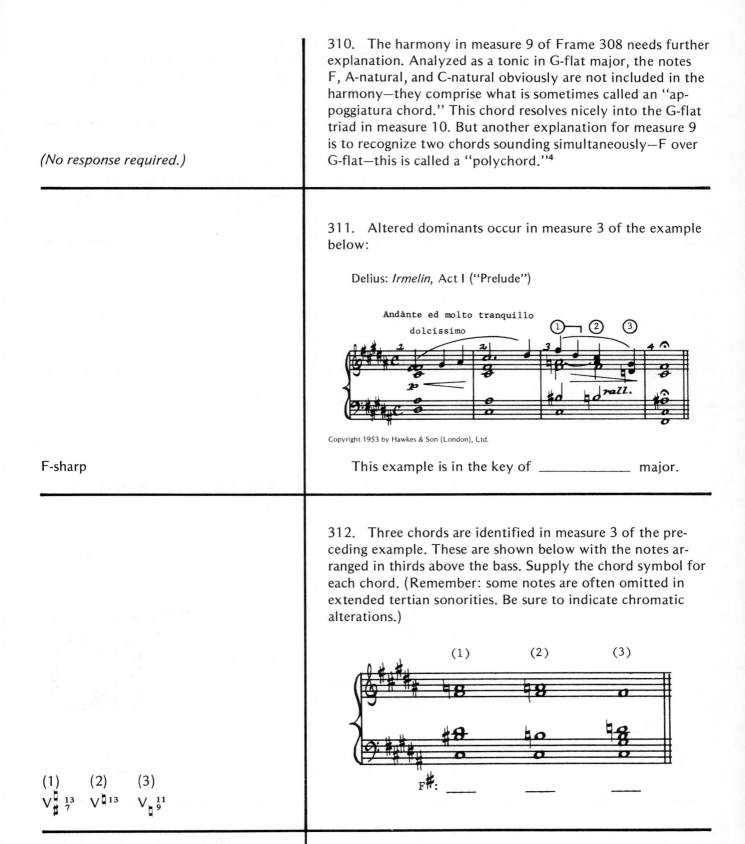

Copyright 1953 by Hawkes & Son (London), Ltd.

F-sharp

This example is in the key of _____ major.

---

312. Three chords are identified in measure 3 of the preceding example. These are shown below with the notes arranged in thirds above the bass. Supply the chord symbol for each chord. (Remember: some notes are often omitted in extended tertian sonorities. Be sure to indicate chromatic alterations.)

F#: _____   _____   _____

(1)   (2)   (3)

$V^{\sharp 13}_{\natural 7}$ $V^{\natural 13}$ $V^{11}_{\flat 9}$

---

313. The analysis above reveals three different alterations of the dominant chord. The result is a colorful elaboration

No. *(Not if functional resolutions prevail.)*	of dominant function. This is a frequent manifestation in impressionist music. Such alterations tend to increase the activity of dominant harmony. Do they also contribute to tonal ambiguity? _____
(No response required.)	314. Altered dominants do not necessarily undermine tonality. But if functional resolution is avoided (as in measures 1-6 of the example in Frame 308), tonality may be ambiguous, or avoided altogether.

Thus far, in exploring the new tonal freedoms of impressionism, we have observed the avoidance of traditional tonic-dominant relations, and the extensive use of altered chords, including chromatic mediants and altered dominants. There remain two features to be noted. These are (1) frequent abrupt changes of tonality, particularly to distant keys, and (2) vaguely defined tonalities. The first of these leads to expanded tonality while the second anticipates the total rejection of functional tonality. The examples which follow will show various features of these two aspects of impressionist music.

	315. The key of G-flat major is established by the plagal cadence in the example below:
	Debussy: *Préludes,* Vol. I, No. 8 ("La fille aux cheveux de lin")

	G♭: IV I
vi⁷	The minor seventh chord outlined in the first two measures would be analyzed as _____ in G-flat major.
	316. The example below is a continuation of the one above. Here we have a sudden shift from G-flat major to E-flat major. Supply a Roman numeral analysis.

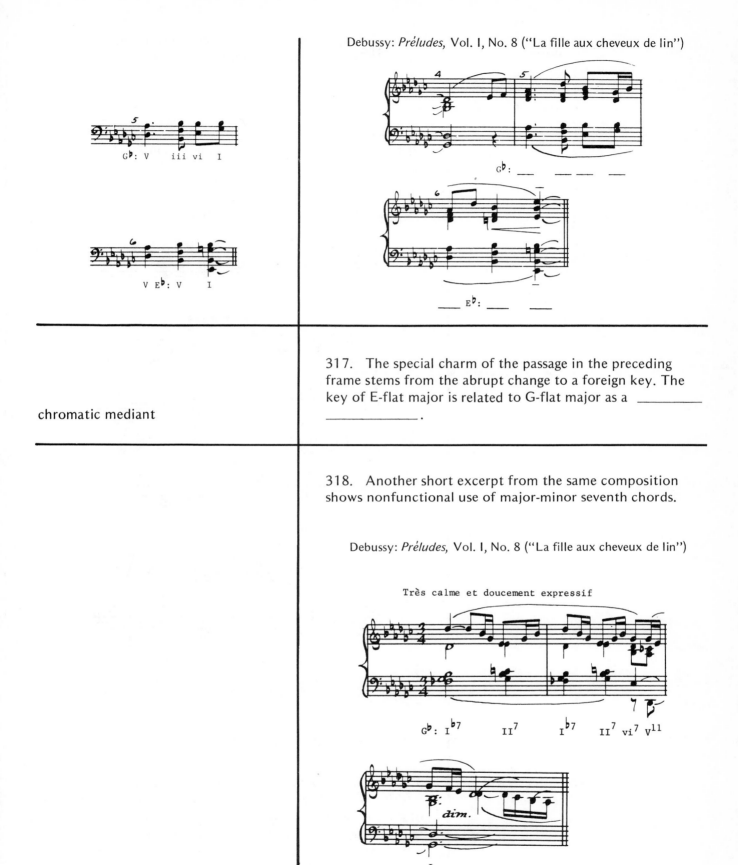

Debussy: *Préludes*, Vol. I, No. 8 ("La fille aux cheveux de lin")

Gb: V   iii vi   I

V   Eb: V   I

Gb: _____ _____

_____ Eb: _____ _____

---

chromatic mediant

---

317.   The special charm of the passage in the preceding frame stems from the abrupt change to a foreign key. The key of E-flat major is related to G-flat major as a _____ _____ .

---

318.   Another short excerpt from the same composition shows nonfunctional use of major-minor seventh chords.

Debussy: *Préludes*, Vol. I, No. 8 ("La fille aux cheveux de lin")

Très calme et doucement expressif

$Gb: I^{b7}$ II^7 I^{b7} II^7 vi^7 v^{11}

Bb:

dim.

I

third

The analysis given above does not show inversions. Actually, each major-minor seventh chord is in _____ inversion.

---

319. Another example of indefinite tonality is shown below:

Debussy: *Pelléas et Mélisande,* Act II, Scene 1

No.

Are the D major-minor seventh chords in the first measure (at the asterisks) resolved functionally? _____

---

320. In the preceding frame, the tones D and A vie for the position of tonal center. Its strong formal emphasis at the end of the passage gives D an advantage, but earlier, the A minor triad is emphasized. At first, the passage seems to lack a functional cadence, but the last three chords could be interpreted as an embellished authentic cadence in D.

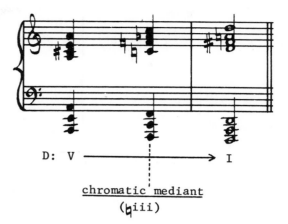

D: V ⟶ I

chromatic mediant
(♮iii)

Regardless of how it is analyzed, the cadence effect is minimized, and the harmony of the entire passage (Frame 319) leaves some doubt as to the tonal center.

Except for the relation pictured above, there is not a single progression which establishes a tonic-dominant axis. (True/False) _____

True.

---

321.   Only hidden tonic-dominant relations exist in the example in Frame 319. One was mentioned in the preceding frame. Notice, too, that the first chord is the minor dominant of the final chord.

D: v   I

Return to Frame 319 to observe the root relations. All chords are in root position, so it is easy to note the intervals involved. Indicate the number of occurrences for each type of movement.

Root Movement	Frequency
by 5th (or 4th)	_____
by 3rd (or 6th)	_____
by 2nd (or 7th)	_____

5th - 3

3rd - 2

2nd - 3

---

322.   The analysis above indicates a relatively high proportion of root movements by seconds and thirds. This is unlike music which is built on functional harmonic principles.

The example in Panel 13 was saved to close this chapter because it sums up a particular aspect of impressionist harmony. In this case tonality is not open to question; the key of D-flat major is clearly established, and most chords are diatonic triads, seventh, or ninth chords.

The chords at the two asterisks (Panel 13) are chromatic mediants which take over the function of the dominant. This passage contains two dominant ninth chords (measures 5 and 6), but each resolves nonfunctionally to the subdominant chord.

(No response required.)

---

323. The tabulation below reveals a concentration of chords on the second and third scale degrees.

Scale Degree	Chords	Occurrences
1 — — —	I	3
2 — — —	⌈ii	1
	⌊II$^{(9)}$	1
3 — — —	⌈iii	4
	⌊III^6	2
4 — — —	IV	2
5 — — —	V^9	2

Of the 15 chords, how many are supertonic or mediant chords (diatonic or altered)? _____

Eight.

---

324. The chord roots of the example in Panel 13 are traced below:

Roots

Tabulate the root movements in the spaces provided. *(List chromatic half-steps as seconds.)*

Root Movements	Occurrences
by 5th (or 4th)	_____
by 3rd (or 6th)	_____
by 2nd (or 7th)	_____

5th - 1
3rd - 5
2nd - 8

---

325. Our analysis of the example in Panel 13 has revealed three significant features:

Yes.

1. The dominant-tonic progression is avoided completely.

2. Chords on secondary scale degrees predominate.

3. Root movement by seconds and thirds greatly outweighs root movement by fifths.

So, in spite of a fairly simple, mostly diatonic chord vocabulary, and unambiguous tonal orientation, harmonic principles are operating here which set this music apart from that ruled by classical tonal order. Instead of tonality based on a structure of perfect fifths, we see here the tonic affirmed by iteration, prolongation, and formal placement—devices all originally associated more with melodic than harmonic tonality. But in spite of this, notice that the second phrase (measure 5 of our example in Panel 13) begins with a dominant ninth chord. Does its formal position give added structural importance to this chord? _____

No.

326. Although no direct tonic-dominant relation exists in this example (Panel 13), the macro-harmonic structure incorporates a hidden underpinning of classical tonal order. Aside from the tonic triad and the dominant ninth chord, do any other chords have structural importance in this example? _____

SUMMARY.

Traditional harmonic order is not abandoned in impressionist music, but new tonal freedoms are asserted which cause features of melodic tonality to be elevated in importance. Thus, when the structural role of harmonic tonality is reduced, the more primitive devices of iteration, formal placement, and rhythm take over. The novel tonal features of impressionist music examined and illustrated in this chapter are summarized below:

1. Traditional tonic-dominant relations are minimized.

2. Tritone and other symmetrical tonal relations are exploited.

3. Extensive use is made of altered chords, especially altered dominants and chromatic mediants.

4. There are frequent abrupt changes of tonality, particularly to distant keys.

5. Tonal centers are not clearly defined.

6. There is less functional harmony (root movements by seconds, thirds, and tritones are prevalent).

7. Dissonant sonorities are often unresolved.

8. Cadence effects are minimized.

(2) √

327. Indicate the correct statement(s) by checking one of the options below:

    1. Impressionism in music helped launch the literary movement called symbolism.

    2. Impressionism developed first as a movement in art.

(1) ____ (2) ____ Both ____ Neither ____

False. *(Tonality is usually rendered ambiguous.)*

328. Symmetrical writing tends to affirm a tonal center. (True/False) _____

True.

329. The following devices are all associated with symmetrical writing. (True/False) _____

    1. Tritone

    2. Real sequence

    3. Use of a single chord type

    4. Palindrome

    5. Alternating major and minor triads

    6. Immediate repetition

    7. Augmented triad

9

Enlarged Scale Resources (I)

In spite of new tonal freedoms harmonic relations associated with the major-minor key system continue to provide the basic—although sometimes hidden—tonal framework of impressionist music. Likewise, traditional scales are by no means given up completely. Much melodic and harmonic material is based on major and minor scales, with more "exotic" structures providing contrast and color. Our concern in this and the following chapter is the exploitation of scales little used in classical and romantic music.

We shall look first at uses made of modal scales. Prior to impressionism, several composers including Berlioz, Gounod, Franck, and Saint-Saens utilized Gregorian melodies in their music, so there was already established a precedent of modal use. Also, Debussy is known to have taken an interest in the work done by the Benedictine monks of Solesmes to restore Gregorian chant.[1] But instead of merely using liturgical melodies as source material, Debussy incorporated modal influences into his music as an integral part of his style. Largely ignored in concert music since the Renaissance, the reintroduction of modal scales evoked an impression of antique remoteness and charm. Actually, extended passages in a single mode are rare. Although pervasive, modal influence is fragmentary, and shows up mainly in melodic lines, with harmonic uses being less obvious.

Unlike medieval and Renaissance liturgical modal practices, the modes are treated merely as other forms of diatonic scales; the aural effect is more or less of "altered" major or minor scales. We shall continue with a brief presentation of modal scales, with particular attention paid to how each differs from traditional scales.

330. The seven modal scales are shown below. The sign ∧ is used to mark the location of half-steps.

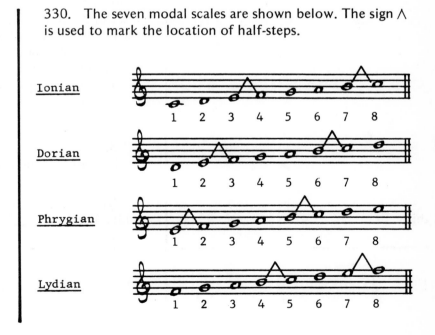

Mixolydian 1 2 3 4 5 6 7 8

Aeolian 1 2 3 4 5 6 7 8

Locrian 1 2 3 4 5 6 7 8

two

All modal scales consist of five whole-steps and _____ half-steps.

---

major

331.   Even though all modal scales consist of the same number of half- and whole-steps, each sounds different from the others because of its unique intervallic structure. Note that the Aeolian mode has the same pattern of half- and whole-steps as the natural minor scale; the Ionian mode sounds the same as the _____ scale.

---

332.   In the preceding frame, the modes are notated with basic (unaltered) notes only—the notes of the C major scale. This suggests an easy way to spell and identify modes on other pitches. *First you must memorize upon which scale degree of the major scale each mode is built.* For example, the Dorian mode is on the second degree of a major scale, the Phrygian mode is on the third, etc. The correct signature for a particular mode may then be supplied without difficulty. Follow the steps for spelling a Mixolydian mode on B:

1.   The Mixolydian mode is located on the fifth degree of a major scale.
2.   B is the fifth degree of the E major scale.
3.   Thus, the Mixolydian mode on B contains the same notes as the E major scale. (The signature is four sharps.)

Upon which degree of a major scale is the Phrygian mode built? The _____ .

third

---

333.   Supply the correct signature for the Phrygian mode on C.

Phrygian

334. Supply the correct signature for the Lydian mode on G.

Lydian

335. Now apply accidentals to the proper notes to produce the Dorian mode on B-flat.

Dorian

336. Apply accidentals to the proper notes to produce the Aeolian mode on F-sharp.

Aeolian

Locrian

337. The facts presented in Frame 332 also make it possible to identify modes. First ascertain the *major* key which results from the accidentals used. Then note upon which degree of this scale the mode is built. The example below shows the _____ mode.

Phrygian

338. The example below shows the _____ mode.

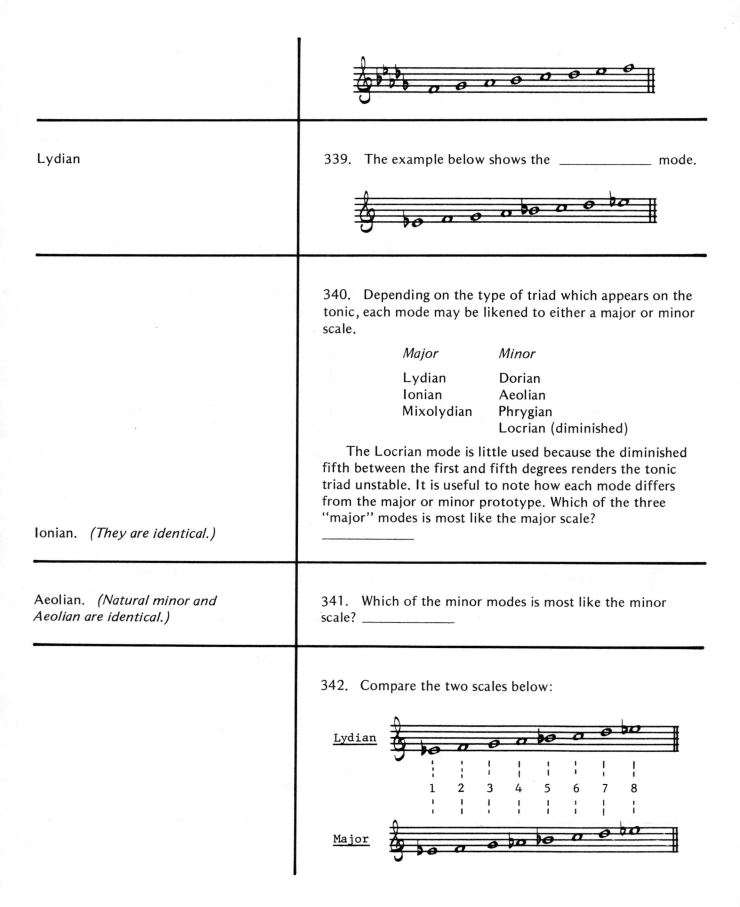

Lydian

339. The example below shows the _____ mode.

340. Depending on the type of triad which appears on the tonic, each mode may be likened to either a major or minor scale.

Major	Minor
Lydian	Dorian
Ionian	Aeolian
Mixolydian	Phrygian
	Locrian (diminished)

The Locrian mode is little used because the diminished fifth between the first and fifth degrees renders the tonic triad unstable. It is useful to note how each mode differs from the major or minor prototype. Which of the three "major" modes is most like the major scale?

_____

Ionian.   *(They are identical.)*

Aeolian.   *(Natural minor and Aeolian are identical.)*

341. Which of the minor modes is most like the minor scale? _____

342. Compare the two scales below:

higher

seventh
lower

higher

second
lower

The Lydian mode is the same as the major scale except that the fourth degree of the former is a half-step _____.

343. The example below shows that the Mixolydian mode is the same as the major scale except that the _____ degree of the former is a half-step _____.

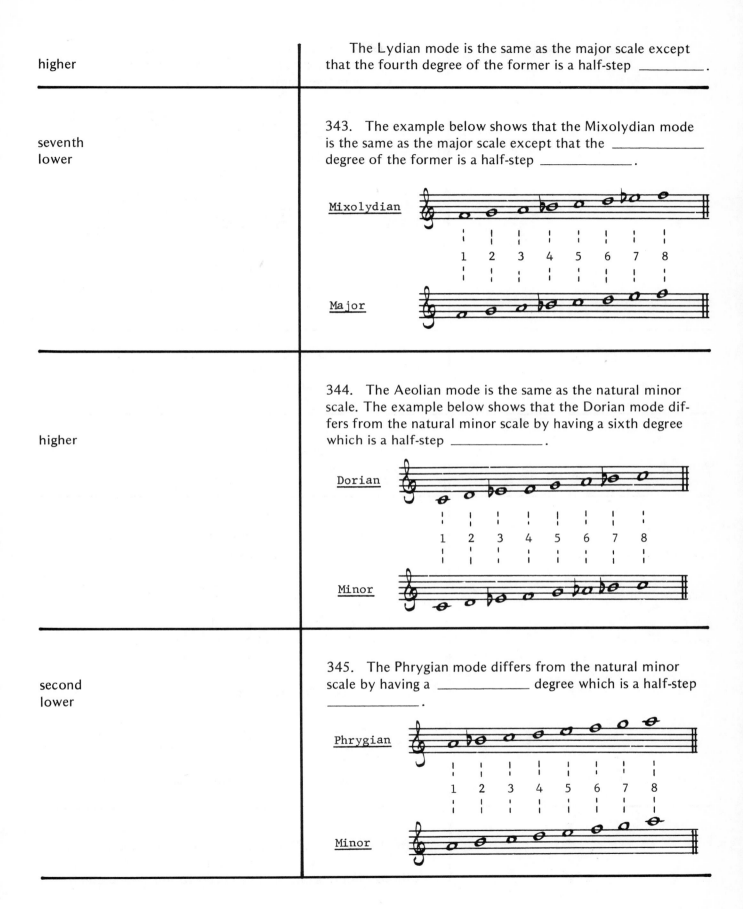

344. The Aeolian mode is the same as the natural minor scale. The example below shows that the Dorian mode differs from the natural minor scale by having a sixth degree which is a half-step _____.

345. The Phrygian mode differs from the natural minor scale by having a _____ degree which is a half-step _____.

Enlarged Scale Resources (I)
153

346. Of all the seven modes, the Locrian is least like either the major or minor scales. It is compared with the natural minor scale in the example below:

Two degrees of the Locrian mode are a half-step lower than in the natural minor scale; these are the _____ and _____ .

2nd (and) 5th

Mixolydian.

347. What mode is like the major scale except that the seventh degree is a half-step lower? _____

Phrygian.

348. What mode is like the natural minor scale except that the second degree is a half-step lower? _____

---

349. The similarity between the modes and major and minor scales is summarized below:

LIKE THE MAJOR SCALE

Ionian	—	identical
Lydian	—	4th degree raised
Mixolydian	—	7th degree lowered

LIKE THE NATURAL MINOR SCALE

Aeolian	—	identical
Dorian	—	6th degree raised
Phrygian	—	2nd degree lowered
Locrian	—	2nd and 5th degrees lowered

(No response required.)

---

350. We shall now look at a few examples of modal influence. The first is a melody by Maurice Ravel (1875-1937). Although impressionism in its purest form is found chiefly in the works of Debussy, Ravel is also intimately associated with this style. Younger than Debussy, Ravel is sometimes referred to as a post-impressionist. Form is generally more firmly delineated in his music than in Debussy's; also his sonorities tend to be more dissonant. Nevertheless, many of the techniques of impressionism distinguish his music, so we shall have occasion to refer to several of his works as we proceed.

The pitch established through iteration and formal placement as the tonal center of the melody below is _____.

Ravel: *Quartet* (1902-3)

A

Phrygian

351.   Although the tones used in the melody above are those of the F major scale, the tonal center is A (the third scale degree). Thus, this melody is in the _____ mode.

Dorian

352.   The tonal center of the next melody is F. The consistent alteration of D-natural changes natural minor to the _____ mode.

Debussy: *Nocturnes*, No. 2 ("Fêtes")

Animé et très rythmé

353.   The next example is by Charles Griffes (1884-1920), an American composer whose music shows influence of impressionism. Though perhaps not apparent at first, the tonal center of this melody is C-sharp.

Griffes: *Poem,* for flute and orchestra

The scale utilized here is notated below (notice that the seventh degree is occasionally lowered to B-natural).

1   2   3   4   5   6   7   8

Disregarding the B-natural, how does this pattern differ from the C-sharp major scale?

_____

_____

The 4th degree is a half-step higher.

354.   The melody in the preceding frame is primarily in the _____ mode.

Lydian

355.   The lowered seventh degree, which appears twice in the melody in Frame 353 shows influence of the _____ mode.

Mixolydian

356.   The melody below centers firmly on the note C. The consistent use of B-flat produces the _____ mode.

Mixolydian

Debussy: *Préludes,* Vol. I, No. 10 ("La Cathédrale engloutie")

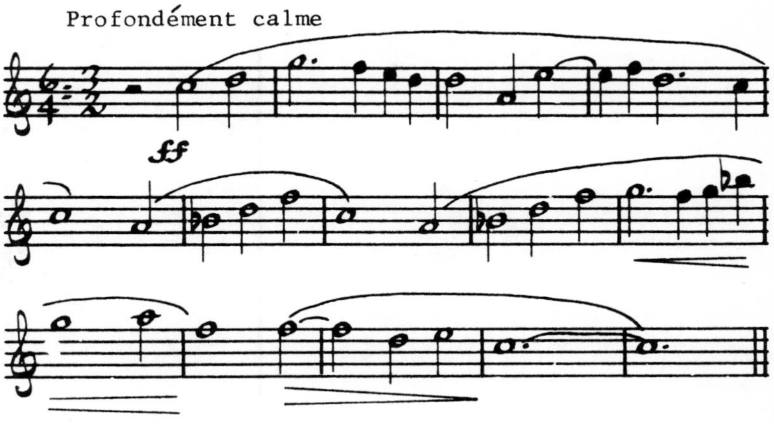

Profondément calme

357. Modal influence shows up most plainly in melodic material. But the singular harmonic effects of impressionism often stem from modal coloration. The brief passage which follows centers on B-flat and ends on an altered dominant chord.

Debussy: *Suite bergamasque* ("Prélude")

Moderato (tempo rubato)

Ignoring the C-sharp in the final chord, write on the staff the scale in use here (begin and end on B-flat).

358. The example in the preceding frame is in the _____ mode.

Lydian

359. The tonal center of the next example is C-sharp.

Debussy: *Nocturnes,* No. 3 ("Sirènes")

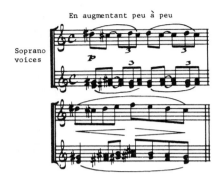

Extract from this example the scale used, and write it on the staff below beginning and ending on C-sharp.

Dorian

360. The example in the preceding frame is in the _____ mode.

361. Extended passages in a single mode are rare in impressionist music, while more typical is a mixture of modal flavor with tones from ordinary major and minor scales. Such is the case in the example below. G is the tonal center, and the next-to-the-last chord contains an F-sharp (this chord is a French-sixth on the lowered second degree).

Debussy: *Quartet,* Op. 10

Except for the F-sharp, all the tones are contained in a single mode. This is the _____ mode.

Phrygian

362. The example below shows the influence of two modes.

Debussy: *Nocturnes,* No. 2 ("Fêtes")

The tonal center is A-flat throughout. On the staff below, notate the scales utilized in the first and second parts as indicated. *(Some notes are supplied because they are not present in the parts.*

(1)

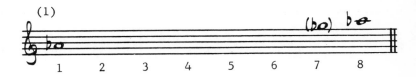

(2)

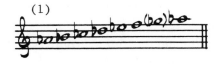

363. Identify each of the modes as notated in the preceding frame.

1. Dorian   1. _____

2. Lydian   2. _____

364.   Other interpretations of the example in Frame 362 are possible, but modal influence is certain. This, along with the orchestral color, accounts for the charm of this passage.

Now we shall turn to the chromatic scale. Actually, most of the chromaticism in impressionist music is built into harmonic relations; the result is expanded, or sometimes suspended tonality. Most melodic movement is diatonic. However, some passages (usually decorative) show deliberate use of the chromatic scale.

Debussy: *Préludes,* Vol. I, No. 12 ("Minstrels")

Modéré (Nerveux et avec humour)

expressif

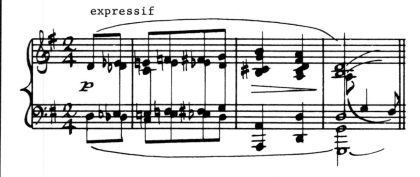

This example shows brief melodic chromaticism which leads to a strong cadence in the key of _____ major.

G

365.   The chromaticism in the next example produces chords which have little functional value. Tonal stability, however, is provided by the pedal tones F and C.

Delius: *Songs of Sunset*

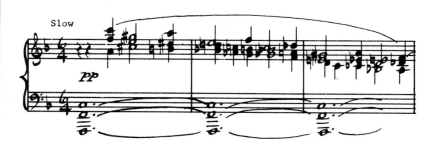

Close examination of the upper voices reveals a rather loose melodic and harmonic sequence. The highest voice does not stray far from the F-major triad. The total effect of this passage is of harmonic (mobility/immobility) _____.

immobility

---

366. Decorative uses of chromaticism usually produce a nonfunctional effect, although not necessarily so immobile as in the preceding frame. The next example conveys a greater sense of motion. It is by Heitor Villa-Lobos (1887-1959), a Brazilian composer, much of whose music is influenced by native folk music, but which also contains many of the impressionist techniques.

Villa-Lobos: *Próle do Bébé No. 1* ("Mulatinha")

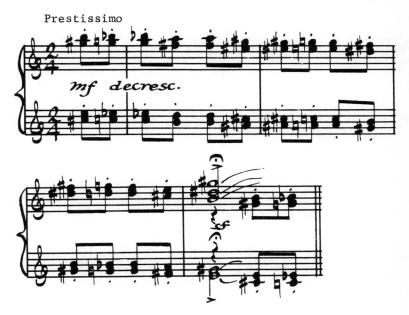

Due to parallel chromatic movement, all the chords are of the same quality. They are _____ seventh chords.

minor

367. Strict chromatic parallelism is featured in the next example, too. This is a brief, one-measure link, which serves to carry the music to a higher pitch level.

Debussy: *Préludes,* Vol. I, No. 7 ("Ce qu'a vu le vent d'Ouest")

Here, the five ascending chromatic lines produce _____ seventh chords.

major

SUMMARY.

Few extended passages are entirely in a single mode. Modal influences are usually melodic, and can often be interpreted as colorations of major or minor scales. Modal influence is sometimes apparent without a particular mode being established. The result is an expanded scale spectrum.

The chromatic scale occasionally is used in a decorative fashion which results in nonfunctional harmonic effects.

10

Enlarged Scale Resources (II)

Although used in new ways by Debussy and other impressionists, modal scales and the chromatic scale are indigenous to Western music. This chapter, however, is devoted to two scales, which, although not unknown in European art music, were little used, and lie mostly outside the standard practices of eighteenth- and nineteenth-century composition. These are the whole-tone, and pentatonic scales, and they were exploited by impressionists as conscious importations from other cultures for the sake of their exotic tonal character.

368. Of all the scales used in impressionist music, none is more characteristic than the *whole-tone scale.* Actually, this scale is rarely the basis for an extended passage let alone an entire composition. Yet its unique color is so easily recognized that even brief exploitation produces an exotic effect— an effect immediately associated with impressionist music. The whole-tone scale consists of six tones (plus octave duplication of the first). Each tone is a major second removed from its neighbor.

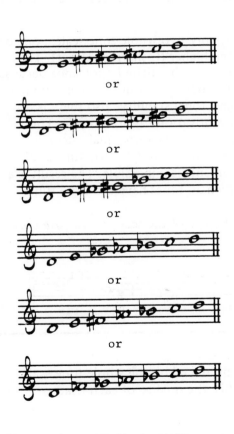

or

*Enharmonic

Because there are only six tones, one of the whole-tones must be written as a diminished third. Notate a whole-tone scale beginning and ending on D.

True.

369.   The preceding frame shows that a variety of spellings are possible for any whole-tone scale. Compare the scale on C with the one on D (above). Discounting enharmonic spellings, these scales consist of the same pitches.   (True/False)

_____

D-flat

370.   Just as the whole-tone scale on D produces the same pitches as the one on C, so do those on E, F-sharp, G-sharp, and B-flat. In fact, *all are the same scale.* There is another whole-tone scale, however, this is shown below:

It follows from what we have observed that the whole-tone scales on E-flat, F, G, A, and B are the same as the one on _____ .

---

371.   There are, in fact, only two whole-tone scales: one on C, and another a half-step higher (C-sharp or D-flat). The note on which the scale begins has little importance because the various tones have no functional value. There is no perfect fifth or fourth to give tonal stability, also there is no leading tone to provide motivation toward a tonic. The whole-tone scale divides the octave into equal intervals (whole-steps), and like all "symmetrical" structures,[1] differentiation between elements is impossible. The result is a static tonal effect in which all tones have the same function.

   Build a triad on each note of the scale below *(use only the notes of the scale).*

---

augmented

372.   All of the thirds produced by the whole-tone scale are major. Because of this, the quality of each triad is

_____ .

---

373.   The whole-tone scale lacks the tonality-defining function of major and minor scales, with their variety of half-

True.

and whole-steps, so its use by Debussy was a radical departure from the harmonic system of traditional music. Although the whole-tone scale can be seen occasionally in works by earlier composers,[2] it appears mostly in modulatory progressions within a prevailing scheme of conventional harmonic relations. Debussy, on the other hand, made conscious use of its inherent lack of tonality to express the vague, indecisive effects appropriate to the impressionist ideal. Debussy may have become acquainted with the whole-tone scale through his contacts with Russian music. Glinka, for example, uses the scale in his opera *Russlan and Ludmilla* (1842).

In the example below, all the tones fall into a whole-tone scale on D.   (True/False) _____ .

Debussy: *Six épigraphes antiques* ("Pour un tombeau sans nom")

---

374.   When a scale structure does not possess tonal implications, the principles of melodic tonality necessarily become determinant factors. The tonality of the first four measures in the example in the preceding frame is D, not because of harmonic factors, but because of stress produced by

a. iteration √
b. form √
c. rhythm √
(See next frame.)

(check one or more)

a. iteration   _____
b. form   _____
c. rhythm   _____

A♭.

(We cannot be so certain here.)

---

375.   All three of the determinants of melodic tonality are in evidence here. Form and rhythm, however, are perhaps the most important. Phrases both begin and end on D, and this note is prolonged in several cases.

What is the tonality established in the final two measures of the example in Frame 373? _____

---

376.   The entire opening section of Debussy's "Pour un tombeau sans nom" is based on the whole-tone scale on D. This is one of the few cases of extended and exclusive use of a single whole-tone scale. Another such case is the prelude entitled "Voiles" (Sails), an example from which is shown below:

Debussy: *Préludes,* Vol. I, No. 2 ("Voiles")

Except for two chromatic embellishments,* the entire opening section of this piece is in the whole-tone scale on C. Due to the lack of differentiation between scale tones, the tonal effect is static, and harmonic function is lacking. What is the source of motivation in this example? _____

_____

*These are in measure 31 (not shown in the example above).

Rhythm.

---

377.   *Expressive rhythmic patterns, and sharply-etched motives are essential when static tonal effects prevail.* Otherwise, the musical effect is likely to be excessively bland and indecisive. Another example from "Voiles" is shown below:

Debussy: *Préludes,* Vol. I, No. 2 ("Voiles")

Like the example in Frame 376, the one above has clearly defined rhythmic and melodic patterns. In this case, however, the rhythm is (more/less) _____ animated.

more

---

378. In the preceding example, the iterated notes in the bass establish a tonal orientation of B-flat. Does the melodic material support this tonal effect? _____

Yes. *(See the next frame.)*

---

379. We wish to stress that although the whole-tone scale itself lacks "centralization," tonality may be produced through the devices of iteration, form, and rhythmic stress. Impressionist composers were rarely willing to give up tonality completely, even when using non-tonal scale resources. The melody of the example in Frame 377 supports the tonal emphasis of B-flat in the beginning because the first two motives end with B-flat in the upper part. But thereafter the melody stresses the note _____ .

A-flat

---

380. Each of the two preceding examples (Frames 376 and 377) features melodic successions of thirds (sometimes spelled enharmonically). In all cases these are _____ thirds.

major

381. Symmetrical scales generate symmetrical intervals and chords. *The result is extremely limited tonal variety.* For this reason, use of the whole-tone scale is usually limited to brief passages, which often include other tonal material. The example below shows such use. Approach this passage by first listing the quality of each chord. *(Use symbols such as C, c, C⁷, etc. Take into account notes on both staves.)*

Ravel: *Sonatine* (1903-5)

Chord quality:

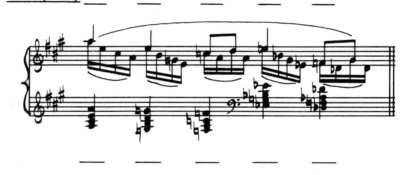

A   e⁷   F   E♭   D♭

A   e⁷   F   E♭   D♭

The lowest voice traces five notes of a whole-tone scale on D-flat.

382. The second measure of the preceding example is merely a restatement of the first an octave lower. Immediate repetition of brief harmonic and melodic fragments (often with slight variation) is a typical impressionist device.³ Except for the second chord in each phrase which is a minor seventh chord, all are major triads. Neither of these two chord types is generated by the whole-tone scale. The melodic line, too, contains intervals not in the whole-tone scale. Where, then, does the whole-tone influence lie? Answer this question in your own words.

_____

_____

_____

383. The example below also shows whole-tone influence, without being entirely in this scale.

Debussy: *Pelléas et Mélisande,* Act IV, Scene 2

On di - rait qu'ils tien - nent

tous à mou-rir sous nos yeux.   Eh bien,

The effect of the first two beats is of a D-flat major triad, and the last chord is a D major triad. The period between, however, consists of "floating" nonfunctional harmony. All of the notes under the bracket fall into the same whole-tone scale. (True/False) _____

True.

384. Here is another example which shows integration of whole-tone and major-minor material.

Debussy: *Prélude à l'après-midi d'un faune*

The harmonic movement is from an A minor triad to a D major ninth chord, and finally to a D-flat major chord with added sixth. Whole-tone influence in this case is exclusively in the melodic line. (True/False) _____

True.

Another scale which has an important place in impressionist style is the pentatonic. Any five-tone division of the octave is a pentatonic scale, and there are many types. Such scales are found in music from every corner of the world, and their origin is very ancient. The type of pentatonic scale exploited by the impressionist is widespread, but is associated especially with Oriental music. Use of this scale probably was suggested by the strong interest in Oriental art and culture generated in European society during the last few decades of the nineteenth century. Just as the flat planes of Japanese prints prompted impressionist painters to rebel against Renaissance perspective by greatly reducing the depth in many of their works,[4] the "tonal space" of harmonic structure was eliminated by the use of static, functionless whole-tone and pentatonic scales.

The pentatonic scale which figures most prominently in impressionist music is the so-called *anhemitonic pentatonic*, a five-tone scale with no semitones. It is known also as the "tonal" or "Chinese" pentatonic, and may be produced merely by playing the black keys of the piano. Because of its importance in impressionist music, a few words devoted to its theoretical basis in Chinese music theory is warranted here.[5]

Because our music study is concerned almost exclusively with Western music, it is easy to acquire the idea that this is the only music supported by a large body of conceptual writing. But, on the contrary, there are four main systems of music theory: the Chinese, Indian, Arab-Persian, and European.

Chinese music theory is heavily encrusted with extra-musical symbolism and allegory; it stems from legends extending back at least to about 2697 B.C., at which time (so the legend goes) Ling Lun was sent by the emperor to the western mountains to make pitch pipes from bamboo tubes *(lüs)*. Establishing a proper standard of pitch was vital because ritual and symbology required that music be in tune with the basic forces of the universe. No less than the well-being of the state was thought to be involved. The influence of music as a vehicle for molding society[6] was recognized by early Chinese writers, and from the time of Confucius, music was used for the social and political education of the people.

The fundamental pitch of the tonal system was called *huang chung* ("the yellow bell"). This was used to produce all other tones by cutting bamboo tubes alternately 2/3 and 4/3 the length of the previous one. The result is a cycle of ascending perfect fifths and descending perfect fourths.

Ex. 18.

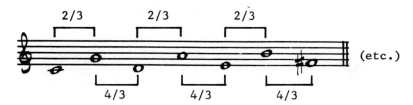

The first five of these tones constitute the fundamental framework of the Chinese tonal system (the anhemitonic pentatonic).

Ex. 19.

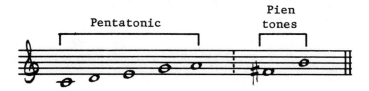

The notes F-sharp and B are called *pien* ("changing") tones, and are used as passing tones, alternate tones, or for modal changes within the basic pentatonic system.

The cyclic process described above was carried out to produce twelve tones.

Ex. 20.

The superior (even-numbered) tones in this cycle were associated with the masculine *(yin)* principle in Chinese metaphysics, and the lower (odd-numbered) tones with the feminine *(yang)*. The male and female portions of the system were sometimes treated as separate entities. Note in Example 20, that the six superior *lüs* and the six inferior ones each produce a whole-tone scale. The complete twelve-note system must not be confused with the chromatic scale with which it has nothing in common. The basic scale in all cases is limited to five tones, but can be transposed by putting the central note *(kung)* on any of the twelve *lüs*.

Over the centuries, Chinese theorists produced ever more elaborate systems. A major concern was the attempt to create a closed system of tuning. The cycle of *lüs* was extended first to 60 fifths (by the musician King Fang in 40 B.C.), and eventually to 360 about 430 A.D. But the attempt was foredoomed because a cycle of just fifths can never produce a perfect octave. It is curious, though, to note that ancient Chinese theorists were concerned with problems of equal temperament much as were musicians in the Western world.

Because any note of the "Chinese" pentatonic scale can be established as the tonal center (through principles of melodic tonality), there are five possible forms.

Ex. 21.

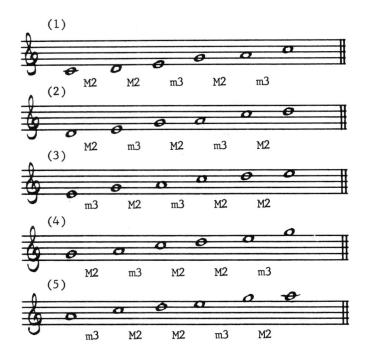

These forms may be written on any note. One way to approach this is to consider a given note as the first, second, third, fourth, or fifth note of a cycle of perfect fifths. Take, for example, the note D as in Example 22.

Ex. 22.

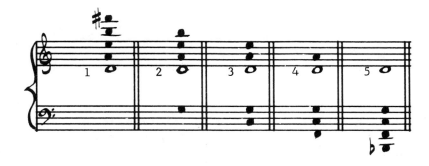

By writing out in scale form the notes contained in each cycle of fifths (always starting and ending on D), the various forms of the "Chinese" pentatonic scale are produced. Another practical approach is to remember that successions of major seconds and minor thirds which correspond to the patterns produced by the black keys of the piano (starting on any black key), will produce these scale forms.

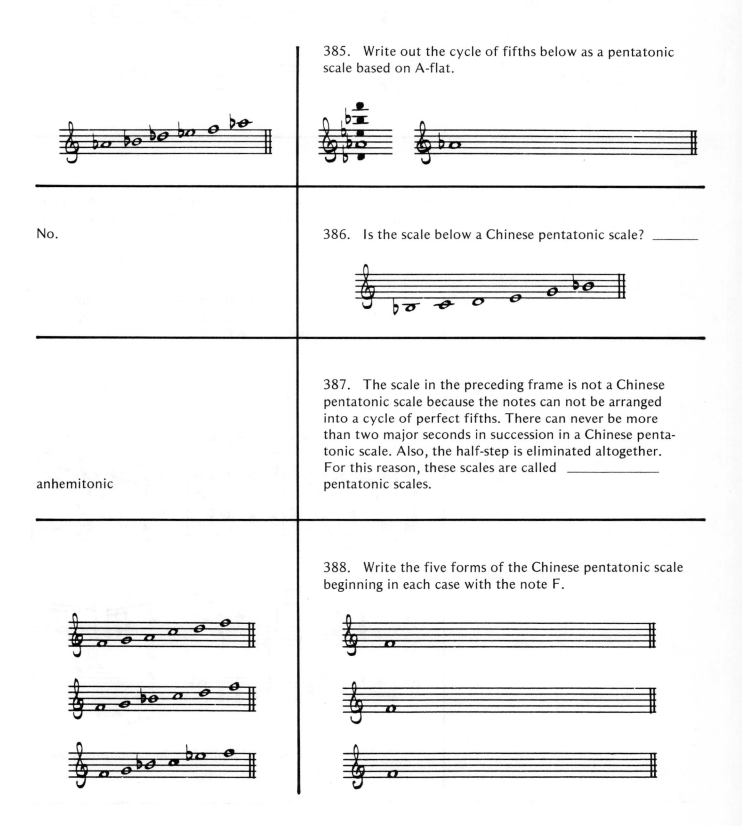

385. Write out the cycle of fifths below as a pentatonic scale based on A-flat.

No.

386. Is the scale below a Chinese pentatonic scale? _____

387. The scale in the preceding frame is not a Chinese pentatonic scale because the notes can not be arranged into a cycle of perfect fifths. There can never be more than two major seconds in succession in a Chinese pentatonic scale. Also, the half-step is eliminated altogether. For this reason, these scales are called _____ pentatonic scales.

anhemitonic

388. Write the five forms of the Chinese pentatonic scale beginning in each case with the note F.

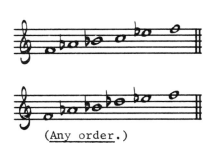

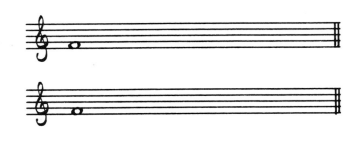

(Any order.)

In impressionist music, pentatonic influence is found in melodic lines harmonized with non-pentatonic material, and also in passages completely dominated by the pentatonic scale. Several examples of each type will be shown in the frames which follow.

389.   Until the last measure, the melody in the example below is entirely in a pentatonic scale which defines a tonal center first on G and later on C.

Debussy: *Six épigraphes antiques* ("Pour invoquer Pan, dieu du vent d'été")

Is the harmonic material limited to the pentatonic scale?

No. _____

_____

Dorian

390.   Although the melody of the example in the preceding frame is pentatonic, the harmony is largely triadic. The tonality defined by the harmony and melody together centers on G. The effect is modal. Specifically, one hears the _____ mode on G.

391.   Another example of a pentatonic melody accompanied by tertian harmony is shown below:

Debussy: *Nocturnes,* No. 1 ("Nuages")

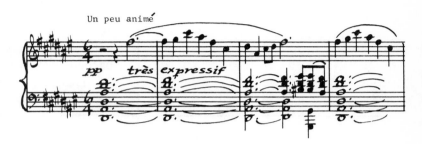

The melody alone traces a pentatonic scale on F-sharp (F♯ G♯ A♯ C♯ D♯), whereas the harmony consists chiefly of the D-sharp minor and G-sharp major triads (the Dorian mode on D-sharp is suggested). Stylistic conflict between the pentatonic melody and the modal harmony contributes to the charm of this passage.

(No response required.)

No.
(See the following frame.)

392.   Is the melody in the example below completely pentatonic? _____

Debussy: *Prélude à l'après-midi d'un faune* (simplified)

---

393.   Except for one note (C in the fourth measure), the melody in the preceding example is derived entirely from the pentatonic scale D♭ E♭ F A♭ B♭. But this note clearly functions as a passing tone, and is incidental to the whole-tone chord with which it is associated. The first four chords exploit a particular tonal relation which is characteristic of impressionist music. This is the _____.

tritone

---

394.   The material under the bracket is derived exclusively from the pentatonic scale.

Ravel: *Valses nobles et sentimentales,* No. 3 (1911)

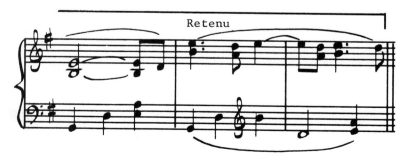

G.

What is the tonal center? _____

395. Write the pentatonic scale employed in the preceding frame. *(Begin and end on G.)*

396. The example below consists entirely of notes in a pentatonic scale on G-sharp.

Debussy: *Estampes,* ("Pagodes")

Modérément animé

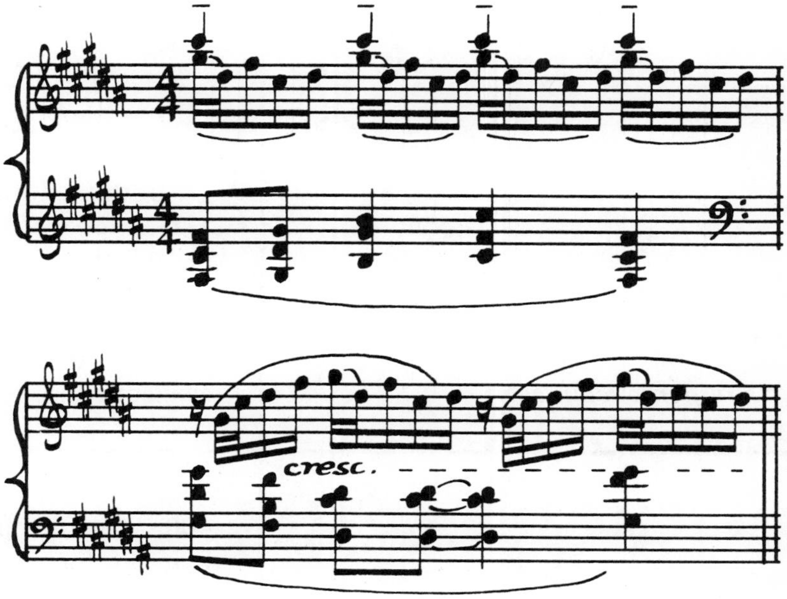

cresc.

Write the scale which is used in the above example. *(Begin and end on G-sharp.)*

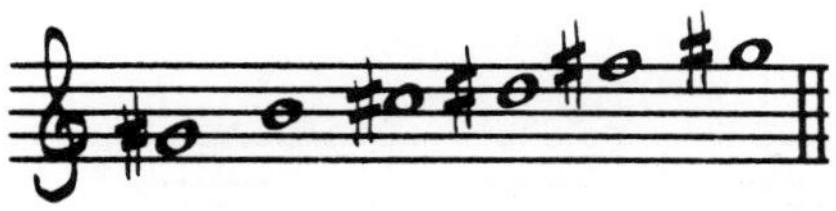

397. Reference has already been made to Debussy's prelude for piano, "Voiles" in connection with the whole-tone scale.* The brief central section of this prelude is shown in Panel 14.

---

*See Frames 377-380.

The B-flat pedal notes in the bass.

What compositional device here establishes the tonality of B-flat? _____

_____

---

398. Write the scale used in the example in Panel 14. *(Begin and end on B-flat.)*

---

399. In Debussy's prelude "Voiles," scale structures contribute to the tripartite form.

A	B	A'
Whole-tone	Pentatonic	Whole-tone

Both the whole-tone and the pentatonic scales create a static tonal effect. This is augmented by the omnipresent pedal B-flats in the bass which appear through all three sections. Tonally, and particularly harmonically, there is practically no feeling of motion in this work. The musical interest resides largely in the melodic and rhythmic elements.

(No response required.)

---

400. The final pentatonic example seems simple enough at first, but there is an interesting feature to discover.

Ravel: *Le Tombeau de Couperin* ("Prélude") (1914-17)

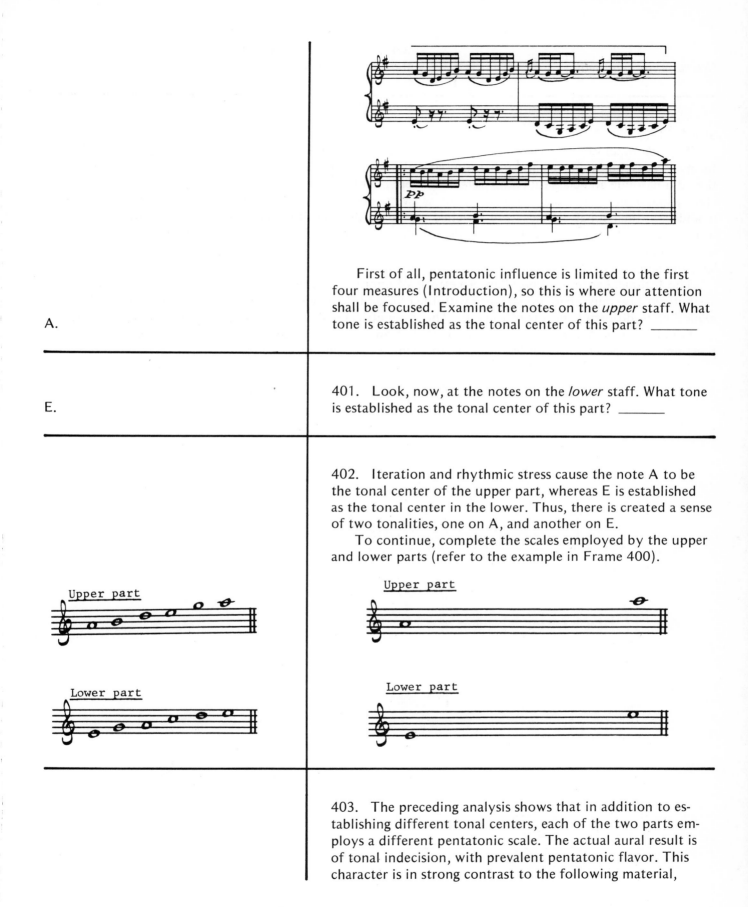

First of all, pentatonic influence is limited to the first four measures (Introduction), so this is where our attention shall be focused. Examine the notes on the *upper* staff. What tone is established as the tonal center of this part? _____

A.

401. Look, now, at the notes on the *lower* staff. What tone is established as the tonal center of this part? _____

E.

402. Iteration and rhythmic stress cause the note A to be the tonal center of the upper part, whereas E is established as the tonal center in the lower. Thus, there is created a sense of two tonalities, one on A, and another on E.

To continue, complete the scales employed by the upper and lower parts (refer to the example in Frame 400).

Upper part

Lower part

Upper part

Lower part

403. The preceding analysis shows that in addition to establishing different tonal centers, each of the two parts employs a different pentatonic scale. The actual aural result is of tonal indecision, with prevalent pentatonic flavor. This character is in strong contrast to the following material,

(No response required.)

which is in the key of E minor, and for a while devoid of pentatonic influence.

SUMMARY.

The rich tonal variety characteristic of impressionist music is due partly to the wide variety of scale forms used. Debussy, Ravel, and other impressionist composers employed a much wider variety of scales than did baroque and classical composers, who were mainly content with relatively impoverished resources—chiefly major and minor scales. Certainly, these two scales were used by impressionist composers too, but in addition, their tonal palettes were enriched by the subtle hues of modal scales, the chromatic scale, as well as the whole-tone and pentatonic scales. Modal scales, through their association with medieval ecclesiastical music, contribute an antique effect, while whole-tone and pentatonic scales have primitive, timeless, and sometimes Oriental connotations.

The antique, exotic, and non-Western effects of impressionist music—vital as they are for opening new aesthetic vistas—must share importance with the crucial influence the use of some of these scales had on exploding traditional concepts of tonality. The symmetrical scales (chromatic, and whole-tone), in particular, but also the pentatonic scale, are functionless in an harmonic sense. Exploitation of these scales by impressionist composers contributed much to the demise of harmonic tonality.

11

Expanded Chord Vocabulary (I)

Fluid melodic and rhythmic patterns, fragmented phrase structure, wide variety of scales, symmetrical tonal and rhythmic elements, as well as new tonal freedoms all contribute to the unique character of impressionist music. The core of this style, however, is harmony. Commenting on Debussy's musical processes, one author states: "All begins and ends with the chord."[1] For Debussy as well as other impressionists, the particular quality of each chord contributes in its unique way to the musical effect, and infinite care is given to selecting the sonority which evokes the desired response. Generally, chords bear less important reference to the tonal scheme than in earlier music—function is secondary to sonority. In impressionist music, emotive and suggestive properties of chords are exploited in a manner which suggests the use by symbolist poets of word sounds for their own sake. So essential is sonority that register, doubling, spacing, and instrumental timbre are patiently selected and manipulated. Impressionism—in spite of its concern for the senses—never suggests a spontaneous outpouring of feeling; it is an art which is painstakingly cultivated, and carefully pruned to yield a varied harvest of tonal nuances. This is a music of refined shades and nuances, and the pastel hues are applied delicately, as with a silk brush.

Compared with classical or even romantic music, impressionism draws on a much wider vocabulary of chord types. All of the chords in traditional music are included, but many new ones are added. The prevalent method of building chords is still the tertian system, and triads are basic to the harmonic style; but expanded tertian sonorities (seventh, ninth, eleventh, and thirteenth chords) are important ingredients. It is with these chords that we shall begin. But first, it is desirable to review briefly some of the chord symbols which will be used in the frames which follow.

---

404.   Extended tertian chords are shown below:

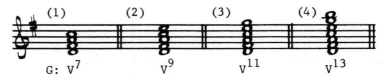

The first chord is the familiar dominant seventh (Mm^7). Chord 2 is called a dominant ninth chord and by applying the same terminology as that used to identify seventh chords the result is as below:

DOMINANT NINTH CHORD

Triad	*Seventh*	*Ninth*
major —	minor —	major

MmM^9 Write the abbreviated symbol for this chord. _____

MmMP¹¹

405. The quality of chord 3 in the preceding frame is indicated below:

DOMINANT ELEVENTH CHORD

Triad   *Seventh*   *Ninth*   *Eleventh*

major — minor   — major — perfect

Write the abbreviated symbol for this chord. _____

MmMPM¹³

406. Write the symbol which expresses the precise quality of chord 4 in Frame 404. _____

---

407. Only rarely is it necessary to indicate so precisely a chord's quality. The purpose of an analysis usually is served by merely showing the extent of tertian extension. As we proceed, the simple method of identifying chords shown below will frequently be used.

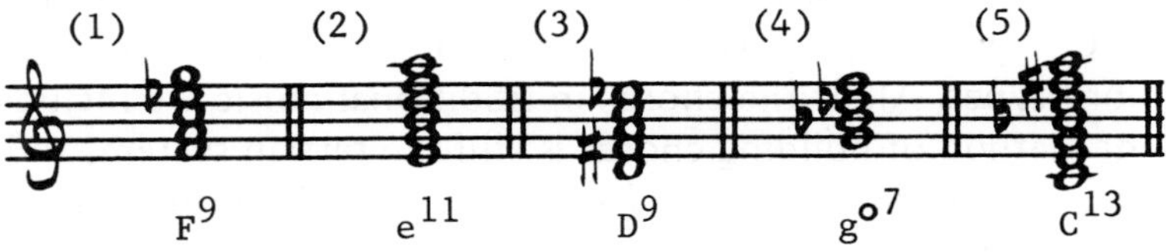

These symbols are used when Roman numerals are not relevant; they are frankly imprecise as only the *chord root,* the *quality of the triad,* and the *extent of tertian extension (7th, 9th, 11th, or 13th)* are identified. But unless vital to the analysis, more elaborate symbols are best avoided.

Which of the above chords is indicated by the symbol

(3).   Mmm⁹ ? _____

---

408. The first example begins and ends with a major ninth chord on F-sharp, and the chords between are all seventh chords.

Debussy: *Pelléas et Mélisande,* Act V

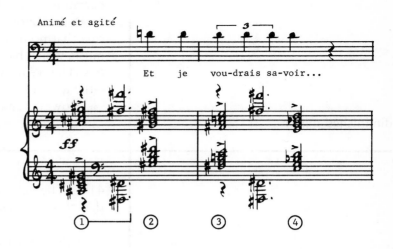

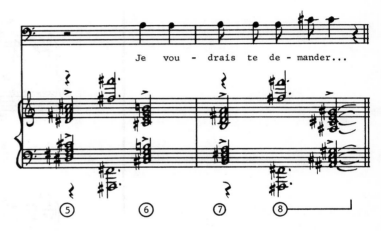

Indicate, now, the quality of chords 2-7. *(Use abbreviations such as Mm⁷, etc.)*

	Chords
1.	MmM⁹
2.	_____
3.	_____
4.	_____
5.	_____
6.	_____
7.	_____
8.	MmM⁹

2. dm⁷
3. dm⁷
4. dm⁷
5. dm⁷
6. dm⁷
7. m⁷

409. Several of the chords in the example in Frame 408 (4 and 6, for instance) can be regarded as nonharmonic (passing) chords. Also, certain notes in the voice part may

diminished-minor

be analyzed as either harmonic or nonharmonic. If treated as harmonic, the voice part causes chord 3 to be a major ninth on D, and chord 6 the same type on A. Such ambiguity of role (harmonic or nonharmonic) is a characteristic feature of music which has a large number of expanded tertian sonorities. The result often is vague, uncertain, and diffuse effects —the quintessence of impressionist harmony.

However analyzed, the prevailing sonority is the

_____ - _____ seventh chord.

410.   The next example contains a variety of extended tertian chords as shown by the analysis.

Debussy: *La plus que lente*

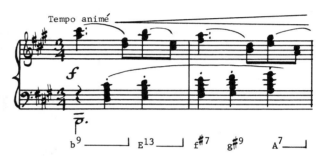

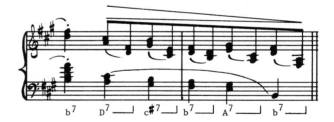

All of these chord types occur in classical and romantic music. But there are two features which set this example apart from earlier music. One is the high incidence of root movement by second; the other is that extended tertian chords are used exclusively.

(No response required.)

411.   Persistent use of seventh, ninth, eleventh, and thirteenth chords is a prominent feature of many passages in impressionist music. Another feature is the lack of resolution supplied for dissonant elements (7ths, 9ths, etc.). Extended tertian sonorities are treated as color entities rather than active chords with consequent need for resolution. Analyze the chords in the spaces provided in the example below. *(Use symbols such as C⁷, etc.)*

Delius: *Sonata,* for violoncello and piano

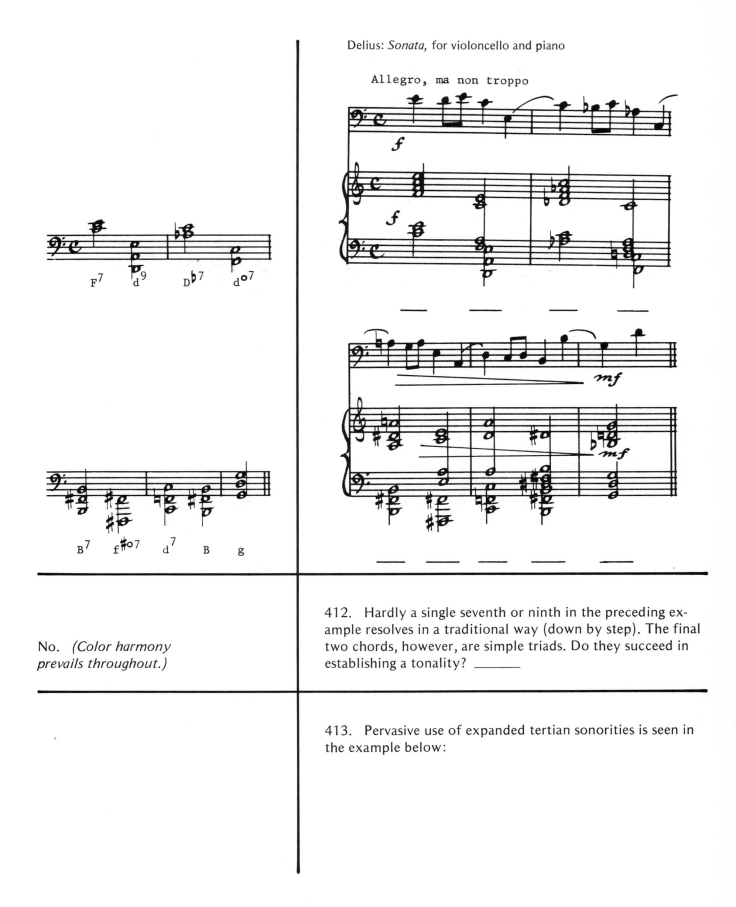

No. *(Color harmony prevails throughout.)*

412. Hardly a single seventh or ninth in the preceding example resolves in a traditional way (down by step). The final two chords, however, are simple triads. Do they succeed in establishing a tonality? _____

413. Pervasive use of expanded tertian sonorities is seen in the example below:

Ravel: *Sonatine* (1903-5)

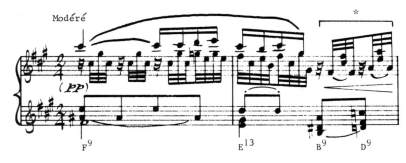

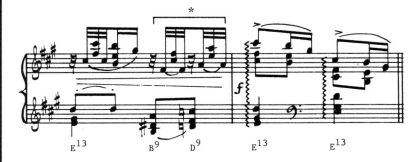

The motion created by the ninth chords at each of the two asterisks can be described as parallel. These parallel chords are major-minor-major ninth chords; they are commonly called _____ ninth chords.

dominant

414. The parallel dominant ninth chords in the preceding frame contrast with "tonal" use of expanded tertian sonorities in which a variety of types occur. Parallel successions of identical chord types are common in impressionist music, and many examples will be seen in Chapter 13, which is devoted to parallelism.

Each chord in the example below is numbered. List those which are dominant ninth chords (MmM^9).

Debussy: *Pelléas et Mélisande*, Act I, Scene 1

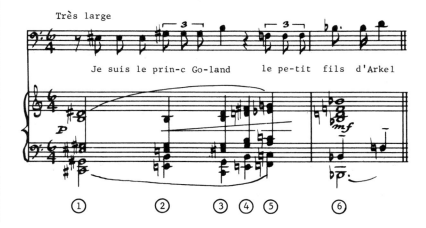

1, 3, 4, and 5.	*Dominant ninth chords:* _____
	415. Except for chords 2 and 6, which are major triads, all the chords in the preceding example are dominant ninth chords. Parallel motion occurs between chords, 3, 4, and 5. These chords cause momentary suspension of tonality, but the final two chords produce a(n) _____ cadence in B-flat major.
authentic	

416. All the chords at the asterisks in the example below are dominant ninth chords.

Debussy: *Pelléas et Mélisande,* Act IV, Scene 4

The second chord is not exactly the same as the other ninth chords. Examine this chord carefully and explain how it differs from the others.

_____

_____

_____

_____

_____

It has a minor rather than a major ninth. *(In your own words.)*

417. In the examples of Frames 414 and 416, parallel ninth chords of identical quality are incorporated into phrases containing other chord types. This prevents the device from becoming cloy, as can so easily happen when used to excess. But brief passages limited to a single sonority do sometimes occur. The sequential writing in the accompaniment below consists of only one type chord.

Debussy: *Pelléas et Mélisande*, Act IV, Scene 4

Dominant ninth chord. (MmM⁹)

Identify the chord type used in this example. _____

---

418. Seventh and ninth chords are prevalent in impressionist music. Although many types are used, the impressionists—Debussy in particular—tended (like Wagner) to favor the diminished-minor seventh chord, and the dominant major ninth chord (MmM⁹). Also favored was the minor seventh chord. Eleventh and thirteenth chords are not so common, but many do occur. The example below contains a seventh chord, an eleventh chord, and a thirteenth chord as well as a simple triad. Since this is a completely tonal passage, Roman numerals may be used. Indicate the analysis in the spaces provided.

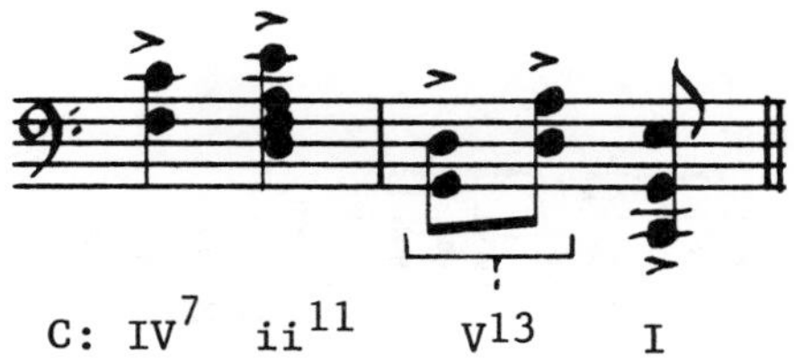

Ravel: *Le Tombeau de Couperin*, No. 6 ("Rigaudon")

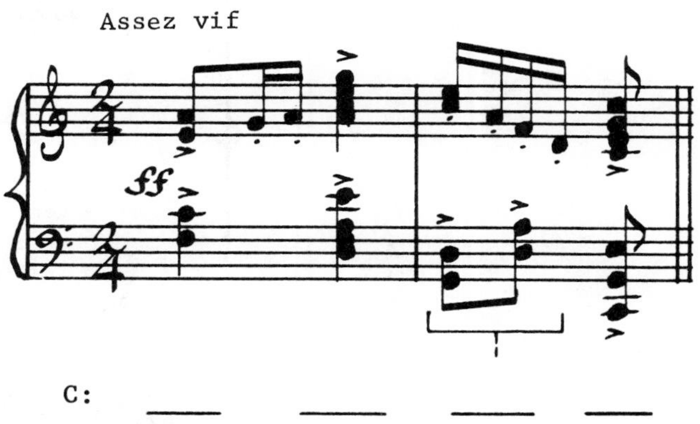

Assez vif

C: IV⁷ ii¹¹ V¹³ I

C: ___ ___ ___ ___

---

419. The next example contains two ninth chords and two thirteenth chords. Supply the Roman numeral analysis. *(Consider all tones to have harmonic status. Show chromatic alterations.)*

Debussy: *Nocturnes*, No. 2 ("Fêtes")

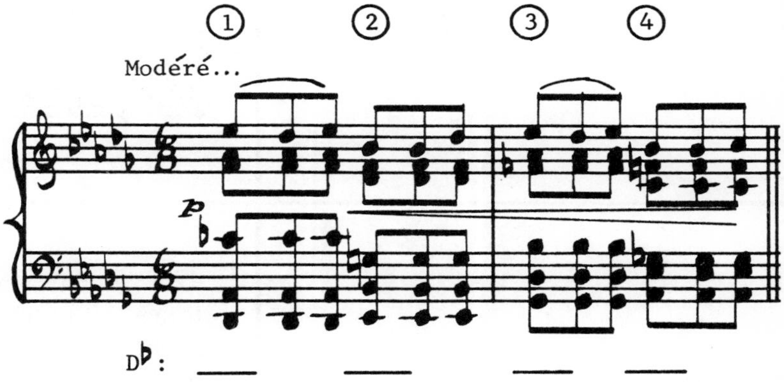

① ② ③ ④

Modéré...

D♭: ___ ___ ___ ___

D♭: I♭⁹₇ II⁹

IV¹³♭₇ V¹³

---

420. Each chord in the preceding example is a "dominant" sonority. Chords 1 and 2 are dominant ninth chords (MmM⁹), and the subdominant thirteenth chord is altered to have the same sonority as the V¹³ which follows. In both of the thirteenth chords one tone is omitted. The omitted tone is the (3rd/5th/7th/9th/11th) _____.

11th

---

421. Another sonority frequently exploited by impressionist composers is the *chord with "added tones."* There are several types; the simplest consists of major or minor triads

minor

with added sixth, second, or fourth. The chord which provides the accompaniment in the first four measures of the example below consists of a sixth added to a (major/minor _____ triad.

Debussy: *Nocturnes,* No. 2 ("Fêtes")

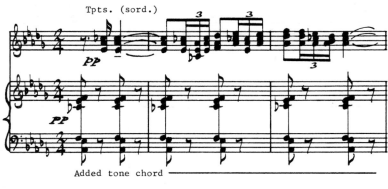

thirteenth

422.   The next example contains several chords with added tones. All tones are analyzed as harmonic except the two B's at the asterisks. These, of course, could be regarded as part of the harmony, and if so, would produce at the time of their appearance dominant _____ chords.

Ravel: *Valses nobles et sentimentales,* No. 3 (1911)

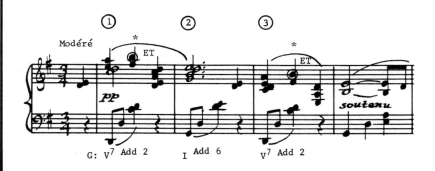

④   Retenu

I Add 2, 6 — — — — — — —

E

423. The preceding example illustrates the delicate decisions which must often be made when choosing an appropriate symbol to represent such chords. Chord 1, which is analyzed as a dominant seventh with added second might well be heard as a dominant ninth chord. Spacing is the determining factor, and here, the prominent seconds (measure one, third beat), tend to produce the effect of added tones. Still, those who hear chords 1 and 3 as dominant ninths (or thirteenths) should identify these chords as such. Chord symbols in all cases should reflect the individual's aural experience, and in music such as this, differences of interpretation are inevitable.

To pursue this matter still further, chord 2 could be regarded as the first inversion of a(n) _____ minor seventh chord.

(See the next frame.)

424. The notes of chord 2 in Frame 422 produce a submediant seventh chord in first inversion. Do you believe this to be a desirable interpretation of this chord? _____

Yes.

425. Because of the prominent perfect fifth (G-D) in the bass, and also the spacing of notes in the upper parts, it is unlikely that many hear chord 2 as other than a tonic with added sixth. Could chord 4 in Frame 422 reasonably be considered a ninth chord with added sixth? _____

---

426. Chord 4 in Frame 422 could also be analyzed as a tonic thirteenth chord (GBD-A-E). From all this it is clear that many interpretations are possible in harmony such as that employed in this example. What factor causes one to analyze chords as having added tones?

Close spacing of tones.
(In your own words.)

_____

427. Check the analysis of the example below which you prefer.

Debussy: *Préludes*, Vol. II, No. 10 *("Canope")*

Très calme et doucement triste
    Plus lent

très doux et très expressif

_____ 1. C major triad with added 2nd and 6th.

_____ 2. C major ninth chord with added 6th.

_____ 3. C thirteenth chord.

_____ 4. C major ninth chord with the note A (in the melodic line) regarded as nonharmonic.

√ 3.
(See next frame.)

428. Actually, choice of any of the options in the preceding frame can be supported. The wide spacing, however, causes all the sustained tones plus the A in the melody to sound as harmonic entities rather than notes added to a simpler sonority. Only one tone in this example is certainly heard as a nonharmonic tone. Name this tone. _____

E♭ *(It is a chromatic passing tone.)*

429. Unlike the preceding example, the one below consists of chords spaced to give the effect of added tones. Only the B major chord is used, but with various spacing and added tones. Complete the analysis below:

Griffes: *Symphony in Yellow*, Op. 3, No. 2

1. 2nd

2. 2nd (and) 6th

3. 2nd

Chord 1:   B major triad with added _____.

Chord 2:   B major triad with added _____ and _____.

Chord 3:   B major triad with added _____.

---

430.   The example below has several interesting chords, some of which may be interpreted as having added tones. The tonality is clearly C major, so Roman numerals may be used. Supply chord symbols for the three chords indicated. *(Use the designations Add 2, Add 6, etc. as part of the chord symbols.)*

Ravel: *Valses nobles et sentimentales,* No. 6 (1911)

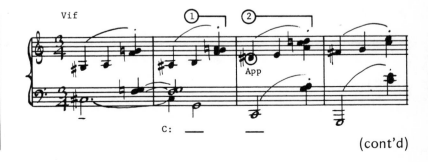

1.   V⁷ Add 2

2.   I Add 2, 6

(cont'd)

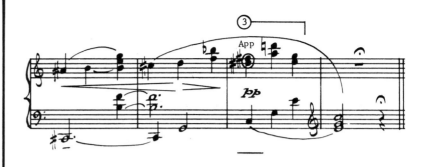

3. |Add 2, 6

---

431. Interpretations other than those given in the preceding frame would be acceptable. Here, as in many other cases, you should weigh in your own mind several possibilities to decide on that which seems most reasonable. Certainly, the chords in the example below are best analyzed as having added tones.

Debussy: *Préludes,* Vol. II, No. 3 ("La puerta del Vino")

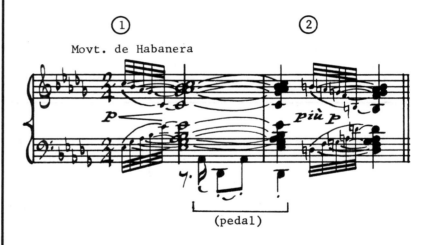

Chord 1:   A-flat major-minor seventh chord with added
—————.

Chord 2:   G major-minor seventh chord with added
—————.

1. 2nd

2. 2nd

SUMMARY.

The two types of chords presented in this chapter are:

1. Extended tertian chords
2. Chords with diatonic added tones

Neither of these types departs radically from earlier practice. The difference is that in impressionist music the proportion of these chords in relation to simpler sonorities is much higher. Also, the dissonant elements in these chords (7th, 9th, 11th, and 13th) are often left unresolved, in contrast to earlier practices which caused most dissonances to result from nonharmonic action, and their tension generally to be dissipated by stepwise resolution to neighboring consonance.

12

Expanded Chord Vocabulary (II)

The chords yet to be examined depart more radically from earlier practices than those presented in the preceding chapter. Many produce more dissonant effects, and some derive from other than major and minor scales.

Chords with added tones were observed in Chapter 11, but these contained "diatonic" added tones. A higher level of dissonance results from *chromatic added tones*; it is with these chords that we shall continue.

1. 2nd

2. 3rd

3. *(No response.)*

4. major

5. root

432.   All the chords in the first example have chromatic added tones. Because the chords are incomplete, there is uncertainty regarding the root in some cases. Nevertheless, the presence of chromatic added tones is obvious. Complete the analysis below the example.

Ravel: *Miroirs,* No. 4 ("Alborada del gracioso")

Chord 1:   D major triad with added minor _____ .

Chord 2:   D major triad with added minor _____ .

Chord 3:   Same as chord 1.

Chord 4:   A diminished triad with added _____ 3rd.

Chord 5:   G major triad with added raised _____ .

433.   An aptly descriptive terminology for the chords in the preceding frame is "chords with split roots or thirds."

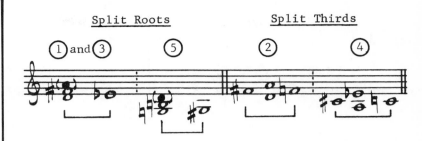

Chromatic added tones also produce split fifths, sevenths, ninths, etc. The example below presents in arpeggiated form several such chords. For your convenience, each is shown in simpler notation. Indicate the chord member (root, 3rd, 5th, etc.) which is split in each case. *(Regard chord 2 as a G-flat minor triad with the third spelled enharmonically.)*

Debussy: *Préludes,* Vol. II, No. 4 ("Les fées sont d'exquises danseuses")

(1) 5th
(2) 5th
(3) 5th
(4) 5th
(5) root
(6) root

seventh

434. In the next example there is both a C-natural and a C-sharp. The result is a chord with split (root/third/fifth/seventh) _____.

Debussy: *Préludes,* Vol. II, No. 10 ("Canope")

Très calme et doucement triste

third

435. The basic aural effect of the chord in the first three measures below is of a D-flat major-minor seventh chord (the seventh is spelled enharmonically); but this chord also contains a split member. The chord member which is split is the (root/third/fifth/seventh) _____.

Debussy: *Préludes,* Vol. II, No. 3 ("La puerta del Vino")

Mouvt. de Habanera

Chapter 12

third

436. The next example contains several interesting chords the first of which warrants close examination. The notes in the first measure alone (over bracket 1) constitute a C-sharp major-minor seventh chord with split _____ .

Ravel: *Valses nobles et sentimentales*, No. 4 (1911)

437. The chord becomes more complex as notes continue to be piled up in beat one of the second measure. When complete (bracket 2), this chord contains seven tones (not including octave doublings). The example below shows this chord in simpler notation.

The lower five notes (bracketed) produce an extended tertian chord. Indicate precisely the nature of this chord. It is a major-minor-_____ ninth chord.

minor

438. The two higher notes in the preceding frame represent chromatic added tones. Specifically the G-natural is a split _____ , and the E-natural is a split _____ .

G-natural = split 5th
E-natural = split 3rd

triad

E

439. Analysis has led to the conclusion that when complete, the first chord in the example of Frame 436 (bracket 2) is a C-sharp ninth chord with split third and fifth. But there is yet another interpretation which may be advanced. Look, again, at the chord as notated in Frame 437 and supply the information needed to complete the statements below:

1. The notes on the bass staff alone produce the C-sharp major _____.

2. The notes on the treble staff alone produce the _____ minor seventh chord.

440. It is possible to regard the entire chord as composed of a combination of two simpler sonorities: an E minor seventh chord above a C-sharp major triad. Such chords are called *polychords*. Debussy, Ravel, and other impressionists made limited use of polychords. An example of a polychord is shown below:

Debussy: *Préludes*, Vol. II, No. 1 ("Brouillards")

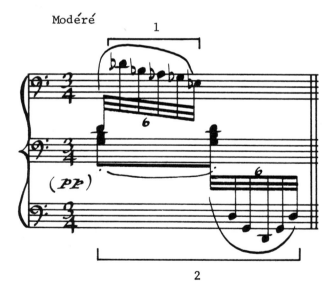

The two chords are identified by brackets. Complete each statement.

1. Chord 1 (arpeggiated) consists of the tones of a _____ scale.

2. Chord 2 is a _____ major triad.

pentatonic

G

441. Another example of polychords from the same composition is shown below:

Debussy: *Préludes,* Vol. II, No. 1 ("Brouillards")

diminished-minor
diminished

Chord 1 consists of a B-flat _____ - _____ seventh chord on the upper staff, and a B _____ triad on the lower.

---

diminished-minor
minor

442. Chord 2 in the preceding frame consists of a D _____ - _____ seventh chord on the upper staff, and an E _____ triad on the lower.

---

pentatonic
major

443. Chord 3 in Frame 441 consists of a chord derived from the _____ scale on the upper staff, and a G _____ triad on the lower.

---

444. We have digressed briefly to observe a few examples of polychords. Chords such as these occasionally are encountered in impressionist music, but their use is limited.

Returning, now, to chords with chromatic added tones, one final example is shown below:

Ravel: *Valses nobles et sentimentales,* No. 1 (1911)

Begin by listing (by number) the chords which contain *chromatic added tones. (All chords are in root position; be alert for enharmonic spellings.)*

1, 3, 4, 6, 7, 9, 10, 12, 13, 15

_____

445.   With reference to the example in the preceding frame complete the information below:

Chord

	1	third
	3	third
	4	seventh
	6	third
	7	seventh
	9	third
	10	seventh
	12	third
	13	third
	15	root

Chord		
1	contains a split	_____
3	contains a split	_____
4	contains a split	_____
6	contains a split	_____
7	contains a split	_____
9	contains a split	_____
10	contains a split	_____
12	contains a split	_____
13	contains a split	_____
15	contains a split	_____

augmented-major	446. Of the chords analyzed in the preceding frame, number 15 is the most complex and dissonant; it is a D _____ - _____ seventh chord with split root.
minor	447. As for the quality of the other chords in the example of Frame 444, number 2 is a D major ninth chord (DF♯ACE). Chords 5, 8, and 11 are all of the same type. These are _____ seventh chords.
sixth	448. Only chord 14 remains to be analyzed. By interpreting the note E-sharp as an F, this chord is a D minor seventh chord with added major _____ .
Roots progress down in perfect fifths to complete the cycle of fifths D-D. *(In your own words.)*	449. The passage in Frame 444 consists entirely of dissonant sonorities, most of which are chords with added tones. There is, however, firm tonal order expressed in two ways: First of all, beginning with chord 2 there is a loose harmonic sequence. The first chord of each of the first four measures is either a seventh or ninth chord. The second and third chords of each measure are chords with chromatic added tones (split thirds or sevenths). The second feature which contributes to tonal order may be discovered by examining the bass notes of chords 2-14 (bracketed). Describe the pattern established by these bass notes, all of which are chord roots. _____ _____ _____ _____ _____
	450. Closely related to chords with added tones are sonorities called CLUSTERS. These are produced by several notes a second apart sounding together.

Villa-Lobos: *Próle do Bébé No. 1* ("O Polichinelo")

When the notes on both staves are sounded together, tight clusters are produced. The chord in the first measure, for example, contains six tones within a major sixth.

It would be possible to regard the chord as a ninth chord on C with split third (CEE♭GB♭D♭). What causes this to be a less desirable term than cluster in this case? _____

Close spacing.

---

451.   The distinction between chords with added tones and clusters is often very small. Indeed, several of the sonorities which have been analyzed as added tone chords could be regarded as clusters (see Chapter 11, Frames 422, 429, 430, and 431). The next example, however, contains some chords for which "clusters" is the more appropriate term.

Debussy: *Préludes,* Vol. II, No. 8 ("Ondine")

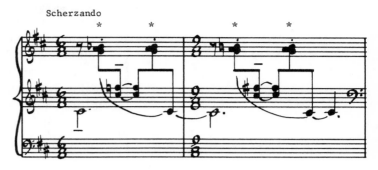

Could the chords at the asterisks also be termed "chords in seconds"? _____

Yes.

---

452.   Especially dissonant clusters occur in the example below:

Debussy: *Préludes,* Vol. II, No. 12 ("Feux d'artifice")

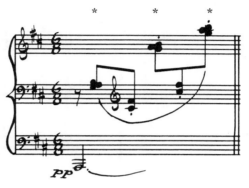

Indicate the intervals contained in each of the chords. *(Observe accidentals carefully.)*

half

half
whole

half

Chords 1 and 3: { _____-step
                    over a
                    _____-step

Chords 2 and 4: { _____-step
                    over
                    _____-step

major

453. One facet of impressionist technique is exploitation of seconds. This has been observed in the examples dealing with added-tone chords and clusters. Sometimes seconds are used as a form of melodic doubling, which is analogous to the doubling of melodic lines in thirds and sixths in earlier music. The harmony below may be analyzed either as an E-flat major triad with added sixth and ninth, or as an E-flat thirteenth chord. The melodic line is given increased density by the use of (major/minor) _____ seconds.

Debussy: *Berceuse Héroïque*

454. Major seconds are used for melodic doubling in the next example too.

Debussy: *Préludes,* Vol. I, No. 12 ("Minstrels")

pentatonic

The scale employed here is a (diatonic/whole-tone/ pentatonic) _____ scale on G.

---

455.   All sonorities are major seconds in the next example.

Debussy: *Préludes,* Vol. II, No. 12 ("Feux d'artifice")

All of the tones in this example are derived from a single whole-tone scale. (True/False) _____

True.

---

456.   It is often difficult to identify precisely the function of seconds. As used in Frame 453, the function seems mainly to be that of lending their special character to the melodic line. The seconds in Frames 454 and 455, however, could well be heard as serving a chordal function. The cumulative effect of the seconds in Frame 454 is a G major triad with added sixth and ninth, whereas the seconds in Frame 455 combine to produce a whole-tone chord.* A single second which has chordal significance may also be called a "cluster." In addition, the term DYAD is sometimes used to refer to a two-note "chord" (usually in seconds).

Whether used chordally, or as melodic doubling, seconds are exploited for their color value often with no regard for their dissonance. One more example of seconds is shown below:

Ravel: *Gaspard de la Nuit,* No. 3 ("Scarbo")

_____   (cont'd)

*Whole-tone chords are presented in Frames 457-460.

The seconds here are used as (check one):

1. harmonic entities _____
2. melodic doubling _____

2. √

457.   Two chord types remain to be explored; these have one feature in common: they arise from symmetrical tonal relations. These two types are *whole-tone chords* and *chords in fourths and fifths.*

In the example below, all chords except the two at the asterisks are whole-tone chords.

Debussy: *Estampes* ("Jardins sous la pluie")

Do all of the whole-tone chords in this example stem from the *same* whole-tone scale? _____

---

458.   Because of the symmetrical structure of the whole-tone scale, whole-tone chords can consist of only three interval types: major second, major third, and the tritone (plus the inversion of each).

```
M2     |___|
M3     |_____|
A4     |_____|
m6=M3  |_____|
m7=M2  |_____|
```

Whole-tone chords tend to be static and rootless because they stem from a symmetrical tonal structure. Passages containing these chords are usually quite brief, because as with all highly distinctive effects, their value diminishes with use. Some tonal variety is obtained when a series of whole-tone chords utilizes both of the two whole-tone scales, rather than being limited to one. Also, a variety of interval combinations may be employed. The example in Frame 457, for instance, contains chords of three, four, and five tones with a variety of spacings and doublings.

Some whole-tone chords have the effect of altered dominants (V, V^7, or V^9 with raised or lowered fifth). In the example in the preceding frame, the two chords which are *not* whole-tone chords (at the asterisks) are thus in good company, for they are both _____ ninth chords.

dominant

---

459.   The passage below consists of a single whole-tone chord. Although the harmony is totally static, there is considerable rhythmic and melodic animation.

Villa-Lobos: *Próle do Bébé No. 1* ("O Polichinelo")

List the notes contained in the whole-tone chord above.

_____

E♭, F, G, A, B   *(Any order.)*

---

four

460. The chord in the previous example consists of all but one of the notes in a complete whole-tone scale (D-flat is missing). Even a complete whole-tone scale may be treated as a chord, all the tones having equal status. Because such chords are static, interest must be supplied by rhythm, melody, and texture. The next example has little melodic interest, but rhythmic motion and textural subtlety supply variety. Chords 4, 5, 6, and 7 are whole-tone chords; each of these consists of _____ (how many) separate tones.

Debussy: *Estampes* ("Jardins sous la pluie")

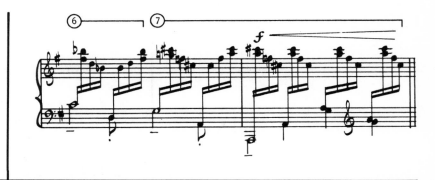

461. Indicate the quality of the first three chords in the preceding example. *(Use abbreviations such as Mm⁷ , etc.)*

Chord

1 dm ^{7}	1 _____
2 MmM^9	2 _____
3 MmM^9	3 _____

462. Like whole-tone chords, those constructed of perfect fourths or fifths produce static harmonic effects. This is due to the symmetrical tonal elements of which they are composed. The example below shows four-note chords in perfect fourths and fifths.

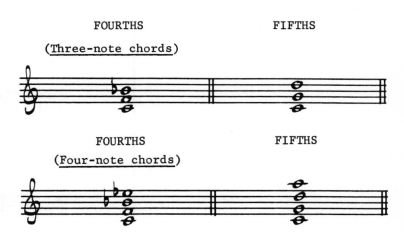

Such sonorities are termed "quartal" or "quintal" chords; the exploitation of such chords (in either fourths or fifths) is generally referred to as "quartal harmony." Chords in fourths or fifths are rarely encountered in impressionist music; the heyday of their use comes somewhat later. But nevertheless, they are part of the impressionist chord vocabulary as the next few examples will show.

(No response required.)

463. The example below contains several quartal chords.

Debussy: *Pour le piano* ("Sarabande")

Except for chords 9 and 10, all the chords in this example are constructed of perfect fourths. In the example below, the quartal chords are somewhat simplified and re-arranged to show their construction.

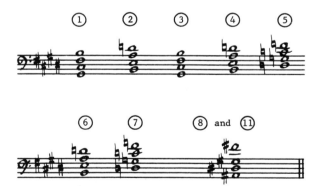

Most of these chords contain *three* perfect fourths. Chords 8 and 11, however, are based on a cycle of *four* perfect fourths with one tone omitted. Name the omitted tone. _____

C-sharp

464. Tertian and quartal chords are mixed in the passage below:

The chords at the asterisks are tertian (triads or seventh chords), all others are three-note quartal chords with octave doublings.

Can chord 1 be interpreted as a ninth chord on C?
_____

Yes. *(See the next frame.)*

465.   Chord 1 in the preceding example may be termed an incomplete ninth chord on C if you desire. Likewise, chord 2 can be regarded as a C thirteenth chord or as a chord with added sixth and ninth. But the question is "how do these chords impress the ear?" Because the third (E) is omitted in chord 1, the quartal construction is audibly evident. But still another approach is to regard all the notes in the first measure as constituting a thirteenth chord on C. The spacing, however, consistently emphasizes the perfect fourth, and the ear picks this out as a primary constructive interval. Obviously, several interpretations are possible; you must choose the one which best expresses what you hear.

(No response required.)

466.   All the notes in the next example can be regarded as constituting a single four-note chord.

Debussy: *Masques*

Très vif et fantasque

Because of the spacing, the tones in this example can be arranged equally well in either fourths or fifths. Using the given note as the bass, arrange the chord as directed.

(1) Fourths   (2) Fifths

(1)   (2)

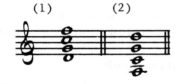

---

quintal

467. Octave displacement and doubling, sometimes makes it impossible to distinguish between chords built in fourths and fifths. As spelled in (1) of the preceding frame, the chord is *quartal*; as spelled in (2) the chord is _____ .

---

468. The chords in the example below are built in fourths, but are unlike those presented thus far.

Debussy: *Préludes*, Vol. II, No. 8 ("Ondine")

Scherzando

augmented	The chords used here consist of two fourths; the upper fourth is perfect, but the lower is _____ .

---

469. Each chord in the preceding example contains a tritone. This produces a more dissonant effect than if only perfect intervals are used. The term "quartal" is not used by some writers unless all intervals are perfect. However, the relation between chords such as those in the preceding frame and quartal chords more narrowly defined is evident.

When all chords are identical in quality (as in the preceding example), the harmony may be called "symmetrical." The influence of tertian harmony is totally lacking in this example. (True/False) _____

True. *(But see the next frame.)*

---

470. The chords themselves (in Frame 468) do not suggest tertian influence, but the succession of chords produces a pattern of intervals which suggests tertian organization. Indicate the interval between each bass note. *(Be specific.)*

(1) m 3rd
(2) m 2nd
(3) m 3rd
(4) m 3rd
(5) m 2nd

SUMMARY.

Preoccupation with harmonic sonorities is a feature of most impressionist music. Chords, and various forms of arpeggiation often carry the burden of expressive content. Even the precise quality of chords, the effect of register, spacing, doubling, and instrumental timbre is of utmost importance, and treated with fastidious care. Impressionist music includes a vastly expanded chord vocabulary as compared with classical and even romantic music. Some chords such as whole-tone chords, clusters, quartal and quintal chords, as well as expanded tertian sonorities produce diffuse harmonic effects, and cause functional distinctions to be blurred.

The list which follows summarizes the chords presented in this and the preceding chapter, and reveals the wide variety of chords which constitute the harmonic materials in impressionist music.

Triads:
　　All types are used.

Seventh chords:
　　All types are used, but diminished-minor, minor, and major-minor seventh chords are especially favored.

Ninth chords:

Dominant ninth types (MmM⁹ and Mmm⁹) are used most frequently, often in nonfunctional (parallel) progressions.

Eleventh and thirteenth chords:

These expanded tertian chords often have dominant function.

Chords with added tones:

The tones most frequently added to simpler sonorities (triads and seventh chords) are diatonic seconds, fourths, and sixths. "Chromatic" added tones produce a higher level of dissonance than "diatonic" added tones.

Chords with split root, third, fifth, or seventh:

Chromatic added tones may be spaced to produce modal mixtures called split roots, thirds, etc.

Polychords:

Combinations of two triads, seventh chords, or other types of chords are used only rarely.

Clusters:

Several notes spaced close together produce clusters; these may sometimes be termed "chords in seconds." Clusters may be chromatic as well as diatonic.

Pentatonic chords:

Three, four, or five notes of a pentatonic scale may be combined to produce a chord.

Whole-tone chords:

Any combination of three, four, five, or six tones from a whole-tone scale produces a whole-tone chord. The tritone is often prominent.

Chords in fourths and fifths:

Three or more fourths produce a "quartal" chord; "quintal" chords are made up of fifths. Ordinarily, only perfect intervals are used; such chords are "symmetrical" because all intervals are the same quality.

13

Parallelism

Perhaps the most remarkable feature of impressionist music is the extensive use of voices moving in parallel planes. This involves not only successions of intervals (seconds, thirds, fourths, etc.), but also entire chords. Parallel harmonies (planed chords—the result of several voices moving in parallel motion) were a radical departure from accepted practice and contributed profoundly to emancipating chords from patterns of relationships established by more than two centuries of tonal harmonic usage. Debussy early showed a predilection for such "unauthorized" harmonies; he delighted in exasperating his professors at the Conservatoire by improvising in this manner. He may have been encouraged to indulge in such audacities by his contact with the eccentric Erik Satie, who, at about the same time, used similar techniques as a pianist in the cabarets of Montmartre. But the use of parallel voices, and even harmonies, is by no means limited to impressionism. On the contrary, parallelism in one form or another occurs in practically all multivoiced music, and in some cases is a prominent feature indeed. A few historical precedents will give a better perspective, and also shed some light on the various forms parallelism may take. First, however, we shall look at the larger problem of relative motion.

The tonal contours of two voices define only four types of relative motion: *contrary, oblique, similar,* and *parallel.* Each of these produces a greater or lesser sense of independence between the two voices.

Ex. 23.

All four types of motion are used in most Western music. But as a heritage of the long evolution of polyphonic music, which extends from about the ninth century to the beginning of the baroque era, motion that contributes to linear independence tends to be favored. Parallel motion in perfect intervals is generally avoided altogether, due to the severe limitation such motion places on melodic individuality. Ironically, though, Western polyphony began with just this kind of motion. Example 24 shows composite organum at the fifth, which produces streams of voices moving in perfect fourths, fifths, and octaves.

Ex. 24. *Musica enchiriadis (ca. 850)*[1]

The style of strict organum was short-lived, however, as the technical evolution of later polyphonic idioms quickly led to preference for greater independence of voices in which first oblique, and then contrary motion were preferred.

Another type of early parallelism is called *gymel*.[2] This style originated in England, possibly under Danish and Norwegian influence; it is two-voice polyphony in which the voices move predominantly in thirds, sixths, or tenths. In Example 25, parallel thirds greatly outweigh other types of motion.

Ex. 25. *Hymn to St. Magnus* (12th century)[3]

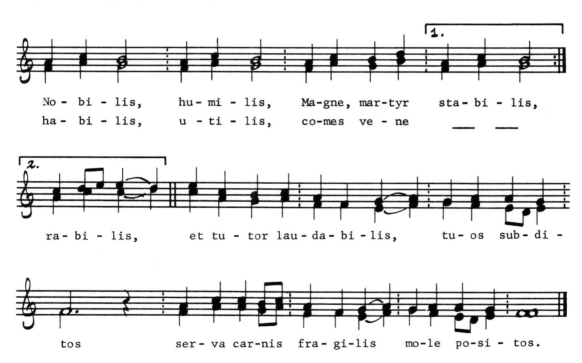

Excessive use of any single type of motion produces monotonous effects, and this is particularly true of parallel motion. Because the ideals of medieval and Renaissance polyphony called for a balance between the competing voices in a musical texture, excessive parallelism was avoided, and parallelism in perfect intervals came to be regarded as either archaic or unschooled. Later composers, however, sometimes wrote passages with prominent parallel perfect fifths, or even complete triads, to suggest rustic, amateurish music making. Such use is shown in Example 26, which dates from the end of the Renaissance, a time in which the very height of refined vocal polyphony was reached. The villanella is a popular genre of the period related to the madrigal; it is a sophisticated parody of rustic life.

Ex. 26 Marenzio: *Villanella* ("Al primo vostro squardo fui d'amoroso dardo")[4]

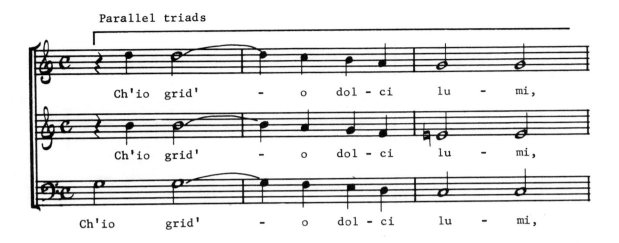

Except when humorous effects are intended,[5] writing such as that shown above is almost completely lacking in "art" music of the baroque, classical and romantic periods. But the coupling of voices in thirds or sixths is quite prevalent in romantic music, and somewhat less so in classical music. Such writing serves merely to enrich the sonority of melodic lines, and makes no pretense of producing independent voices.

This brings us to the vital distinction between "tonal" and "real" parallelism. Our first step is to assert that *the streams of thirds and sixths so familiar in nineteenth-century music actually do not consistently produce parallel motion.* The seeming contradiction of this statement will be unraveled in the frames which follow.

471. The melody in the example below is tonally enriched by coupling in thirds.

Brahms: *Sonata No. 1*, Op. 1

Coupled voices such as these commonly are considered to be moving in *parallel thirds.* But is this really true? In search for the answer to this question, first indicate the quality (major or minor) of each third in the first phrase as notated below:

M3 m3 M3 m3 m3 m3   m3

m3 m3 M3 M3 M3 m3   m3

No. *(See the next frame.)*

472. The analysis in the preceding frame reveals that the coupled voices produce a mixture of major and minor thirds. The next question is this: *is movement from a major to a minor third truly parallel motion?* State your opinion:

_____

minor

473. When consecutive thirds are of different quality, the voices do not move by the same interval. Notice below that the upper voice moves a major second from the first to the second chord, whereas the lower voice moves a _____ second.

M2

M3   m3

---

similar

474. Voices which move in the same direction, but by different intervals move not in parallel motion, but in _____ motion.

Both. *(See the next frame.)*

475. Thus, movement of voices which forms unequal intervals (as in Frame 473) actually should be called similar rather than parallel. *Established terminology, however, overlooks this imprecision.* So we shall refer to streams of intervals as "parallel" even though the quality may vary. Of course, the *numerical* interval type (2nd, 3rd, etc.) must be consistent, otherwise the term "similar motion" must be used.
 Which is an example of *parallel motion?* (1, 2, both, or neither) _____

(1)   (2)

m6   M6   M3   M3

---

476. The preceding frame shows that the term "parallel motion" applies to the *unequal* sixths in (1) as well as to the *equal* thirds in (2). This means that some motion is "more parallel" than others—a highly illogical position. Clearly, some distinction needs be made, and for this purpose the terms REAL and TONAL are used.
 Real parallelism: voices move in identical intervals.

P5   P5   P5   P5   m3   m3   m3   m3

Tonal parallelism: voices produce the same basic interval type, but the quality varies.

m6   M6   M6   m6   P4   A4   P4   A4

The coupled thirds in the example of Frame 471 produce (real/tonal) _____ parallelism.

tonal

2.

477. Which is an example of *real* parallelism? (1, 2, both, or neither) _____

(1)   (2)

Both.

478. Which is an example of *tonal* parallelism? (1, 2, both, or neither) _____

(1)   (2)

---

479. Write notes which produce *real* parallelism in major sixths above the given notes.

---

480. Prior to impressionism, most parallelism is tonal because the coupled voices are in the same tonality. This is the reason for calling inexact parallelism "tonal." In (1) below, both voices use tones contained in the key of E-flat major. In (2), however, each voice is at least potentially in a different key. Indicate the key suggested by the lower voice.

Chapter 13

(1) Tonal Parallelism

Eb: (both voices)

(2) Real Parallelism

Eb:

G:

___

---

1. √ *(Tonal parallelism enriches sonority, but does not necessarily expand tonality.)*

481. Real parallelism introduces a new tonal dimension: the suggestion of polytonality. If not actually polytonal, passages which include real parallelism are tonally expanded by including tones outside the diatonic scale. These tones are justified merely by moving in planes parallel to diatonic voices.

Indicate the correct statement(s) by checking one of the options below:

1. Extensive use of real parallelism is likely to produce tonal ambiguity.

2. Tonal parallelism expands tonality by providing richer sonorities.

(1) ____   (2) ____   Both ____   Neither ____

Now that a background has been established by noting a few historical precedents, and also by distinguishing between tonal and real parallelism, it remains to observe how various kinds of parallelism are incorporated into impressionist music. Most of the examples which follow are taken from works by Debussy. This is because parallelism (particularly planed chords) was in modern times first widely exploited by him. This mannerism remains a virtual trademark of his music, so much so that such writing is yet looked upon as a "Debussy formula."

A number of previously quoted examples contain prominent use of parallelism. You may wish to refer to Frames 291, 300, 308, 366, 376, 381, 414, 417, 456, and 468.

482. The example below contains a type of parallelism which is reminiscent of strict organum.[6] In the first measure, the voices move in perfect fourths with octave doubling.

Profondément calme

(dans une brume doucement sonore)

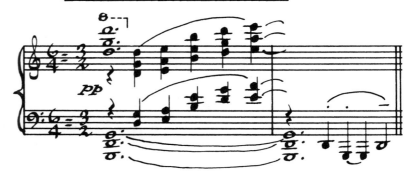

No doubt the pictorial subject of this prelude ("the engulfed cathedral") suggested the technique used. The result is a solemn, antique flavor with liturgical overtones. Another factor which adds to the archaic character of this passage is the scale used. All the notes added together (GABDE) form a _____ scale.

pentatonic

483.   Parallelism such as that in the preceding frame can be regarded as *melodic coupling*; the resulting sonorities have little harmonic status. But the intervals chosen are instrumental in producing the tonal character of the passage. Similar treatment is used in the next example.

Debussy: *Images,* Series 2 ("Poissons d'or")

Animé

Whereas parallelism in fourths was exploited in the example in Frame 482, here the voices are coupled in fifths (with octave doubling). There is another difference, too: The example immediately above contains both perfect and imperfect fifths. So instead of real parallelism, this is an example of _____ parallelism.

tonal

real

484. Parallelism in thirds may be seen in Frame 376. Because of the whole-tone scale, all the thirds in this example are major; the result is (real/tonal) _____ parallelism.

---

no

485. Parallel seconds frequently occur in connection with other intervals, but rarely by themselves. Two such examples may be seen in Frames 453, and 456. In both cases, voices are coupled in major seconds to "thicken" the sonority of the melodic line.

Two-voice planing in fifths, fourths, thirds, or seconds generally has (no/some/much) _____ harmonic value.

---

486. All parallelism is a form of melodic coupling. But when the coupled voices form complete chords, harmonic connotations are inescapable. The role of each chord, however, is ambiguous as the voices are locked into the same pattern of movement; thus, root movements are dictated solely by melodic action, not by pre-established patterns of harmonic relations. Root relations, then, are melodically, not harmonically determined. This is the radical effect of planed harmonies: *chords escape from the role previously determined for them by their sonority (type) and position within an harmonic tonal structure.*

In the example which follows, a C tonality is clearly established by the melody which cadences frequently on C, and gives rhythmic stress to both G and F. In addition, the recurrent C's in the bass provide a tonic pedal. But by moving only in parallel motion, the chords play a largely coloristic role. Except for the tonic (C major), "chord function" is lacking.

Debussy: *Préludes,* Vol. I, No. 10 ("La Cathédral engloutie")

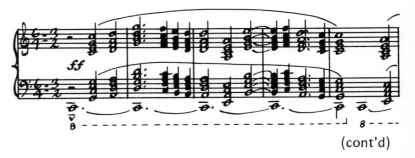

Profondément calme (dans une brume doucement sonore)

Sonore sans dureté

(cont'd)

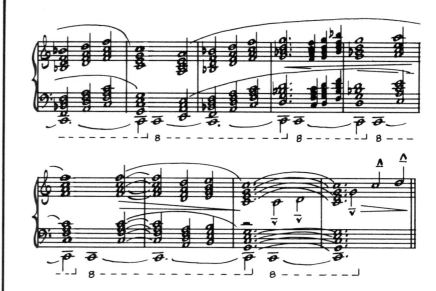

tonal

The parallelism in this example is (real/tonal) _____.

487. The passage in the preceding frame was chosen for our first example of planed chords because it contains many features which link it to traditional harmonic practice. The unequivocal tonality, and stress on tonic, dominant, and subdominant have been mentioned. Also significant is the use of *tonal* parallelism. Later examples will show that tonality is more seriously threatened by *real* parallelism.

Like the preceding example, the one below contains a variety of major and minor triads.

Debussy: *Préludes*, Vol. II, No. 10 ("Canope")

Yes.

The tonality clearly is based on D. Would it be correct to claim that the first three measures are a combination of the Dorian and Aeolian modes? _____

488.   The parallel triads in the example below appear over a G pedal which is often at odds with the harmony sounding above.

Ravel: *Le Tombeau de Couperin,* No. 5 ("Menuet") (1914-17)

tonal

The parallelism here is (real/tonal) _____.

489.   Like the preceding few examples, the fragment below consists of triads moving in parallel motion. Indicate in the spaces provided the quality of each chord.

Debussy: *Danse sacrée,* for harp and strings

(All are major triads.)

____ ____ ____ ____ ____ ____ ____

real

490. Because each voice in the preceding example moves exactly parallel to the others, every chord has the same quality. Such writing is called _____ parallelism.

491. Real parallelism as in Frame 489 causes tonal uncertainty, or at least modal ambiguity. As in all cases where functional distinctions are erased by identical tonal entities, tonality is produced (if at all) through principles of melodic tonality. Because the triads in Frame 489 are in root position, the lowest note of each chord has pre-eminent status. This, plus the rhythmic stress given the first chord in each of the first two measures, causes E-flat to assume a tonic role. But what is the mode? The passage as a whole defies analysis as only two notes of the chromatic scale are missing (E-natural, and B-natural). All that can be said with regard to mode is that each voice, considered by itself, can be analyzed as being in either a Dorian or an Aeolian mode.
      Can the term "symmetrical harmony" be applied to real parallelism such as that in Frame 489? _____

Yes. *(See the next frame.)*

492. Any harmony which makes use of identical tonal relations, or a consistent pattern of relations can be termed "symmetrical." We already have encountered several types. Some chords, for example, have symmetrical structure: augmented triads, diminished seventh chords, and chords derived from the whole-tone scale are symmetrical, as are quartal and quintal chords, as well as chords constructed of a consistent interval sequence. Chords whose roots are related by identical intervals produce symmetrical harmony, as do successions of chords which have the same quality, or a consistently alternating pattern of qualities.
      The next example contains two types of parallelism (shown by brackets). In the first, major triads are used exclusively. Continue the chord analysis in the third and fourth measures as begun in the first two.

Chapter 13

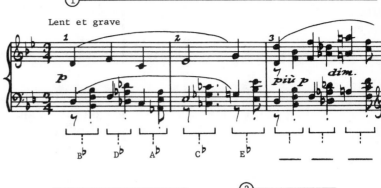

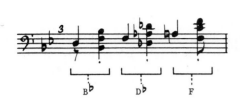

(No response required.)

493. By tracing the chord roots in the form of a tonal diagram, we reveal the initial tonal emphasis of B-flat, and the subsequent ascending series of thirds (mostly major), which quickly reaches E-natural—a tritone removed from the tonal center.

(3rds)

494. The second type of parallelism in Frame 492 (under bracket 2) is symmetrical in three ways:

1. Parallelism is real.

2. Chords move up by half-steps only.

Augmented triads are symmetrical
structures.
(In your own words.)

The third feature concerns the type chord used. Identify
this feature.

3. _____

_____

---

495.   Parallelism may be limited to a few chords, or carried
on for a considerable time. The brief passage below contains
parallelism which is tempered by some counter motion in
the upper voices.

Ravel: *Valses nobles et sentimentales* ("Epilogue") (1911)

Lent, un peu plus las

Cédez

tonal

This parallelism is (real/tonal) _____.

---

496.   Much more extensive parallelism is shown in the next
example.

Mouvt. de Habanera

In the first three measures the parallelism on the upper staff consists entirely of major triads; thereafter, major and minor triads are mixed. The bass notes (D♭-A♭) constitute a multiple _____.

pedal

497. Thus far all the examples have shown only planed major, minor, and augmented triads. But more complex chords are treated in this fashion too.

Debussy: *Estampes* ("La Soirée dans Grenade")

Mouvt. de Habanera
Tempo giusto

(cont'd)

All the chords in this example are _____ - _____ seventh chords.

major-minor

---

498.   Another example of planed major-minor seventh chords is shown below:

Ravel: *Daphnis et Chloé*, Suite No. 2

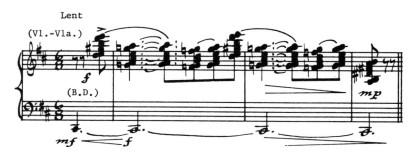

It is clear that as used here (and also in Frame 497), the major-minor seventh chord has lost completely its usual functional value. In terms of traditional music, no other chord has a more clearly-defined role than the "dominant seventh" chord. When locked into parallel streams, however, it is merely one of many possible sonorities, and is exploited solely for its color potential, and affective value.

(No response required.)

---

499.   The parallelism in the first measure of the example below consists of chromatically descending major thirds. There is a variety of chords thereafter, but the last four (accompaniment only) are all major-minor seventh chords with fifth omitted.

Ireland: *Sonata,* for violoncello and piano

The totally chromatic accompaniment contributes little toward establishing a tonality. The melody, on the other hand, contains no chromatic movement, and produces a tonal center of _____ .

C

500. Arpeggiated ninth chords are used in parallel motion below:

Debussy: *Images,* Series 1 ("Reflets dans l'eau")

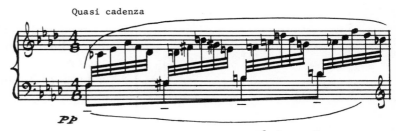

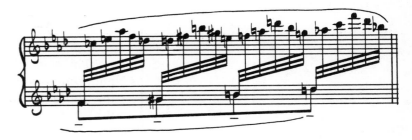

The chords are in first inversion, and move up exclusively in _____ thirds (or equivalent).

minor

501.   The chords in the preceding frame are major-minor-major ninth chords.[7] The next example is considerably more complex.

Debussy: *Six épigraphes antiques* ("Pour un tombeau sans nom")

The parallel chords all have the same quality. Notation makes the interpretation of these chords difficult, so the one on beat three is shown below with the notes respelled and spaced in thirds to make more evident the actual aural effect.

This shows that the chord may be interpreted as a major-minor-minor ninth chord. As actually spaced in the music, this chord is in an unusual inversion: the (root/3rd/5th/7th/9th) _____ is in the lowest voice *(consider the moving voices only)*.

9th

502.   The chords in the last two measures of the preceding example are more dissonant than one expects to find in im-

pressionist music. At first glance these chords appear to consist of a random association of notes. There is a logic behind their construction, however, which is revealed by examining closely the intervals contained in the sonority at the asterisk. Indicate the precise quality of each interval in the spaces provided below:

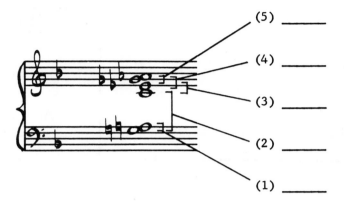

(5) _____

(4) _____

(3) _____

(2) _____

(1) _____

(5) M2
(4) m3
(3) m3
(2) m3
(1) M2

---

503.   The series of intervals analyzed above reads the same either upward or downward. The resulting chord is thus "symmetrical," and this aspect is picked up (perhaps unconsciously) by the ear. The final chord of the example is the same as the one in the preceding measure except that a perfect fifth (D-A) is added below.

The fragment in Frame 501 is a notable example of symmetricality. This kind of writing is a significant aspect of some impressionist music, but other twentieth-century styles, in which rational approaches are still more consistently applied, carry these techniques much further.

(No response required.)

---

504.   As an adjunct of the expanded chord vocabulary of impressionist music, parallelism sometimes involves sonorities more complex than triads, seventh, and ninth chords.

Debussy: *Préludes*, Vol. II, No. 2 ("Feuilles mortes")

Lent et mélancolique

(cont'd)

Most of the chords in this passage are triads with
_____ tones.

added

---

505.   The chords below result from melodic coupling and
can be analyzed variously, but perhaps the simplest is as
chords in fifths with octave displacement. *(The last two
chords are constructed differently.)*

Debussy: *Images*, Series 2 ("Et la lune descend sur le temple qui
fut")

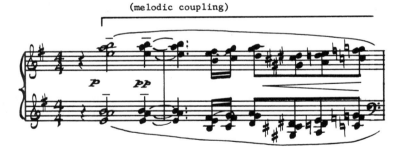

If analyzed as suggested above, the first chord would be
a series of perfect fifths based on the note _____.

A

506. The planed voices below produce chords built in fourths.

Debussy: *Six épigraphes antiques* ("Pour l'Egyptienne")

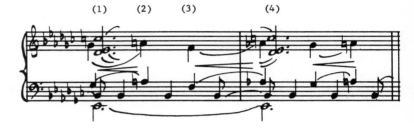

The parallelism in the first two measures is (real/tonal) _____.

tonal *(Sonorities vary.)*

507. Other than simple octave doubling, there is no parallelism in the final two measures in Frame 506. These measures are included to show an intriguing chord structure. This chord is an E-flat minor seventh chord (E♭ G♭ B♭ D♭), which is adorned by several added tones. At (1), the C-natural in the highest voice is an added major sixth, whereas the A-natural at (2)—taken melodically by leap—is an added augmented _____.

fourth

major

508. At (3), the note F is an added _____ second.

fourth

509. At (4), the A-flat—also approached by leap—can be analyzed as an added perfect _____.

SUMMARY.

The examples of this chapter show various types of parallelism found in impressionist music. In addition to melodic coupling of intervals (seconds, thirds, fourths, etc.), most of the sonorities contained in the expanded chord vocabulary are used in parallel streams. Such use causes chords to lose the functional value associated with their quality and position in the tonal structure; tonality is thus rendered ambiguous. This is particularly true when parallelism is real. Impressionist composers, however, countered the tonality-dissolving effect of parallelism with pedal tones. A glance over the examples contained in this chapter will indicate the prevalence of this device (see Frames 486, 488, 495, 496, 497, 498, and 506). This testifies to an unwillingness to give up tonality as a formal and expressive force.

14

Form in Impressionist Music

Coherence in music results from the manipulation of rhythm, melody, harmony, tone color, and texture. The manner in which these elements are handled varies with the purpose of the music, its style, medium, and the aesthetic out of which it grows. Particular formal designs, and approaches to the elements which constitute them are associated with various periods and styles. For example, rhythmic characteristics such as a steady pulse, constant meter, and motoric patterns, all of which are associated with baroque music, are much less evident in impressionist music. The rhythmic idiom of impressionism is richly varied. But perhaps the most characteristic features are fluctuating meters, an implicit rather than an explicit pulse, and subtle combinations of rhythmic patterns—including syncopation and irregular divisions of the beat—which veil the meter. But this is not to say that impressionist music is pulseless. A slow, implicit beat is still a beat, and fluctuating meters do provide patterns of temporal organization.[1]

In much vocal music, the text is sufficient to provide continuity and meaning. Purely instrumental music, on the other hand, may lack coherence unless musical events occur in intelligible sequences of repetitions and contrasts. This, at any rate, is the concept of form which guided composers of the classical period, whose music tends to be ordered by easily-perceived and evenly-balanced phrases, periods, sections, etc. The result is architectonic forms in which the constructive element of composition often is thrust to the fore.

Although still willing to exploit formal patterns inherited from the classical period, nineteenth-century composers under the influence of romanticism drifted toward freer and more complex forms. The portrayal of emotional stress, and the expression of individualism, both of which are characteristic of romantic music, led to the expansion and loosening of existing forms. The grip of formal rigidity was further loosened in impressionist music. The evocative and suggestive character of this music would be stifled by the predictability of regular phrase structure and stereotyped cadence formulas. The expression of fleeting, insubstantial impressions naturally requires less clearly-defined phrases and sharply-etched motives than does a more objective, classical-influenced style. For these reasons impressionist composers made little use of formal development; instead, they favored short self-contained fragments strung together to suggest a free stream of associations and impressions.

Debussy once made a clear statement regarding form:

> "I should like to see the creation—I, myself, shall achieve it—of a kind of music free from themes and motives, or formed on a single continuous theme, which nothing interrupts and which returns upon itself. Then there will be a logical, compact, deductive development. There will not be, between two restatements of the same characteristic theme, a hasty and superfluous 'filling in'! The development will no longer be that amplification of material, that professional rhetoric which is the badge of excellent training, but it will be given a more universal and essential psychic conception."[2]

A clearer statement could hardly be made. The ideal enunciated in Debussy's credo is no less than the freedom of music from external formal constraints; this obviously is miles removed from the concept of classical order. The rejection of established attitudes toward form implicit in the above statement, and at least partially realized in some impressionist music, was revolutionary at the time, and continues to be an important feature in much twentieth-century music. For many of today's composers, formal symmetry and order have given way to "structureless," fluid, or even "random" expressions. Impressionism had a hand in this development. It is easy to be blinded by the dazzling sonic features provided by expanded scales and harmonic resources, and thus lose sight of the impetus furnished by impressionism for redefining the role of form in music. The remainder of this chapter will be devoted to examining the more important features of form in impressionist music.

510. In spite of Debussy's desire to create a "music free from themes and motives," his melodic style often involves extensive use of motives, and motives are also used to integrate entire compositions. But before citing a few examples, it is necessary to consider the ways motives are varied.

Any melodic unit may be subjected to either *tonal* or *temporal* variation. This means that the two aspects which may be altered are *pitch* and *rhythm*.[3] First, we will consider variations of pitch. An original motive and three derivative forms are shown below:

Retrograde causes the same notes to be sounded in reverse order. Inversion, on the other hand, produces some new pitches, and the direction of intervallic motion is changed. Which of the three variants above seems *least* like the original? _____

_____

*The terms "cancrizans" and "crab" are also used.
**This is also called "mirroring."

Retrograde-inversion

511. Because two operations are used, retrograde-inversion is least like the original motive. Often it is difficult to discern aurally the relation between motives which have been so extensively altered. But in spite of this, a germinal identity exists which helps unify the music, perhaps at a subconscious level of perception.

Note the symbols for the variation forms shown in the preceding frame.

Original	- O
Retrograde	- R
Inversion	- I
Retrograde-inversion	- RI

These symbols are widely accepted and used, and they will appear occasionally as we proceed. Use these symbols to identify each of the derivative forms below:

Original (O)

(1) _____

(2) _____

(3) _____

(1) RI

(2) I

(3) R

512. You may have found the RI version to be the most difficult to identify. At any rate, it is the form least like O.

Varied forms of a motive may be either *real* or *tonal* depending on whether or not intervals are answered precisely (M3-M3), or merely generally (M3-m3). Both I and RI in the preceding frame are (real/tonal) _____ variations.

real

513. Another variation of pitch is this: *The original or any of the forms mentioned thus far may be transposed to different pitches.* This is a very useful manipulation because it

produces both unity and sonic variety. Sequence is a common result of motive transposition, but transpositions which are not immediate (as in sequence), are often even more effective for creating melodic unity without the obvious, sometimes mechanistic effect conveyed by sequence.

514. The original motive in Frame 510 is shown below with still other variations of pitch.

Of course, these variations may be used with the R, I, and RI forms, too.

Interval expansion and contraction alter the ambitus of a motive, but the melodic shape remains the same. The addition or deletion of tones, however, may cause more drastic change because the rhythm is altered.

515. The addition or deletion of tones causes partial alteration of rhythm. More systematic rhythmic alteration which often affects the entire motive occurs two ways as shown below:

(1) Original

(2) Diminution

(3) Augmentation

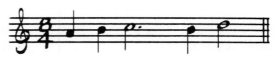

Assuming a common quarter-note beat, the three fragments above move at different speeds. In (2), the notes are half the value of the original; in (3), the notes are double the value of the original. When augmented or diminished in this manner, the rhythmic identity of the original motive is preserved; but when some notes are varied differently than others, greater change results.

The original motive is subjected to extensive rhythmic variation in the next example. Indicate how each note of the original is altered.

Original

Varied

1. 3

2. (unaltered)

3. 3 - shorter

4. 3 - longer

5. 2 - longer

Note 1 is _____ times longer.

Note 2 is unaltered.

Note 3 is _____ times _____ .

Note 4 is _____ times _____ .

Note 5 is _____ times _____ .

516. Much of a motive's character is conveyed by its rhythm; thus, variations which change rhythmic configuration generally cause greater change than do tonal variations. But still more drastic variation occurs when both rhythm

and pitches are changed simultaneously. By combining several of the processes of motive variation, transformation may be so drastic that a totally new motive appears to have been created. Still, when such manipulations are used, some generic relation must exist, and this imparts hidden unity to the music.

One final point: Application of the techniques of motive variation facilitates composition. Even a few notes can serve as source material for extended musical forms, and seemingly new ideas can be created with relative ease.

(No response required.)

---

517.   It is time now to see to what extent motives are used to integrate melodies in some impressionist music. The melody below is built of very limited motivic material:

Debussy: *Préludes*, Vol. I, No. 8 ("La fille aux cheveux de lin")

This melody grows from a three-note motive. The use of this motive in the first phrase is shown below:

	The original motive (1) is altered in each of the subsequent occurrences. Variation in (2) is by alteration of intervals. Complete the analysis below: *Occurrence* *Intervals* (1) m3 followed by M2 (2) _____ followed by _____
M2 - m3	
augmentation	518. Occurrence (3) has the same sequence of intervals as (2); the variation in this case is rhythmic. Because the duration of each note is increased, the term for this type of variation is _____ .
inversion	519. Version (4) of the motive has the same rhythm as (1) and (2), but the notes move in a downward direction. This is called _____ .
seconds	520. In addition to being inverted, the intervals in version (4) are both major _____ .
diminution	521. Version (5) of the motive also moves in descending seconds. Compare the rhythm of (5) with that of the original motive (1). Not only is the motive placed in a new metric position, but the third note is shortened. This latter process is called _____ .
	522. The second phrase of our melody shows further exploitation of the motive.

No.	

Slightly different interpretations could be made, but the pervading influence of the original motive is inescapable. Each of the occurrences above shows rhythmic variation. Does the original sequence of intervals (m3-M2) recur in any of the units as indicated above? _____

---

523. The final phrase is analyzed below:

Compare the original motive (1) with occurrence (14).

(1)

(14)

Analyze the succession of intervals in each of these.

Occurrence	Intervals
(1)	____ followed by ____
(14)	____ followed by ____

(1) m3 - M2

(14) M2 - m3

---

524. Not only do the intervals occur in reverse order (retrograde), but in the opposite direction. The latter process is called _____ .

inversion *(or mirroring)*

---

525. Occurrence (14) has been shown to be a retrograde-inversion (transposed) of the original motive. Although this process is rather complex, the rhythmic identity, and also the simplicity of the three-note melodic unit assures aural association of the two forms.

(No response required.)

Far from being "free from . . . motives," Debussy's deceptively simple, unassuming melody (Frame 517) is built up entirely from a single three-note melodic unit.

526.   Three brackets are drawn in the example below. Each indicates a melodic unit which is exploited as the melody develops.

Ravel: *La Valse*

Mouvt. de Valse vienoise

Although other terms might be used, the notes under bracket 1 will be called a motive. Brackets 2, and 3 indicate submotives. Draw a bracket to indicate the recurrence of the complete motive (1).

transposition

527.   The two-measure motive (1) is restated immediately, but two intervals are altered; also the motive begins on a different pitch. This latter device is called _____ .

528.   Bracket 2 drawn below the notes in Frame 526 indicates a smaller melodic unit which can be called a submotive. Draw brackets (in Frame 526) to show the recurrence of this submotive (2). *(There are six appearances altogether; try to find them all.)*

529. The appearances of submotive (2) as analyzed in the preceding frame contain considerable intervallic variation. The direction of movement, however, is consistent (a leap downward followed by an ascending interval). Rhythm also contributes to establishing the identity of this melodic unit.

Check the factor you consider to be most important for preserving motivic identity.

1. Pitch similarities   _____

2. Rhythmic similarities _____

2. √   *(See the next frame.)*

530. Of course both pitch and rhythmic similarities contribute to preserving the character of a motive, but rhythm is usually a stronger binding feature than pitch. *Unity and coherence in music are due largely to the exploitation of relatively few rhythmic patterns.*

Ravel's melody is reproduced again below. This time show with brackets each occurrence of the smallest submotive (3). *(Continue the analysis as begun.)*

Ravel: *La Valse*

Mouvt. de Valse vienoise

531. The analysis in the preceding frame shows that practically the entire melody is constructed from a single two-note unit. From this unit larger motives and phrases grow. It is the variation devices of transposition, inversion, interval alteration, etc. which permit such a simple melodic unit to serve as the basis for more extended formal divisions.

In the next melody a motive is stated four times *(each is numbered and bracketed)*.

Ravel: *Trio*, for piano, violin, and 'cello

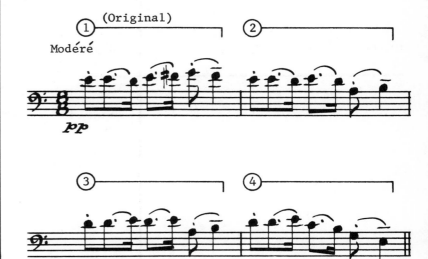

True.

No.

---

532. Recurrence of a single rhythmic pattern as in the preceding frame is called ISORHYTHM.[4] Unity is virtually guaranteed by this device because of the ease with which the ear recognizes rhythmic entities. Look, now, at the tonal characteristics of the melody. Are any two statements identical in this respect? _____

---

533. Let us compare some of the tonal variation devices exploited in the melody in Frame 531. Notice that the first four notes in (1) and (2) are the same, but thereafter variation occurs.

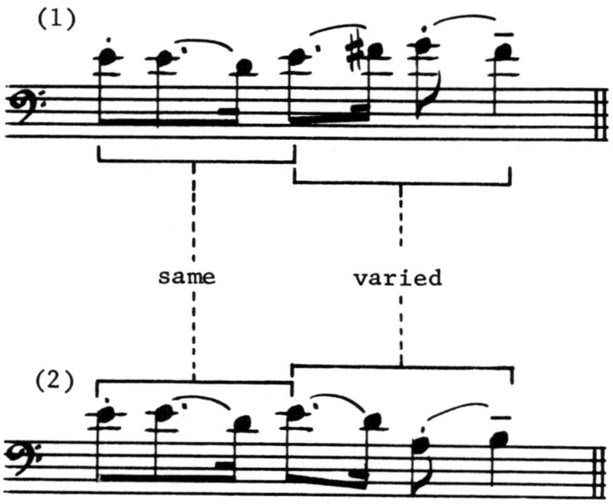

(1)

same   varied

(2)

Inversion *(or mirroring)*

Name the variation device used in the latter part of (2) above. _____

---

534. The inversion observed in the preceding frame is "free," because, although the direction of movement is reversed, two intervals are changed (by expansion).

Versions (1) and (3) are compared in the next example.

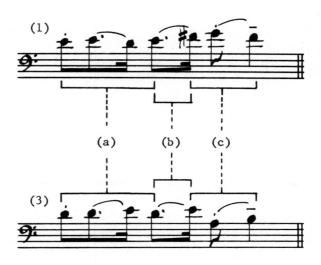

Three manipulations are singled out. Describe each of these in the spaces below:

a. Inversion   *(transposed)*

a. _____
    _____

b. Transposition

b. _____
    _____

c. Inversion
    (with interval expansion)

c. _____
    _____

535. Versions (1) and (4) of Frame 531 are compared below:

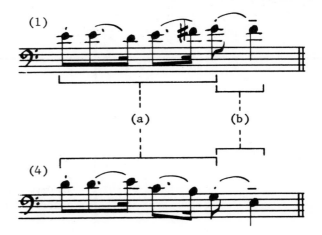

Two manipulations are singled out. Describe each of these.

a. Inversion
(transposed, with interval
expansion)

a. _____
_____
_____
_____
_____

b. Interval expansion

b. _____
_____
_____

536. One final set of analyses will close our brief examination of melodic writing in impressionist music. Refer, now, to Panel 15. The five fragments contained in this panel constitute not all, but most of the melodic material of the composition. In the first fragment, three motives are identified. We shall trace their fate as the melodic material evolves in subsequent phrases. As the first step, indicate with brackets how each of the three motives identified in ① appear in ②.

537. Although considerably altered, the phrase as a whole—as well as each of the three motives—retains its essential character. The overall contour is similar in each case, and the rhythmic patterns are enough alike to assure recognition. Motive 1 is rhythmically and melodically extended; motive 2 is slightly altered rhythmically, and some of the intervals are expanded; motive 3 is also slightly altered rhythmically. In addition, it is transposed, and the interval has been changed from a _____ to a _____ third.

minor (to a) major

538. Fragment ③ is still more extensively altered, but nevertheless, its generic relation to the original is evident. Use brackets to identify the motives as before.

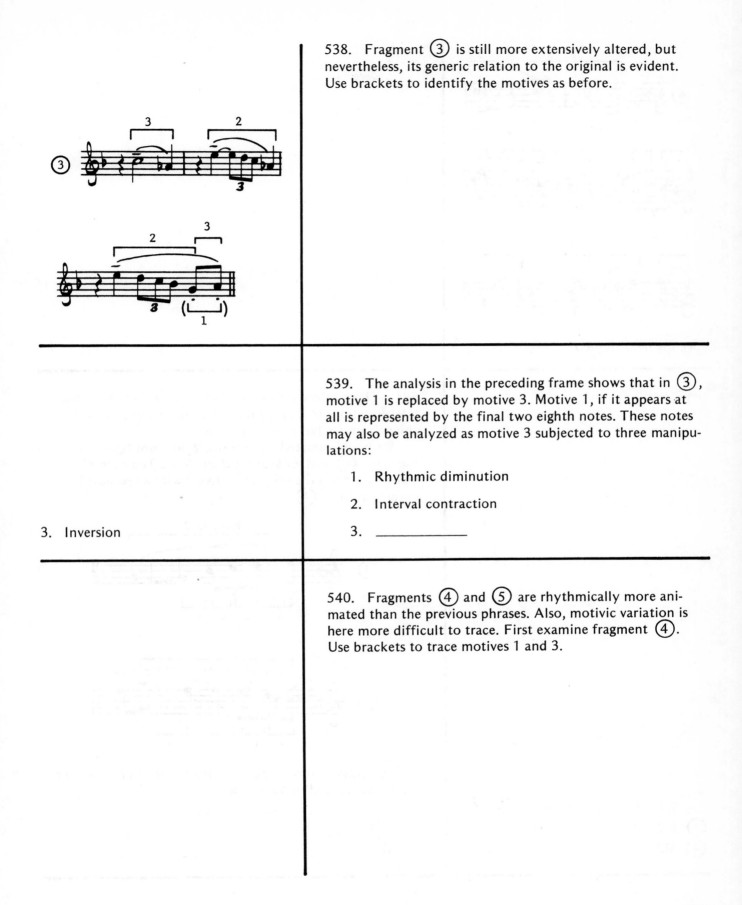

539. The analysis in the preceding frame shows that in ③, motive 1 is replaced by motive 3. Motive 1, if it appears at all is represented by the final two eighth notes. These notes may also be analyzed as motive 3 subjected to three manipulations:

1. Rhythmic diminution

2. Interval contraction

3. _____

3. Inversion

540. Fragments ④ and ⑤ are rhythmically more animated than the previous phrases. Also, motivic variation is here more difficult to trace. First examine fragment ④. Use brackets to trace motives 1 and 3.

(See the next frame.)

541. The motives are so varied and interwoven that other interpretations of ④ are possible. The analysis supplied above is suggestive, but not definitive.

We have intimated that motive 2 does not figure in fragment ④, but let's take a closer look. The example below compares the original motive 2 with a few notes excerpted from ④.

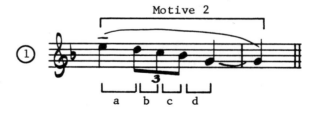

Your task in this frame is to analyze precisely the intervals (a, b, c, and d) in each case.

	(a)	(b)	(c)	(d)
①	___	___	___	___
④	___	___	___	___

	(a)	(b)	(c)	(d)
①	M2	M2	M2	m3
④	M2	M2	M2	m3

inversion

542. The intervals occur in the same order, but the direction is reversed. Thus, the device used here is _____ .

---

543. The two versions of motive 2 in Frame 541 are difficult to relate aurally even though the intervals are identical. This is because of the lack of rhythmic similarity.

Fragment ⑤ is much like ④. Motive 3 is the most evident of the three motives. The example below, however, will reveal another hidden relationship involving motive 2.

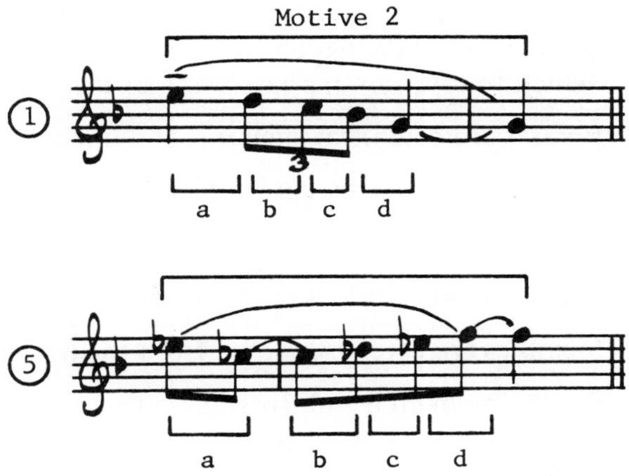

Motive 2

Complete the analysis by listing the intervals (a, b, c, and d) which occur in the excerpt from ⑤.

	(a)	(b)	(c)	(d)
①	M2	M2	M2	m3
⑤	____	____	____	____

(a) (b) (c) (d)

⑤ M3 M2 M2 M2

---

544. The analysis in the preceding frame reveals that the intervals occur in reverse order.

Thus, the device of retrograde is in use here. The retrograde is inexact, however, for two reasons: not only is the direction of interval (a) in ⑤ reversed, but this interval should be not a major but a _____ third.

minor

---

545. It is possible that such extensive variation as that demonstrated in the preceding few frames is neither con-

sciously written nor perceived. It may result merely from exploiting relatively few intervals (in this case seconds and thirds). But in spite of this, these hidden relations produce coherence no less valid for being perceived at a subconscious level of experience.

In music so chord-dominated as impressionism, it is not surprising that melodies should be mere elaborations of the harmonic background. But chord-generated melodies are common in older music, too. The special character of such melodies in impressionist music is due to the harmonic style out of which it grows. The feature of impressionist music which has been stressed in this chapter is the use of short, fragmentary motives. This, too, is a part of other styles. In impressionist music, however, motives (and their variants) often provide the chief unifying device.

The list which follows summarizes some of the more characteristic features of impressionist melodies:

1. Phrases are often fragmentary, and unequal in length.

2. Stereotyped cadences are avoided.

3. Immediate repetition of a short melodic fragment is common.[5]

4. Vocal melodic style is strongly affected by the rhythm and inflection of the spoken words.

5. Melodies are often extracted from the harmonic background.

6. Short, fragmentary motives serve to unify the whole. These motives are often subjected to transformations by embellishment, rhythmic variation, change of intervals, register, or instrumental color.

Because impressionist music appeals to the senses rather than the intellect, formal developmental processes are inappropriate. The working out of themes as in sonata form is replaced by the even more sophisticated techniques of motive variation. These techniques provide a kind of atomistic unity, and the thematic metamorphoses are apprehended at more nearly a subconscious level. Part forms are favored for the larger formal units in impressionist music; but in contrast to such forms in earlier music, sections are often indistinct, and not clearly set off from one another. Also, recurring sections may be greatly altered in length, thus producing designs lacking in balance. Ternary form (ABA) occurs very frequently, especially in the works of Debussy, who seemed to have special interest in tripartite forms. He tended even to write pieces in sets of three (the *Nocturnes*, *La Mer*, *Images*, and *Estampes*, for example).

Still another formal mannerism is the frequent use of pedals and ostinatos. These devices contribute not only formal coherence, but also provide tonal stability. Pedals, for example, are almost always present in passages which feature parallelism.[6]

We shall turn now to two examples of complete compositions.[7] These have been selected as especially pure demonstrations of impressionist formal practices. The first is contained in Panel 16. The music here is reduced to its essential melodic and motivic material. You should refer, also, to the complete work, which contains many stunning harmonic devices, including chords with split sevenths, and parallelism. Notice in Panel 16 that two motives are identified (measures 1, and 7-8). We shall trace the transformations of these motives and also note the organization of the whole composition.

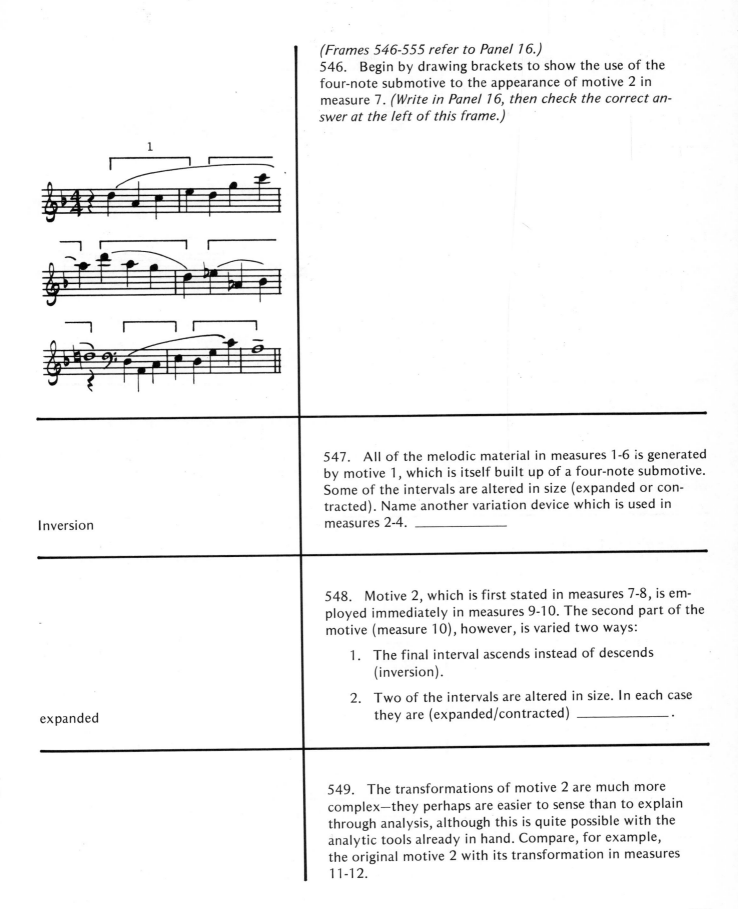

(Frames 546-555 refer to Panel 16.)
546. Begin by drawing brackets to show the use of the four-note submotive to the appearance of motive 2 in measure 7. *(Write in Panel 16, then check the correct answer at the left of this frame.)*

Inversion

547. All of the melodic material in measures 1-6 is generated by motive 1, which is itself built up of a four-note submotive. Some of the intervals are altered in size (expanded or contracted). Name another variation device which is used in measures 2-4. _____

expanded

548. Motive 2, which is first stated in measures 7-8, is employed immediately in measures 9-10. The second part of the motive (measure 10), however, is varied two ways:

1. The final interval ascends instead of descends (inversion).

2. Two of the intervals are altered in size. In each case they are (expanded/contracted) _____ .

549. The transformations of motive 2 are much more complex—they perhaps are easier to sense than to explain through analysis, although this is quite possible with the analytic tools already in hand. Compare, for example, the original motive 2 with its transformation in measures 11-12.

Form in Impressionist Music

257

Original Motive 2

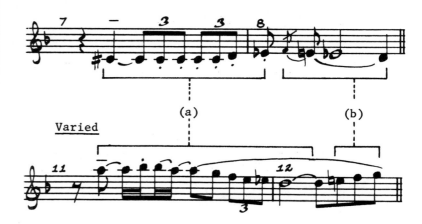

Varied

The motive is divided into two parts (a and b) to make clear various relations. Part (a) is varied by change of rhythm, addition of tones and also by _____ .

inversion

550. Part (b) is varied by inversion too, but also by the deletion of a grace note, and rhythmic change. Still another change in part (b) may be identified: the final interval of the original is a half-step; in the varied form, this interval is a _____ - _____ .

whole-step

551. Note the relation of the original motive 2 to its varied form in measures 13-14.

Original Motive 2

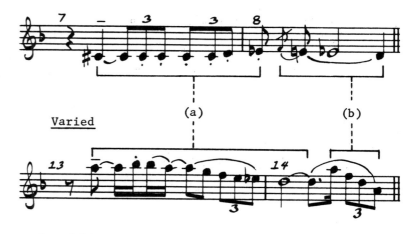

Varied

Part (a) is varied exactly the same as in measure 11. Part (b), however, is treated differently. In this case, all

expanded	rhythmic values are altered (the grace note, for example becomes a sixteenth note, and triplet eighths replace the eighth, half and quarter notes). The direction of intervallic movement is the same, so there is no inversion as before, but each interval is altered by being (expanded/contracted) _____ .
Motive 2, part (b).	552. Look, now, at measure 14 in Panel 16. The lower voice in this measure is derived from previous material. Identify its source. _____
The grace-note figure from motive 2, part (b).	553. The melodic material in measure 14 consists of two variants of motive 2, part (b). Measure 15 is an immediate repetition of this material. Such repetitions have already been noted as a mannerism in impressionist music. Now state the source of the material in measure 16. *(Be as specific as you can.)* _____ _____ _____ _____
It is one-half as long.	554. The grace-note figure continues to be exploited for some time. Notice, too, the appearance of the complete motive 2 in measures 20-23. Thus, motive 2 plays a vital role in this part of the composition. Although this section (measures 17-25) consists of material derived from motive 2, there are features which set it off from prior measures. First of all, there is a new tempo *(Animez un peu),* and the perfect fourth is notably exploited for the first time. Because of these two features, measures 17-25 may be termed the middle part (B) of a three-part form, in spite of the fact that no new thematic material is introduced. The validity of this interpretation is reinforced by the prominent reappearance in measure 26 of the original material built up of motive 1. Further, it is in measure 26 that the original tempo is resumed. Thus, the section from measure 26 to the end is the final part of the form, and contains prominent use of motives 1 and 2. How does the length of this section compare with the first? _____ _____

555. Our analysis of the composition in Panel 16 has shown how a few small motives are used to build an entire composition. It has also revealed the blending of one formal unit into another—the second section is not clearly set off from the first, and the thematic material is not new. The chart below summarizes the form and content; notice particularly the unequally balanced sections.

Section	A	B	A'
Tempo	*Très calme*	*Animez un peu*	*1er Mouvt.*
Length	16 measures	9 measures	8 measures
Material	Motive 1 Motive 2	Motive 2	Motive 1 Motive 2

The contrast in B is not due to new thematic material, but to the new tempo, and also the way motive 2 is used. As analyzed, this is a tripartite form, which in musical terminology is known as _____ form.

ternary *(or three-part)*

The melodic material in Debussy's prelude for piano "Canope" (Panel 16) consists mainly of short, fragmentary motives. Balanced, rhetorical phrases so familiar in classical music are lacking—instead, there is a sense of inner affinity, and nearly organic metamorphosis. These features are typical of impressionist form in its purest state. The next composition which we shall examine is by Ravel, who generally took a more traditional approach to form than Debussy. Turn now to Panel 17.

The reduction of Ravel's composition in Panel 17 facilitates our examination of the formal design, but it is highly desirable that you refer to the complete work. Otherwise, subtle harmonic effects—extended tertian sonorities abound—will be missed. Also, tonal ambiguity as opposed to tonal certainty, which has an affect on form, is not evident in the reduced version.

(Frames 556-568 refer to Panel 17.)
556. The major divisions of the form are shown by the letters ABA', and a two-note motive is identified in the first measure. Our concern is to observe the construction of each section, and to note how the motive is exploited.

To begin, the first 12 measures constitute a period, which can be analyzed as consisting of two phrases (4+8 measures). Draw brackets to show each exploitation of the two-note motive (to measure 12). *(Write in Panel 17, then check the answer on the next page.)*

(See the next frame.)

Addition of a tone.

557. Interpretations other than those given in the preceding frame may be made. Clearly, though, the motive plays a dominant generative role in the construction of this melody. Name the type of motive variation used in measure 2.

_____

2. √

558. Check the correct item(s) below:

The motive variation used in measure 4 is

1. diminution _____

2. Interval contraction _____

3. inversion _____

4. √

4. change of phrasing _____

559. The second section begins after the first double bar and extends to measure 27. This section is actually merely further exploitation of the material in the initial period, but there is enough contrast to justify the analysis below:

A ⌐————————————————————┐
a (1-12) --------➤ b (13-26) -------➤

Within section (b), there are two obvious appearances of the original motive. The first is in measure 13; the second is in measure _____ .

560. The example below shows the similarity between the opening measures of sections (a) and (b).

(a)

(b)

In addition to ornamentation, section (b) contains considerable variation. The motive in the first measure is merely transposed up a third, but in the second measure there is rhythmic change, and interval contraction. In the third measure, there is, in addition to ornamentation, change of phrasing and alteration of the intervals.

(No response required.)

561. Measure four in (b) of the preceding frame is the result of five variation techniques. Complete the list of these five techniques.

    1. Ornamentation

    2. Change of phrasing

    3. Transposition

4. Inversion

5. Interval contraction *(Any order.)*

    4. _____

    5. _____

562. In addition to the relations observed in the preceding three frames, notice that measures 17, 19, 21, 22, and 25 are clearly related to measures 3 and 9. Because of the identity between the thematic material contained in measures 13-26, one could analyze this section as a variant of section (a). But the variation is extensive, and the accompanying harmonic and textural writing (not shown in Panel 17) provides further contrast.

Measures 27-38 constitute a third section which closes part A of the form. This section consists of three phrases (identified in Panel 17), and the melodic material contrasts significantly with what has gone before. The complete sectional analysis of part A is shown below:

A ──────────────────────────────────┐
a(1-12) -------►b(13-26) -------►c(27-38) --►

Now turn to Panel 17 and look more closely at the "c" section (measures 27-38). The organization of this section into three phrases is quite clear. Complete the comments on the relation of phrases two and three to the first.

1. Phrase 2 (measures 30-32) is exactly the same as phrase 1 (measures 27-29) except that it is

_____

_____

transposed an octave higher

2. Phrase 3 (measures 33-38) is extended; it begins like phrase 1, but is varied in the second measure. Describe this variation.

_____

_____

Intervals are changed.

563. The final four measures of the part just analyzed (c) serve as a transition into the next part of the form (B). The interval exploited in these measures is a major third (C-A♭), and the relation between this interval and the original motive is obvious.

We shall move on now to the middle section (B). This section is short compared to the first; it consists of measures 39-52. The melodic material features a descending perfect fourth (C♯-G♯), which is the inversion of the original motive (D♭-A♭). In all, there are 14 appearances of this interval (either ascending or descending). Many appearances are in the same rhythm as the original motive (♪♩), which makes the relationship especially clear. List the measures in which the motive is used in this obvious fashion. _____

_____

45, 47, 49, 50, 51, 52.

564. The entire B section consists basically of a dominant thirteenth chord in A major. The tonic note (A) never appears, yet the dominant function of the harmony establishes the tonality by implication. The third section of the ternary form begins in measure 53. Here the original key of D-flat is reestablished. The tonal relation of the middle section to the principal tonality is shown below:

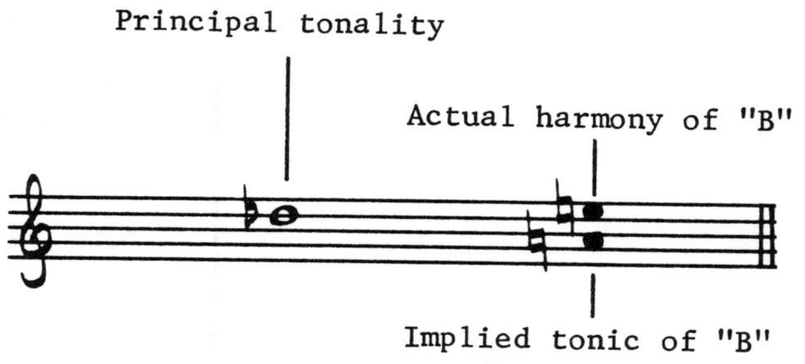

Principal tonality

Actual harmony of "B"

Implied tonic of "B"

chromatic

Both the actual harmony (E^{13}), and the inferred tonic (A) are related by thirds to the tonic key of D-flat. The relation in each case is that of a _____ mediant.

D-flat

565. Not only is the B part short in relation to A, but it is limited tonally and harmonically. It does, however, provide colorful tonal contrast to the principal tonality of D-flat because of the chromatic mediant relationship. The melodic material is clearly derived from the original motive.

Our final concern is to see how the last principal section (measures 53-end) is constructed. The first twelve measures (53-64) are much like the initial section of the composition; but whereas the cadence in measure 12 is on F (Aeolian), the cadence in measure 64 is on _____.

C-sharp

566. The next section (measures 65-78) is a variant of the preceding one, much like the corresponding one in the first part (measures 13-22). But instead of the tonality of F, here the tonality is _____ minor.

27-28 (etc.)

567. The final four measures serve as a coda. From whence is this material derived? It comes from the melodic material in measures _____.

---

568. Ravel's composition contains motive exploitation as does Debussy's prelude—a single two-note motive generates most of the melodic material. Still, we found that phrases are quite clearly defined, as are the three parts of the ternary form; this produces more easily perceived formal structures.

The basic organization of the composition in Panel 17 is shown below:

Chapter 14

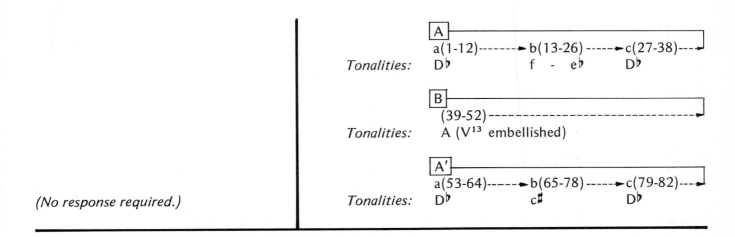

A
a(1-12)-------►b(13-26) -----►c(27-38)---┘
Tonalities: D♭   f - e♭   D♭

B
(39-52) ------------------------------┘
Tonalities: A (V¹³ embellished)

A'
a(53-64)-----►b(65-78) -----►c(79-82)---┘
Tonalities: D♭   c♯   D♭

(No response required.)

SUMMARY.

Debussy's goal of creating "music free from themes and motives" was not realized, even by himself. The desire for coherence was still strong, and impressionists—influenced by traditional training, and the conventional musical world about them—were unable to invent truly new formal methods to serve the identity-establishing function of melodic and rhythmic motives. Nevertheless, the rejection of sonata form —with its formal development processes and intellectual-dramatic character—in favor of the exploitation of very small motives, did redirect formal practices toward a more nuclear type of coherence, more felt than heard, and appropriate to the expression in sound of subjective sense perceptions.

The outline which follows recapitulates the principal points made in this chapter.

I.   *The Function of Form*

1.   The chief function of form is coherence. The means to achieve this varies with the style, aesthetic, and purpose of the music.

   a.   Order of a symmetrical, architectural nature is favored in classical music.

   b.   Form is freer, more expanded, and adjusted to dramatic, programmatic needs in romantic music.

   c.   The evocative nature of impressionist music leads to less clearly-defined phrase structure and sections. Preference is shown for short, self-contained fragments which are strung together to suggest a free association of impressions.

II.   *Larger Formal Units*

1.   The formal developmental processes associated with sonata form are avoided.

2.   Part forms are favored, but sections are often integrated by the use of similar material.

3.   Motivic variation is often the chief unifying device.

Notes

1. THE PERSISTENCE OF TONALITY

1. For a description of an African harmonic tonal system see John Blacking, "Tonal Organization in the Music of Two Venda Initiation Schools," *Ethnomusicology* 14 (1970): 1-56, esp. 11-19.
2. Max Wertheimer, "Musik der Wedda," *Sammelbände der Internationalen Musik-Gesellschaft* 11 (1909-10): 304.
3. Erich M. von Hornbostel, "Musik der Makuschí, Taulipáng und Yekuaná," in Theodor Koch-Grünberg, *Vom Roroima zum Orinoco*, 5 vols. (Stuttgart: Verlag Stecker und Schröder, 1923), 3:437.
4. Alan P. Merriam, *Ethnomusicology of the Flathead Indians*, Viking Fund publications in anthropology, no. 44 (Chicago: Aldine Publishing Co., 1967), p. 305.
5. For additional information on approaches to tonality in primitive music see Bruno Nettle, *Theory and Method in Ethnomusicology* (London: The Free Press of Glencoe, 1964), pp. 146-47.
6. Jaap Kunst, *Music in Java; its History, its Theory and its Technique*, trans. Emil van Loo, 2nd ed., 2 vols. (The Hague: Martinus Nijhoff, 1949), 2:512.
7. Jaap Kunst, "Songs of North New Guinea," Musicologisch Onderzoek, No. 2, in *Oudheidkundige Dienst in Nederlandisch-Indie* (1931), p. 10.
8. Curt Sachs, "Primitive and Medieval Music: A Parallel," *Journal of the American Musicological Society* 13 (1960): 45-46.
9. E. de Coussemaker, *Oeuvres Complètes du Trouvère Adam de la Halle* (Paris: A Durand & Pédone-Lauriel, 1872; facsimile ed., New York: Broude Brothers, 1964), p. 28.
10. Guido Maria Dreves, *Aurelius Ambrosius, "der Vater der Kirchengesanges"* (Freiburg im Breisgau, St. Louis, Mo., etc.: Herder, 1893), p. 111.
11. Monte Cassino, MS. q. 318, fo. 291. Facsimile in *New Oxford History of Music*, vol. 2, 2nd ed. rev., ed. Dom Anselm Hughes (London: Oxford University Press, 1955), p. 221.
12. F. Gennrich, ed., *Troubadours, Trouvères, Minne- und Meistergesang*, in *Das Musikwerk; eine Beispielsammlung zur Musikgeschichte*, 31 vols., ed. K. G. Fellerer (Cologne: Arno Volk-Verlag, 1951), 2:14.

2. TONALITY AS ORDER

1. Fétis' chief works are *Traité complet de la théorie et de la pratique de l'harmonie* (Brussels, 1884), and *Esquise de l'historie de l'harmonie considerée comme art et comme science systematique* (Paris, 1840).
2. Gioseffo Zarlino, *L'istitutioni harmoniche* (Venice, 1558).
3. Zarlino, *L'istitutioni*, pp. 296-97.
4. Thomas Morley, *A Plaine and Easie Introduction to Practicall Musicke* (London, 1597), pp. 129-30. See the facsimile edition of this work with an introduction by Edmund H. Fellowes published by the Shakespeare Association (Warwick Square: Humphrey Milford, Oxford University Press, 1937).
5. "Number mysticism" is evident in a good bit of theoretical speculation about music. The number 6,

for example, has special appearl for those seeking mathematical explanations because it results from both the addition and multiplication of the first three numbers $(1 + 2 + 3 = 6; 1 \times 2 \times 3 = 6)$.

6. *Senario* (It.) base of six, pertaining to six.

7. These proportions represent the relation between the frequencies of the two tones constituting each interval. They also represent lengths of strings, because the fundamental pitch of a string is directly proportionate to its length, providing all other factors are equal.

8. Rameau's principal theoretical works are *Traité de l'harmonie réduite a ses principes naturels* (Paris, 1722); *Nouveau système de musique théorique* (Paris, 1726); *Génération harmonique* (Paris, 1737); *Demonstration du principe de l'harmonie* (Paris, 1750). These and other writings by Rameau may be seen in Jean-Philippe Rameau, *Complete Theoretical Writings*, ed. Erwin R. Jacobi, 5 vols. (Dallas: American Institute of Musicology, 1967-69).

9. Rameau was one of the greatest French organists of his time, and he wrote much keyboard music. His greatest successes, however, were in the field of dramatic music. He brought to French opera a new emphasis on musical content, and his music is characterized by harmonic and orchestral idioms, which then were relatively rich and varied. He was involved in several Parisian "war of words," the most notorious of which was his controversy with Rousseau and the "Encyclopedistes." This bitter struggle was known as "la guerre des bouffons," and concerned the relative merits of French and Italian music.

10. Rameau, *Traité*, p. 36.

11. Rameau, *Traité*, p. 212.

12. For additional information regarding Rameau's theories see Joan Ferris, "The Evolution of Rameau's Harmonic Theories," *Journal of Music Theory* 3 (1959): 231-56.

13. Rameau, *Nouveau Système*, p. 38.

14. See Mathew Shirlaw, *The Theory of Harmony* (London: Novello & Company, Limited, 1917; reprint edition, New York: Da Capo Press, 1969), pp. 201-05.

15. Guiseppi Tartini, *Trattato di Musica secondo la vera scienza dell'armonia* (Padua, 1754; facsimile ed., New York: Broude Brothers, 1966).

16. Ibid., fold-out leaf (unnumbered).

17. For more information regarding Tartini's speculations see Alejandro Enrique Planchart, "A Study of the Theories of Jiuseppe Tartini," *Journal of Music Theory* 4 (1960): 32-61.

18. Moritz Hauptmann, *Die Natur der Harmonik und der Metrik* (Leipzig: Breitkoff und Härtel, 1853).

19. Translated into English by Alexander J. Ellis and published under the title *On the Sensations of Tone as a Physiological Basis for the Theory of Music* (London: Longmans, Green, and Co., 1875); reprint ed. (New York: Dover Publications, Inc., 1954).

20. Helmholtz, *On the Sensations of Tone*, p. 249.

21. Fétis, *Traité complet*, p. 249.

22. Rameau insisted that melody originates in harmony, not the reverse. See *Traité*, Book II, Chapter 19, pp. 138-41.

3. CLASSICAL TONALITY

1. Thomas Morley, *The First Book of Canzonets to Two Voices* in *The English Madrigalists* ed. Edmund H. Fellowes, rev. Thurston Dart, 36 vols. (London: Stainer and Bell, Ltd., 1956), 1:6-7.

4. EXPANDED TONALITY

1. See Rousseau's philosophical essay, *Discours sur l'origine et les fondements de l'inégalité parmi les hommes (Discourse on the Origin and Bases of Inequality among Men)*, 1754, in which he lauds the "natural man," and points to private property and the state as causes of inequality and oppression.

2. Major or minor chords other than the tonic may be tonicized by means of a chord having dominant function (V, V^7, vii$^\circ$, vii$^{\circ7}$, and vii^{d7}) within the tonal area of the tonicized chord. See Paul Harder, *Harmonic Materials in Tonal Music*, 2 vols. (Boston: Allyn and Bacon, Inc., 1968), 2:62-79.

3. Chromatic mediants are altered chords related by the interval of a third to diatonic chords (mostly tonic, dominant, or subdominant). For more information see Harder, *Harmonic Materials*, Part 2, Chapter 8.

5. ULTRACHROMATICISM (I)

1. See Ernst Kurth, *Romantische Harmonik und ihre Krise in Wagners "Tristan,"* second edition (Berlin: Max Hesses Verlag, 1923). But for an account which stresses identity with classical tonal usages see Harold Truscott, "Wagner's Tristan and the Twentieth Century," *Music Review* 24 (February 1963): 75-85.

6. ULTRACHROMATICISM (II)

1. The conductor Hans von Bülow dubbed Strauss "Richard the Second."
2. Franck scrawled the word "poison" on the cover of his copy of *Tristan und Isolde.*

7. DENIAL OF HARMONIC FUNCTION

1. Scriabin's theosophic speculations and their affect on his music are detailed in Faubion Bowers, *Scriabin, A Biography of the Russian Composer*, 2 vols. (Tokyo and Palo Alto, Calif.: Kodansha International, Ltd., 1969), 2:47-71.
2. Much has been made by some writers of Scriabin's use of serial methods in his later works. See, for example, George Perle, *Serial Composition and Atonality* (Berkeley and Los Angeles: University of California Press, 1963), pp. 37-40; Oliver Neighbour, "The Evolution of Twelve-note Music," *Proceedings of the Royal Musical Association* 81 (1955): 49-61.
3. The mystic chord consists of tones which approximate partials number 8, 9, 10, 11, 13, and 14 of the natural harmonic series.
4. Neighbour, "Twelve-note Music," p. 56.

8. NEW TONAL FREEDOMS

1. See Boris Kochno, *Diaghilev and the Ballets Russes*, trans. Adrienne Foulke (New York and Evanston: Harper & Row, Publishers, 1970), pp. 80-81.
2. Chords with added tones are presented in detail in Chapters 11 and 12. For information about chords with added sixths see Frame 421.
3. From *palindromus* (Lat.), "turning backwards." A word or phrase which reads the same both forward and backward. The word MADAM is an example of a palindrome.
4. For more information about polychords see Frames 439-443.

9. ENLARGED SCALE RESOURCES (I)

1. Refer to Julia D'Almendra, *Les Modes grégoriens dans l'oeuvre de Claude Debussy* (Paris: Librairie Gabriel Enault, 1950).

10. ENLARGED SCALE RESOURCES (II)

1. Other symmetrical divisions of the octave are the tritone, augmented triad, diminished seventh chord, and chromatic scale.
2. See Frames 147-149, and 152-153. The whole-tone scale is used by Mozart in *Ein Musikalischer Spass* (A Musical Joke), second movement, measures 74-75 as a humorous transgression of style.
3. See, for example, Debussy, *Nocturnes* No. 1 ("Nuages"), measures 1-4, 11-12; *Nocturnes* No. 2 ("Fêtes"), measures 27-28; *Préludes,* Vol. I, No. 1 ("Danseuses de Delphes"), measures 1-2, 6-7; *Préludes,* Vol. II, No. 2 ("Feuilles mortes"), measures 10-11, 32-35, 37-40.
4. So strong was the influence of oriental art on impressionist painters that at one time they were called "the Japanese of painting." Manet's portrait of Emil Zola (1868) has very shallow depth, and in the background are represented various objects of interest to the artist including a Japanese print and a painted oriental screen. The same artist's "The Fifer" (1866) portrays a flat figure silhouetted on a flat background; all perspective and depth are eliminated.
5. For additional information see William Malm, *Music Cultures of the Pacific, the Near East, and Asia* (Englewood Cliffs, N. J.: Prentice-Hall, Inc., 1967), pp. 107-111; see also Curt Sachs, *The Rise of Music in the Ancient World East and West* (New York: W. W. Norton & Company, Inc., 1943), pp. 114-119.
6. This parallels the concept of *ethos* in ancient Greek philosophy. See Gustave Reese, *Music in the Middle Ages* (New York: W. W. Norton & Company, Inc., 1940), pp. 44-46.

11. EXPANDED CHORD VOCABULARY (I)

1. Oscar Thomson, *Debussy, Man and Artist* (New York: Dodd, Mead & Co., Inc., 1967), p. 241.

13. PARALLELISM

1. Martino Gerbert, *Scriptores ecclesiastici de musica,* 3 vols. (1784; facsimile ed. Milan: Bollettino bibliografico musicale, 1931), 1:167.
2. From *cantus gemellus,* "twin song." See Reese, *Music in the Middle Ages,* pp. 387 ff.
3. Guido Adler, ed., *Handbuch der Musikgeschichte,* 2d ed., 2 vols. (Berlin: W. H. Keller, 1930), 1:167.
4. Luca Marenzio: *Il 3° libro delle Villanelle a 3* (1585), p. 18.
5. See, for example, Mozart's "Musical Joke," K. 522, I, measure 66; II, measures 59-60; III, measures 1, 2, 4, and 26.
6. Cf. Example 24, page 319.
7. For other examples of this type chord used in parallel motion see Frames 413, 414, 416, and 417.

14. FORM IN IMPRESSIONIST MUSIC

1. See Curt Sachs, *Rhythm and Tempo* (New York: W. W. Norton & Company, Inc., 1953), p. 360 f. For an analysis of rhythmic vagueness in Debussy's prelude for piano "Des pas sur la neige" see Grosvenor W. Cooper and Leonard B. Meyer, *The Rhythmic Structure of Music* (Chicago & London: The University of Chicago Press, 1960), pp. 171-74.
2. Thomson, *Debussy, Man and Artist,* p. 103.
3. Timbre is an important expressive element in music which could be included as a factor in motive variation. But since this is properly a concern of orchestration, it is outside the scope of this study.
4. Iso-. From the Greek *isos,* equal: a combining form meaning equal, alike, identical. Thus, the term "isorhythm" denotes the use of identical rhythms.

5. See Frames 272-273.
6. For examples of the pedal device see Frames 486, 488, and 497.
7. The limitation of space prohibits detailed analysis of more music. For other published analyses of impressionist music see the following: Debussy, *Préludes,* Vol. I, No. 5 ("Les collines d'Anacapri") in William Christ, *et alii, Materials and Structures of Music,* 2 vols. (Englewood Cliffs, New Jersey: Prentice-Hall, Inc., 1967), II:411-415; Debussy, *String Quartet,* Op. 10 (third movement) in Wallace Berry, *Form in Music* (Englewood Cliffs, New Jersey: Prentice-Hall, Inc., 1966), pp. 115-119; Debussy, *Préludes,* Vol. I, No. 10 ("La Cathédrale engloutie") in Douglass M. Green, *Form in Tonal Music* (New York: Holt, Rinehart and Winston, Inc., 1965), pp. 289-291.

Discography and Films

Records:

Most of the compositions referred to in the text are included in this list. Additional items are supplied for those who wish to expand the scope and increase the depth of study. To aid in making appropriate selections, information is given regarding other words contained in each item. Listings following the dagger (†) indicate other selections on the same record, or in the same album.

Afghanistan
See Nos. 58, 59
Ambrosian Hymn: "Aeterne rerum conditor"
   1. A Treasury of Early Music (vol. I, side 1, bd. 1)—Haydn HSE 9100. For other Ambrosian chants *see* Nos. 2, 3
   2. Ambrosian Chants, Cho. of the Polifonica Ambrosiano—Vox DL 343
   3. History of Music in Sound (vol. II, side 1 [Pre-Gregorian Music], bd. 7)—RCA Vic. LM-6015

Brahms, Johannes
   Sonata No. 1, Op. 1
   4. Katchen—Lon. 6410
Burundi
   See No. 63

Chopin, Frédéric
   Preludes, Op. 28
   5. Freire—Col. M-30486
   6. Novaes—Vox 510940
   7. Slenczynska—Dec. 710059
Congo
   See No. 65

Debussy, Claude
   Berceuse Heroïque
   See Nos. 8, 9, 10
   Complete piano music
   8. Frankel—Vox SVBX-5432/3
   9. Haas—Phi. (World Series) PHC-5-012
   10. Webster—Desto 7111/5
   Danses sacrée et profane, for Harp and Orch. (1904)
   11. Chailifoux, Boulez, Cleveland Orch.—Col. MS-7362
   12. Zabaleta, Kuentz Chamber Orch.—DGG 139304
   Epigraphes antiques (1915)
   13. Ansermet, Orch. Suisse Romande †*Jeux*—Ev. 3285

   14. R. & G. Casadesus †*En blanc et noir*—Col. MS-6641
   Estampes (1903)
   15. Regules—Count. 53003
   16. Richter—DGG 138849
   Images pour piano, Books 1 and 2 (1905; 1907)
   17. Entremont †*Children's Corner; Pour le piano*—Col. MS-6567
   Masques
   See Nos. 8, 9, 10
   Nocturnes, for orchestra (1893-9)
   18. Ansermet, Orch. Suisse Romande †Ravel: *Ma Mère l'Oye*—Lon. 6023
   19. Boulez, New York Phil. †*Première rapsodie,* for clarinet; *Printemps*—Col. M-30483
   20. Ormandy, Phila. Orch. *Danse*; Ravel: *Rapsodie espagnole*—Col. MS-6697
   Pelléas et Mélisande (1892-1902)
   21. Soederstrom, Minton, Shirley, Ward, McIntyre, Wicks, Britten, Boulez, Covent Garden Orch. (complete opera)—Col. MS-30119
   22. Spoorenberg, Maurane, London, Ansermet, Orch. Suisse Romande (complete opera)—Lon. 1379
   La plus que lente
   See Nos. 8, 9, 10
   Pour le piano (suite) (1896-1901)
   23. Entremont †*Images pour piano; Children's Corner*—Col. MS-6567
   Prélude à l'aprèz-midi d'un faune (1892-4)
   24. Ansermet, Orch. Suisse Romande †*La Mer*; Ravel: *Rapsodie espagnole*—Lon. STS-15109
   25. Boulez, New York Phil. †*Jeux; La Mer*—Col. MS-7361
   26. Karajan, Berlin Phil. †*La Mer*; Ravel: *Daphnis et Chloé,* Suite No. 2—DGG 138923
   Preludes, for piano, Vols. 1 and 2 (1910; 1910-13)
   27. Vol. 1, no. 8 "La Fille aux cheveux de lin," no. 10 "La Cathédrale ingloutie," no. 11 "La Danse de Puck," no. 12 "Minstrels" in Time-Life

Records, *The Story of Great Music* (series)
"Prelude to Modern Music"
    28. Pennario—RCA Vic. LSC-7036
Quartet, Op. 10 (1893)
    29. Budapest Quartet †Ravel: *Quartet in F*—Col.
        MS-6015
    30. Juilliard Quartet †Ravel: *Quartet in F*—RCA
        Vic. LSC-2413
Suite bergamasque, for piano (1890-1905)
    31. Vàsàry †*Arabesque; Pour le piano*—DG 139458
Delius, Frederick
Irmelin, "Prelude" (1932)
    32. Barbirolli, London Sym. †*Walk to the Paradise
        Garden*; Ireland: *London Overture*—Ang. S-36415
Songs of Sunset (1906-7)
    33. Liverpool Phil. Cho., Baker, Shirley-Quirk,
        Groves, Royal Liverpool Phil. *Cynara & Arabesk*
        —Ang. S-36603

Flathead Indians
See No. 74
Franck, César
Symphony in D Minor
    34. Ansermet, Orch. Suisse Romande—Lon. 6222
    35. Bernstein, New York Phil.—Col. MS-6072
    36. Karajan, Orch. Paris—Ang. S-36729
    37. Monteux, Chicago Sym.—RCA Vic. LSC-2514

Ghana
See No. 62
Griffes, Charles
Poem, for flute and orchestra (1918)
    38. Mariano, Hanson, Eastman-Rochester Orch.—
        Mer. 90379
    39. Wanausek, Hendl, American Recording Soc.
        Orch.—Desto 6424
Guiraut de Borhelh
"Reis glorios" (Alba)
    40. Troubadour and Trouvère Songs (side 1, bd. 1)—
        EA 0012
        See also Troubadour songs

Hymn to St. Magnus
    41. Musical Heritage Society (side 1, bd. 2, Ex. 25c)
        —OR 350

Indonesia
See No. 77
Ireland, John
Land of lost content (Song Cycle) (1920-1)
    42. Pears—Argo 5418
London Overture (1936)
    43. Barbirolli, London Sym. †Delius: *Irmelin: Walk*—
        Ang. S-36415

Japan
See No. 78
Java
See No. 79

Kyrie "fons bonatatis"
    44. Ruhland, Capella Antiqua Munich—Tele. (Das
        Alte Werk) SAWT 9493
Other chant recordings:
    45. World Library of Sacred Music—WLSM 8S.SD
    46. Masterpieces of Music before 1750—Haydn HSE
        9038
    47. St. Thomas Abbey Monks—Vox 516420
    48. Treasury of Early Music—Haydn HSE 9100

Liszt, Franz
Sonetti (3) del Petrarca
    49. Arrau (Nos. 104, 123)—Phi. 802906
    50. Gunnar Johansen (complete works of Franz
        Liszt; individual albums available)—Art.-Dir.
Trois Etudes de Concert
See No. 50

Marenzio, Luca
Various compositions:
    51. History of Music in Sound, vol. IV—RCA Vic.
        LM-6029
    52. Insbruck Vogelweide Chamber Cho.—Mace
        S-9062
    53. Italian Madrigals of the Renaissance—Ev. 3179
Morley, Thomas
Canzonet: "Sweet Nymph Come to Thy Lover"
    54. Duets for Countertenor Alfred Deller and Mark
        Deller—Van. (Cardinal) VCS 10022
Mozart, W. A.
Sonata No. 17, in D major, K. 576
    55. Ashkenazy—Lon. 6659

Organum
Various examples:
    56. Organum, Motets, Conductus and Other Early
        Polyphony—Tele. (Das Alte Werk) SAWT 9530/1
    57. Sequence: "Rex caelik Domine" (9th century)
        (vol. 1, side 1, bd. 6)—Haydn HSE 9038

Pakistan
See No. 81
Papua (Northwest New Guinea)
See No. 76
Primitive and ethnic music
Numerous recordings of primitive and ethnic music are
now available. Those listed here are appropriate for sup-
plemental listening related to the study of melodic
tonality as presented in Chapter 1.
Afghanistan
    58. Music of Afghanistan. Documentary recording
        by Radio Kabul—Folk. FE 4361
    59. The Music of Afghanistan, 4 vols.—Anth. AST-
        4001, 4004, 4007, 4010
Africa
    60. African Music. Sudan, Nigeria, Cameroons—
        Folk. LC R-57-1367
    61. Folk Music of the Western Congo. Bapindi,
        Bakwesi, Bapende—Folk. FE 4427

Etude, Op. 56, No. 4
    106. Richter—MK 1582 LP
Preludes, Op. 74
    107. Kuerti †*Etudes*, Op. 65; *Sonatas* Nos. 4, 6;
           Berg: *Piano Sonata*—Mon. S-2134
    108. Lewenthal—ABC (number not assigned)
Sonatas, Nos. 1, 2, Op. 6, 19
    109. Laredo—Conn. S-2035
Sonata No. 3, Op. 23
    110. Laredo †*Sonatas Nos. 4, 6, 10*—Conn. S-2034
Sonata No. 4, Op. 30
    See Nos. 107, 110
Sonata No. 5, Op. 53
    111. Laredo †*Sonatas Nos. 7, 9; Etudes*, Op. 42—
           Conn. S-2032
    112. Richter †*Debussy: Estampes*—DGG 138849
    113. Szidon †*Sonatas Nos. 6, 7, 8, 9, 10*—DG
           2707 053
Sonata No. 6, Op. 62
    See Nos. 107, 110, 113
Sonata No. 7, Op. 64
    114. Somer †*Sonata No. 9*—Mer. 90525
        See also Nos. 111, 113
Sonata No. 8, Op. 66
    See No. 113
Sonata No. 9, Op. 68
    See Nos. 111, 113
Sonata No. 10, Op. 70
    See Nos. 110, 113
Symphony No. 4 (The Poem of Ecstasy), Op. 54
(1907-8)
    115. Johanos, Dallas Sym. †*Symphony No. 5*,
           (Prometheus: Poem of Fire)—Can. 31039
    116. Stokowski, Houston Sym.—Ev. 3032
Strauss, Richard
Don Quixote, Op. 35 (1897)
    117. Fournier, Karajan, Berlin Phil.—DGG 139009
    118. Janigro, Reiner, Chicago Sym.—RCA Vic.
           LSS-2384
    119. Munroe, Lincer, Bernstein, New York Phil.—
           Col M-30067
Till Eulenspiegels lustige Streiche, Op. 28 (1895)
    120. Bernstein, New York Phil. †*Debussy: Prélude à
           l'après-midi d'un faune*—Col. MS-6441
    121. Karajan, Vienna Phil. *Tod und Verklärung;
           Salome: Dance*—Lon. 6211
    122. Ormandy, Phila. Orch. †*Rosenkavalier Suite;
           Salome: Dance*—Col. MS-6678

123. Time-Life Records, *The Story of Great Music*
    (series) "Prelude to Modern Music"
Sudan
    See No. 71

Tibet
    See No. 82
Troubadour songs
    124. Chansons der Troubadours. Songs and Instru-
           mental music of the 13th Century. (Includes
           several works by Guiraut de Bornelh.)—Tele.
           (Das Alte Werk) SAWT 9567
    125. French Troubadour Songs—West. 9610, 9620
    126. History of Music in Sound, vol. II—RCA LM-6015
    127. Music of the Middle Ages.—Lyr. 85

Vedda (Ceylon)
    See No. 76
Villanellas
    128. Madrigals, Villanellas, Chansons. Jürgen Jürgens,
           Hamburg Instrumental Ensemble—Tele. (Das
           Alte Werk) SAWT 9462

Wagner, Richard
Die Götterdämmerung (1876)
    129. Dernesch, Janowitz, Ludwig, Brilloth, Stewart,
           Ridderbusch, Karajan, Berlin Phil.—DGG
           2716001
    130. Nilsson, Watson, Ludwig, Windgassen, Fischer-
           Dieskau, Frick, Solti, Vienna Phil.—Lon. 1604
Tristan und Isolde (1865)
    131. Nilsson, Ludwig, Windgassen, Wächter, Talvela,
           Böhm, Bayreuth Festival Orch.—DGG 2713001
    132. Nilsson, Resnik, Uhl, Krause, Van Mill, Solti,
           Vienna Phil.—Lon. 1502
Watusi
    See No. 70
Wolf, Hugo
Goethe-Lieder
    133. Ludwig, Berry †*Schumann: Liederkreis*—DG
           139386
Mörike-Lieder
    134. Evelyn Lear—DGG SLPM 138979
    135. Prey—Lon. 25946

Yecuaná Indians (Brazil)
    See No. 73

Abbreviations and Sources   (Records)

ABC (ABC/Dunhill), also dist. for Westminister
    ABC/Dunhill Records
    8255 Beverly Blvd.
    Los Angeles, Calif. 90048
Afrot. (Afrotone)
    International Record Industries, Inc.

    135 West 41st Street
    New York, N. Y. 10036
Das Alte Werk
    See Argo
Ang. (Angel) also dist. for Seraphim
    Capitol-Angel Records, Inc.

1370 Avenue of the Americas
New York, N. Y. 10019
Anth. (Anthology)
Anthology Record and Tape Corp.
32 Oxford Street
Lynn, Mass. 01902
Argo, also dist. for Telefunken "Das Alte Werk," & London
Argo Sight and Sound Ltd.
539 West 25th Street
New York, N. Y. 10001
Art-Dir. (Artist Direct)
Artist Direct Recordings
Blue Mounds, Wisconsin 53517
Bären. (Bärenreiter)
Audio Research Services, Inc.
739 Boylston Street
Boston, Mass. 02116
Can. (Candide)
See Vox
Cardinal
See Vanguard
Col. (Columbia)
CBS Records
51 West 52nd Street
New York, N. Y. 10019
Conn. (Connoisseur Society)
Connoisseur Society, Inc.
470 West End Ave.
New York, N. Y. 10024
Count. (Counterpoint/Esoteric)
See Everest
Dec. (Decca)
MCA Records, Inc.
100 Universal City Plaza
Universal City, Calif. 91608
Desto
Desto Records
Loch Road
Franklin Lakes, N. J. 07417
DG or DGG (Deutsche Grammophon Gesellschaft)
Polydor Inc.
1700 Broadway
New York, N. Y. 10019
Dover
Dover Publications, Inc.
180 Varick Street
New York, N. Y. 10014
EA (Expériences Anonymes)
See Lyrichord
Ev. (Everest), also dist. for Counterpoint/Esoteric
Everest Records Group
10920 Wilshire Blvd.
Los Angeles, Calif. 90024
Folk. (Folkways/Scholastic)
Folkways/Scholastic
906 Sylvan Ave.
Englewood Cliffs, New Jersey 07632
Haydn (Haydn Society)
Haydn Society
P. O. Box 321

East Hartford, Conn. 06108
Lon. (London)
See Argo
Lyr. (Lyrichord), also dist. for Experiences Anonymes
Lyrichord Discs, Inc.
141 Perry Street
New York, N. Y. 10014
Mace
Scepter Records, Inc.
245 West 54th Street
New York, N. Y. 10019
Mer. (Mercury), also dist. for Philips
Mercury Records Corp.
35 East Wacker Drive
Chicago, Illinois 60601
M.H.S. (Musical Heritage Society)
The Musical Heritage Society, Inc.
1991 Broadway
New York, N. Y. 10023
M.K. (Melodiya)
Not available at present
Mon. (Monitor)
Monitor Records, Inc.
156 Fifth Avenue
New York, N. Y. 10010
Ocora (Disques Ocora)
Audio Research Services, Inc.
739 Boylston Street
Boston, Mass. 02116
Phi. (Philips)
See Mercury
RCA Vic. (RCA Victor)
RCA Records
1133 Avenue of the Americas
New York, N. Y. 10036
Sera. (Seraphim)
See Angel
Tele. (Telefunken) "Das Alte Werk"
See Argo
Time-Life Records
Time-Life Records
Time & Life Building
541 North Fairbanks Court
Chicago, Illinois 60611
Turn. (Turnabout)
See Vox
Van. (Vanguard), also dist. for Cardinal
Vanguard Recording Society, Inc.
71 West 23rd Street
New York, N. Y. 10010
Vox, also dist. for Candide, and Turnabout
Vox Productions, Inc.
211 East 43rd Street
New York, N. Y. 10017
West. (Westminster)
See ABC/Dunhill
WLSM (World Library of Sacred Music)
World Library of Sacred Music
2145 Central Parkway
Cincinnati, Ohio 45214

Films:

These films are useful for supplementing ordinary learning experiences. Some provide a view of non-Western music and culture, which can heighten appreciation for the persistence of tonality throughout the world, and emphasize the contrast between melodic and harmonic tonality. Films may be rented, or (in some cases) purchased from the distributors listed.

African Musicians (C.C.M. Films)
15 min. b/w
Shows a variety of instruments including drums, xylophone, nail piano, and end-blown flute.

L'Amitié Noire (MMA)
20 min.
Conceived and narrated by Jean Cocteau. Photographed by François Villiers. A document of Chad culture, the film shows the arts, handicrafts, and ceremonial dances.

Annual Festival of the Dead (Dogen People—Africa) (IFF)
14 min. color
Sham attacks and war games performed in the village square. With dance movements, the warriors enact the accomplishments, or what might have been accomplishments, of their departed comrades. Much use is made of percussion instruments.

Bali Today (HP)
18 min. color
Includes background music by gamelan orchestras and temple singers.

Ballets of the Atlas (MMA)
9 min.
Communal dances of the Atlas Mountains of North Africa.

The Bilo (MMA)
10 min.
Funeral of a tribal chief in southern Madagascar, with emphasis on the taboos, fetishes, and sacrificial blood rites of the ceremony.

Dance Contest in Esira (MMA)
11 min.

A dance contest held between tribes in southern Madagascar, with an explanation of the meaning of the dances.

Discovering the Music of Japan (FAC)
22 min. color
Demonstration of music for various Japanese instruments, including the *koto* and *shamisen*.

Images From Debussy (AF)
14 min.
An impressionistic visual interpretation of "En bateau," "Arabesque en mi," "Reflets dans l'eau," and "Arabesque en sol."

Impressionism (Bailey)
7 min. color
Basic characteristics of impressionism in art; simplification of form by comparative analysis; textures and heavily painted surfaces; generalization of objects; broken color techniques.

Men's Dance (Pushtu—Afghanistan) (IFF)
11 min. color
Rugged Pushtu tribesmen are shown against a backdrop of snow capped peaks in an unusual national dance, which portrays man's endless combat with evil.

Suite of Berber Dances (MMA)
10 min.
Directed by Serge Kebecove. Photographed by Jean Leherisser. Produced by the Centre Cinématographique Marôcain.

Trance and Dance in Bali (TF)
20 min. b/w
Produced by Margaret Mead. Chiefly of anthropological interest. There is little music, but the film shows a fascinating facet of Balinese culture.

Abbreviations and Sources   (Films)

AF (Association Films)
  Distributed by:
  Radim Films
  220 West 42nd Street
  New York, N. Y. 10036
Bailey
  Bailey Films Association
  11559 Santa Monica Blvd.
  Los Angeles, Calif. 90025
C.C.M. Films
  C.C.M. Films, Inc.
  866 Third Avenue
  New York, N. Y. 10022
  Distributed by:
  Brandon Films
  200 West 57th Street
  New York, N. Y. 10019
FAC (Film Associates of California)
  Film Associates of California
  11559 Santa Monica Blvd.
  Los Angeles, Calif. 90025

HP (Hartley Productions)
  Hartley Productions
  279 East 44th Street
  New York, N. Y. 10017
IFF (International Film Foundation)
  International Film Foundation
  475 Fifth Avenue
  New York, N. Y. 10017
MMA (Museum of Modern Art)
  The Museum of Modern Art
  Department of Film
  11 West 53rd Street
  New York, N. Y. 10019
TF (Todd Films)
  Available from:
  New York University Film Library
  26 Washington Place
  New York, N. Y. 10003

Index of Musical Examples

(Except where indicated otherwise, numbers refer to frames.)

General Index

Reference is to both frames and pages (f. = frame; p. = page).
Thus, the entry "Modulation, f. 104; p. 36, 40, 72" indicates
that information may be found in frame 104, and also on
pages 36, 40, and 72.

Projection of colored lights, p. 105
Próle do Bébé No. 1, Villa-Lobos
    "Mulatinha," f. 366
    "O Polichinelo," f. 450, 459-460
Promethius: The Poem of Fire, Scriabin, f. 242; p. 105
Pulse, p. 239
Punctuation, p. 36
Pythagoras, p. 24

Quartal chords, f. 462-469 (*see also* Chords, quartal)
Quartal harmony, f. 462
Quartet, Debussy, f. 361
Quartet, Ravel, f. 350-351
Quintal chords, f. 462, 466-467 (*see also* Chords, quintal)

Rameau, Jean-Philippe, f. 57, 59, 66, 67, 77; p. 26-32, 34-35
Ravel, Maurice, f. 350, 440; p. 105, 180, 260
Real parallelism (*see* Parallelism, real)
Real sequence (*see* Sequence, real)
Register, p. 215
"Reis glorios," (Alba), Guiraut de Bornelh, f. 37-40; p. 18
Relative motion, p. 217
Renaissance period, p. 9-10, 36
Renaissance polyphony, p. 218-219
Renoir, Auguste, p. 123
Repetition, f. 273, 329, 382, 553; p. 36, 133, 256
Resolution of active tones, f. 411-412
Resolution of dissonance, f. 280
Retrograde, f. 510-511, 514 (*see also* Motive variation, retrograde)
Retrograde inversion, f. 510-512, 514 (*see also* Motive variation, retrograde-inversion)
Rhythm, p. 239
Rhythmic stress (*see* Tonality, rhythmic stress; *see also* Stress, rhythm)
Riemann, Hugo, p. 34
Rimbaud, Arthur, p. 124
Ritter, Alexander, p. 92
Roman numerals, f. 407; p. 80
Romantic music, f. 122, 410; p. 104, 265
Romantic period, p. 65, 219
Romanticism, p. 57-58, 239
Root, p. 27-30
Root movement, f. 184, 321-322; p. 72
Root relations, f. 69; p. 30-31, 40, 58
Rosenkavalier, Der, Strauss, p. 92
Rousseau, Jean Jacques, p. 26, 58
Rule of the octave, p. 30
Russlan and Ludmilla, Glinka, f. 373

Sachs, Curt, p. 9
Saint-Saëns, Camille, p. 149
Salieri, Antonio, p. 65
Salome, Strauss, p. 92
Satie, Erik, p. 217
Scales:
    chromatic, f. 364, 499; p. 74, 86, 162-163, 171, 180
    diatonic, f. 97, 481
    intervallic structure, f. 331

    major, f. 332, 340, 342-343, 349, 373; p. 26, 30, 180
    minor, f. 340, 349, 373; p. 26, 180
        natural, f. 331, 344-346, 348-349, 352
    pentatonic, f. 385-403, 440, 454, 482; p. 163, 170-174, 180
    symmetrical, p. 180
    whole-tone, f. 148-149, 152-153, 308, 368-373, 376-384, 455, 460, 484; p. 163, 170-171, 180
Schiller, Friedrich von, p. 58
Schoenberg, Arnold, p. 122
Schubert, Franz, p. 97
Schumann, Robert, p. 97
Scriabin, Alexander, p. 105, 119, 122
Second Viennese school, p. 122
Secondary dominant, f. 96, 120-122, 131-132; p. 62
Seconds, f. 450, 453-456
Senario, f. 45-51; p. 24
Sequence, f. 136-137, 174, 417 (*see also* Motive variation, sequence)
    harmonic, f. 175-177, 365, 449
    melodic, f. 365
    real, f. 177-178, 187, 297-299, 329; p. 87
Seurat, Georges, p. 123
Seventh chords (*see* Chords, seventh chords)
Similar motion (*see* Motion, similar)
Simultaneous contrast, p. 123
Sisley, Alfred, p. 123
"Sit gloria Domini" (Musica enchiriadis), p. 217 f
Six épigraphes antiques, Debussy,
    "Pour invoquer Pan, dieu du vent d'été," f. 389-390
    "Pour l'Egyptienne," f. 506-509
    "Pour un tombeau sans nom," f. 373-376, 501-503
Solesmes monks, p. 149
Sonata No. 1, Op. 1, Brahms, f. 471-472
Sonata, for violoncello and piano, Delius, f. 411-412
Sonata No. 15 "Menuetto," Haydn, f. 101-116
Sonata, for violoncello and piano, Ireland, f. 499
Sonata, k. 576, Mozart, f. 78-100
Sonata No. 5, Op. 53, Scriabin, f. 238-241
Sonata No. 6, Op. 62, Scriabin, f. 251-259
Sonata No. 7, Op. 64, Scriabin, f. 244-250
Sonata form, p. 256, 265
Sonatine, Ravel, f. 381-382, 413, 556-558
"Sonetto 104 del Petrarca," Liszt, f. 136-149; p. 65
Songs of Sunset, Delius, f. 365
Sous-dominante (*see* Subdominant)
Spacing, f. 423, 426, 428-429, 450; p. 215
Split chord members (*see* Chords, split chord members)
Square, p. 32-33
Stage (of sequence), f. 177
Strauss, Richard, p. 88, 92, 104, 122
Stress, p. 20 (*see also* Tonality, formal stress, iteration, rhythmic stress)
    contribution to tonality, f. 1, 3
    form, f. 325, 350, 374-375, 379; p. 6, 10, 20, 22, 147
    iteration, f. 325, 350, 374, 378-379, 402; p. 3, 6, 10, 20, 22, 147
    prolongation, f. 325
    rhythm, f. 35, 374, 375, 379, 402; p. 6, 20, 22, 147

Sweet Nymph Come to Thy Lover

Morley

Sonata K.576

Mozart

Sonata K.576 (cont.)

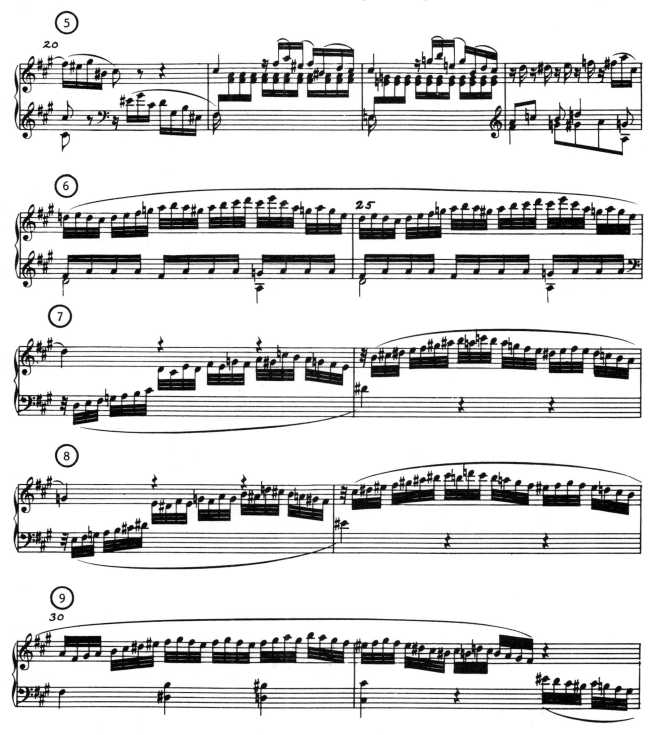

Sonata K.576 (cont.)

Sonata K.576 (cont.)

Sonata in D Major

Haydn

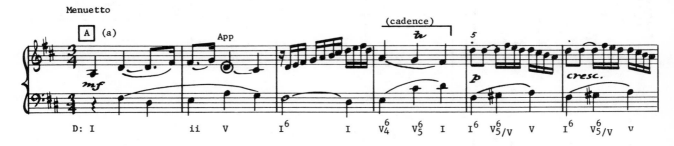

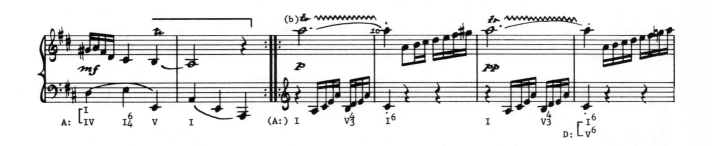

Sonata in D Major (cont.)

Papillons, Op. 2

R. Schumann

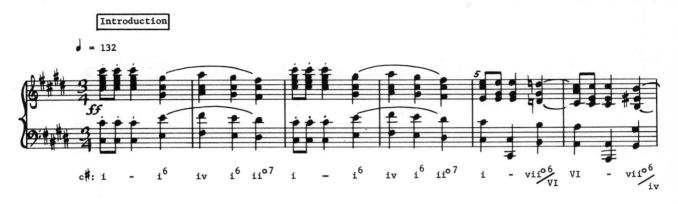

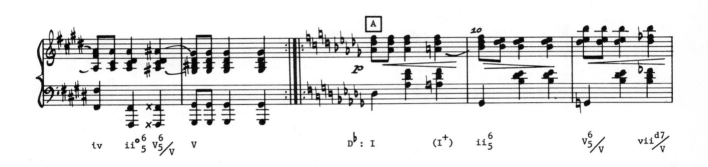

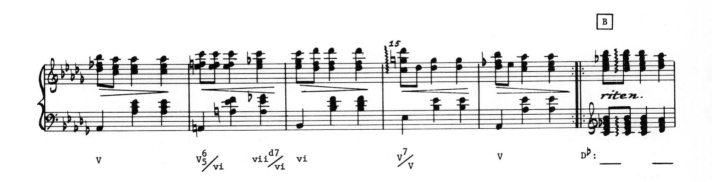

Papillons, Op. 2 (cont.)

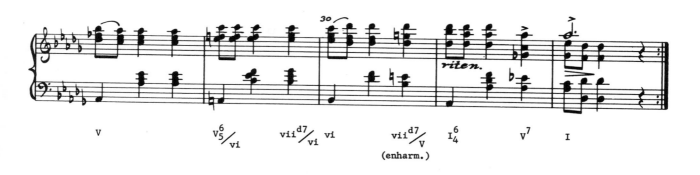

(Answer to Frame 121)

Prelude No. 9, Op. 28

Chopin

Sonetto del Petrarca

Liszt

(Answer to Frame 140)

Sonetto del Petrarca (cont.)

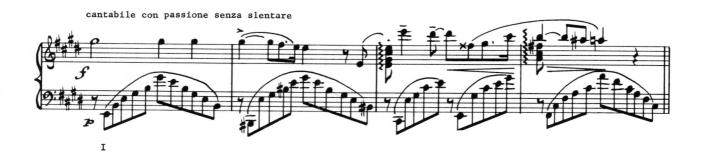

Tristan und Isolde (Prelude)

Wagner

Tristan und Isolde (Prelude – cont.)

Ex. b

Tristan und Isolde (Act II, Scene 2)

Wagner

Ex. a

(Prelude to Act III)

Ex. b

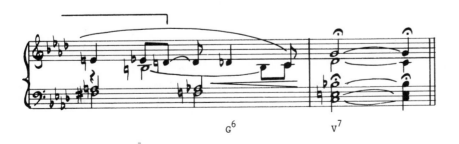

Die Götterdämmerung (Prelude — voices omitted)

Wagner

Ex. a

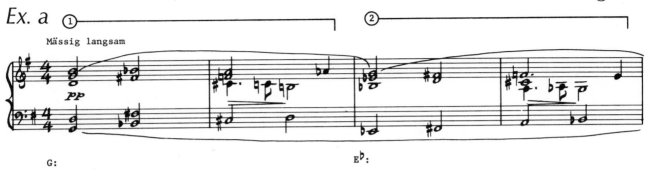

(Act II, Scene 4 — voice part omitted)

Ex. b

Sonata No. 6, Op. 62

Scriabin

Ex. a

Ex. b

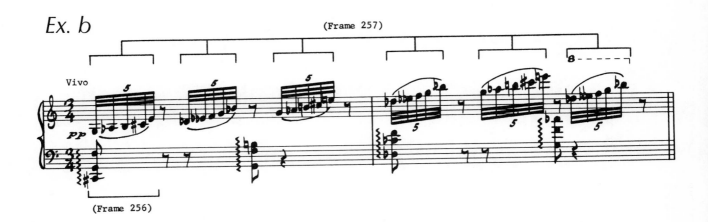

Prelude No. 1, Op. 74

Scriabin

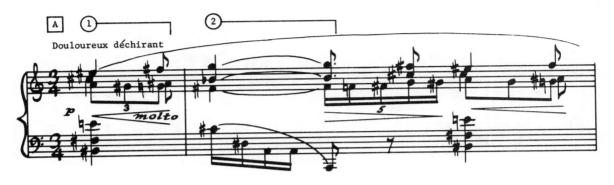

Prelude No. 1, Op. 74 (cont.)

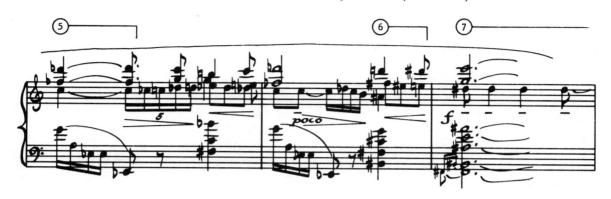

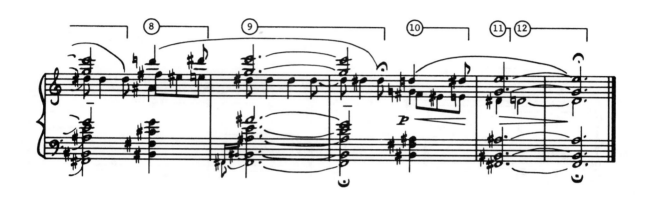

Prélude à l'après-midi d'un Faune

Debussy

(Answer to Frame 283)

1. C#7   2. A#7   3. C#7   4. A#7   5. C#7   6. C   7. a

8. c7   9. c7   10. f#   11. d#°7   12. B13   13. E

Suite bergamasque ("Clair de lune")

Debussy

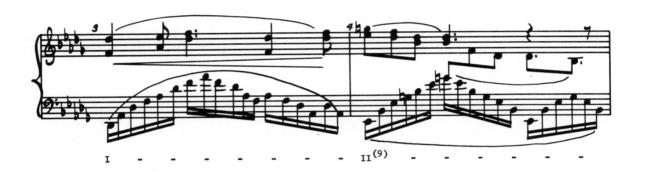

Prelude, Vol. I, No. 2 ("Voiles")

Debussy

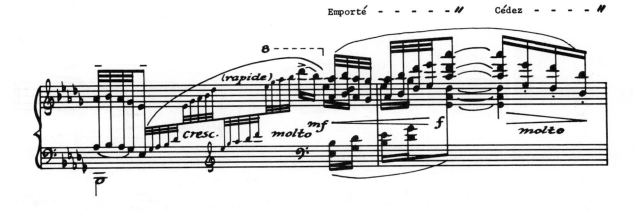

Prelude, Vol. I, No. 6 ("Des pas sur la neige")

Debussy

Prelude, Vol. II, No. 10 ("Canope")

Debussy

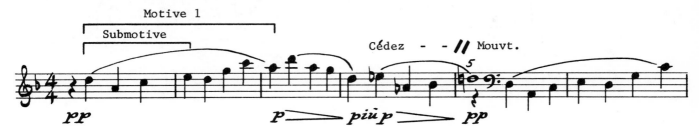

Prelude, Vol. II, No. 10 ("Canope" — cont.)

Sonatine (1905)

Ravel

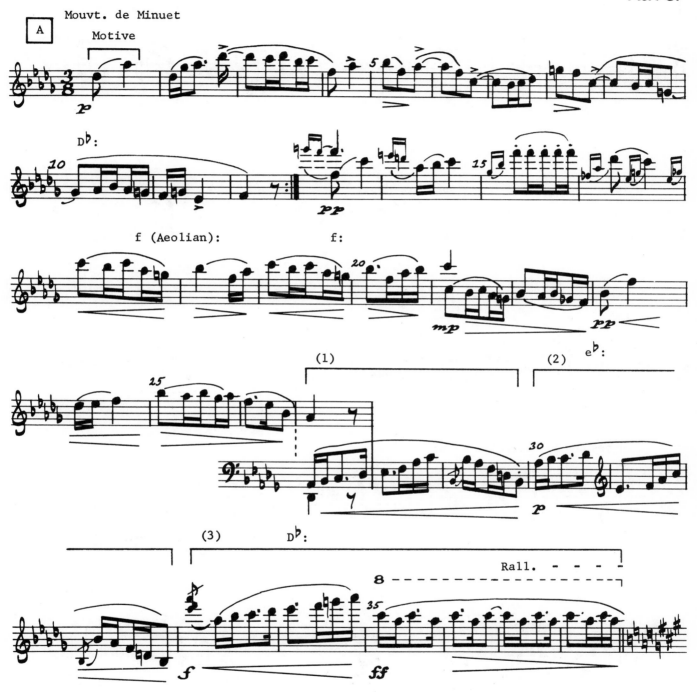

Sonatine (1905 — cont.)